I0086095

HEY! NIETZSCHE! LEAVE THEM KIDS ALONE!

HEY! NIETZSCHE! LEAVE THEM KIDS ALONE!

THE ROMANTIC MOVEMENT, ROCK & ROLL, AND
THE END OF CIVILISATION AS WE KNOW IT.

WITH ILLUSTRATIONS BY BRAD COOK

CRAIG SCHUFTAN

ABC
Books

Published by ABC Books for the
AUSTRALIAN BROADCASTING CORPORATION
GPO Box 9994 Sydney NSW 2001

Copyright © Craig Schuftan 2009

First published April 2009

All rights reserved. No part of this publication
may be reproduced, stored in a retrieval system
or transmitted in any form or by any means,
electronic, mechanical, photocopying, recording
or otherwise, without the prior written permission
of the Australian Broadcasting Corporation.

National Library of Australia
Cataloguing-in-Publication entry

Schuftan, Craig.
  Hey! Nietzsche! : Leave them kids alone / Craig Schuftan;
  illustrated by Brad Cook.
  1st ed.
  978 0 7333 2402 4 (pbk.)
  Popular culture – History
  Social movements – History
  Civilization, Modern
  Art and society – History
  Music – Social aspects – History
  Cook, Brad.
  Australian Broadcasting Corporation.
306

Cover designed by Brad Cook
Illustrated by Brad Cook
Typeset in 10.5/14pt Sabon by Kirby Jones

For Marissa and Shane,
and the new kid on the block.

Thank You

Hey, Nietzsche! first began to resemble a book in November last year. At that point, my wife and I had been travelling for almost nine months, and I had accumulated six notebooks full of ideas and an ipod full of emo. In Thailand, we met an Australian girl called Chrissie, and one night I tried (for the first time) to explain my idea for this book to her. When I'd finished my spiel, she thought for a moment and said, 'You know, when you first told me you were writing a book, I thought, "What a waste of time". But now that you've explained it, I reckon it might actually be really good.' This was the second most valuable piece of encouragement I received while writing *Hey! Nietzsche!*—the first being something my father-in-law, Peter Lynch said to me twelve months later. I was, by this point, a little emo myself—the combination of the looming deadline and over a year's worth of exposure to angst-y poetry was taking its toll. Was I, I wondered out loud, attempting too much? Pete told me that I was, but that he believed this was the secret to success. 'Bite off more than you can chew', he said, 'and chew like fuck.' (I think this is more or less what Rainer Maria Rilke was getting at in his *Letters to a Young Poet*.)

Along with Pete and Chrissie, I have a few other people to thank. Zan Rowe, Dan Buhagiar, Marc Fennell, Chris Scaddan and Linda Bracken at triple j; Wendy Were for having me to the Sydney Writer's Festival; Jenny Valentish at J*mag*; Keith Hurst for legal business; Jase Harty and Michael Agzarian for their continuing support; and the amazing Brad Cook for his portraits of 'old dudes' and guys with names nobody can pronounce. I'd also like to thank everybody who helped to make the *Culture Club* book launch such a roaring success— The Devoted Few, Dr Lindsay McDougall, Sam Simmons, Brendan Doyle, Nina Las Vegas, and the Pemmell Pad crew; and everybody at ABC Commercial for their hard work on *Hey! Nietzsche!*, including Louise Cornege, Jacquie Kent, Megan Johnston, and especially Susan Morris-Yates—for her unwavering support and saint-like patience.

Speaking of which, my friends and family—Michael 'Timmy' Rosenthal, Ben and Jess, the girls (and their boys), Pete and Lyn, Marissa and Shane and Mum and Dad—have been listening to me say 'it's nearly finished' for over a year now. As I type this, I think I can safely say that this time I *really* mean it. Thank you all for putting up with me.

And thank you, Kirileigh Lynch. You have confounded my thesis by being the least emo person I know *and* the most romantic (in a good way). I promise to come out of the tower of doom and have some real fun.

*And why are you so firmly and triumphantly certain
that only what is normal and positive—in short, only
well-being—is good for man? Is reason mistaken about
what is good? After all, perhaps prosperity isn't the
only thing that pleases mankind, perhaps he is just as
attracted to suffering...whether it's a good thing or a
bad thing, smashing things is also sometimes very
pleasant. I am not here standing up for suffering, or
for well-being either. I am standing out for my own
caprices and for having them guaranteed when
necessary.*

Fyodor Dostoyevsky
Notes From Underground

Introduction

This book began with a song I heard on the radio about two years ago. It was a five-minute rock epic in three acts, a sincere denial of modern life, an affirmation of the power of dreams, and a conflation of corny melodrama and gut-wrenching personal confession the likes of which had not been heard since 'Bohemian Rhapsody'.

I ranted and raved about this song and how great it was to everyone I knew, and quickly discovered that nobody liked it as much as I did. Or they liked it, but were unwilling to make any greater claim for it than that. I, on the other hand, was full of great claims. I believed this song had the power to change the world. I leaped to its defence. I argued, in all sincerity, that it was one of the Greatest Songs of All Time.

I was becoming unreasonable—but I liked the feeling of being unreasonable. It was a feeling I remembered from when I was about fifteen years old, when I blundered into many similar arguments with my friends. I tried to convince them that Supertramp's 'The Logical Song' was the Greatest Song of All Time. My proclamations were met with embarassed silence or outright scorn. I was an outcast—a heretic. But my almost religious devotion to Supertramp allowed me to weather this isolation—my faith would sustain me.

This was the irrational love I felt for my new favourite song, 'Welcome to the Black Parade' by New Jersey five-piece My Chemical Romance. And this, I soon discovered is the love that My Chemical Romance's fans feel for the band and their music. It's how the band themselves would like to be loved, as singer Gerard Way once explained to his audience:

> *If for one minute you think you're better than a*
> *sixteen-year-old girl in a Green Day T-shirt, you are*
> *sorely mistaken. Remember the first time you went to a*
> *show and saw your favourite band. You wore their*
> *shirt and sang every word. You didn't know anything*
> *about scene politics, haircuts or what was cool. All you*
> *knew was that this music made you feel different from*
> *anyone you ever shared a locker with. Someone finally*
> *understood you. This is what music is about.*

This is one of the many Gerard Way quotes I began collecting around this time. I read every interview I could find. I listened to *The Black Parade* album over and over again, I studied the lyrics intently. I told people I was doing 'research'—but I wasn't fooling anyone. I was collecting pictures of the band and gluing them in my notebooks. I had crossed over to the other side.

I was entering the advanced stages of pop obsession. 'Gerard Way and I really do have a lot in common,' I thought to myself. This is actually true. The bands Way talks about in interviews, the singers he says changed his life, are all the same ones I like. Queen, Bruce Springsteen, The Cure, The Smiths, and David Bowie. I realised that all of these artists share something in common—a quality that is present in 'Born to Run', 'Heroes', 'How Soon is Now' and 'Welcome to the Black Parade'—but that I was hard pressed to say exactly what that was. I started making graphs and charts, looking for the missing link in all of this music. My notebooks started to accumulate more collaged fragments—Bowie, Bruce, and Morrissey shared space with Gerard and the band. I was preparing a case—a passionate defence of My Chemical Romance and their music—and I knew I would need evidence to back up my claims. But I was also trying to explain something to myself. I wanted to understand what it was in these songs that moved me so much, and where that something came from.

With my last book, I had attempted something similar. I had gone looking for the ideas that informed certain songs and albums of the last ten years, and had found them in the dimly lit corners of the twentieth-century avant-garde. I found Dada in Beck, Artaud in Gnarls Barkley, Walter Benjamin in The Scissor Sisters and Andre Breton in The Mars Volta. But I quickly realised that in this case, the twentieth century would be of no use to me. The ineffable something that connected the songs in my new lists could not be explained by any twentieth-century idea. So I took a leap back another hundred years—into the period bookended by the French Revolution in 1789 and the death of Friedrich Nietzsche in 1900. Here, I immediately found what I was looking for.

Self-expression, the rejection of institutions, individualism, questing spirituality, the desire to escape society, the strong identification with criminals and madmen, the divinity of sin, the tragic view of nature, ideal love, dying young, solitude, melancholy, medievalism and an unhealthy obsession with death. These were the ideas that connected the songs in my list to one another. But they're also, I learned, the ideals and characteristics of romanticism, the artistic and philosophical movement that dominated much of the nineteenth century. As I learned more about the romantics, I began to realise how widespread their influence in rock and roll really was. Every poem I read reminded me of a song lyric, every letter of an interview with a musician. The collaged portraits in my notebooks became festooned with spidery lines. I began to see how Bowie was linked to Byron, what Freddie Mercury owed to Friedrich Nietzsche, and what put the romance in My Chemical Romance. For years I'd been reading that a singer's looks are 'Byronic', that an album is 'Wagnerian', that the singer's philosophy is 'Nietzschean', that the song's mood is 'gothic' and that the band are hopelessly 'romantic'. Behind these words I had always sensed a story that was not being told—now I realised I had an opportunity to tell it. My speech in defence of 'Welcome to the Black Parade' had grown to the point where no-one would have time to listen to it all. I imagined myself calling up a radio request show:

> 'And what do you like about this song, Craig?'
> 'I'm glad you asked. See, about two hundred years
>   ago...'

2.

One of the hurdles I knew I would have to face in presenting my argument was the Emo Factor. My Chemical Romance is considered emo. And emo is not considered acceptable. In fact, if you're into indie rock and over the age of twenty-five, there are few things less cool on the planet than emo. It is, almost by definition, un-cool. Cool implies a certain amount of detachment, an ironic attitude to life, a refusal to show too much feeling, a preference for playing with signs and surfaces without becoming too attached to their meanings. Emo has no truck with cool. Emo is about private passion, and its success is judged on how much passion is produced and how nakedly it's exposed. Emo wants avalanches of feeling, tragic romances, explosive rage, bottomless self-pity and gordian knots of self-absorption. Its symbols are fire, blood, churning thunderstorms, endless oceans and cold, dark earth. What do these symbols represent? Emotions—my emotions, not yours. Emo is first person—and for most of the songs the first person is the only person. Politics does not exist, society barely registers. In emo, the singer's emotional world is the whole world—nothing else is as big, nothing else is as important.

Emo, I began to realise, is the most unashamedly romantic sub-culture in rock today. It represents the outer extreme of romanticism, its purest and most dangerous strain, the romanticism of Goethe's young Werther, of Frankenstein, of Byron and Nietzsche—a philosophy which rejects the idea of the greater good, which says that what is good is simply what's good for me. One of the extraordinary things about emo is the panic it's created in the media and society at large. It's been a long time since youth culture was this frightening to grown-ups. But behind the squawking over self-harm, 'suicidal messages' and school shootings is one, big dangerous idea—that emotions, my emotions, are the most important thing in the world, and the only justification I need for my actions, however extreme. Emo culture is a threat to society because it's irrational—and it knows this, which is why it looks a bit like goth. Emo, like goth, has a preference for horror imagery—hence the fondness for Nightmare Before Christmas merchandise and Misfits T-shirts. This too, I discovered, leads back to romanticism. The romantics' desire to escape from a de-valued, meaningless present frequently led them into the arms of the Gothic Revival, and the close kinship between these two early nineteenth-century ideas would eventually produce the founding work of the modern horror genre, Mary Shelley's *Frankenstein*. Shelley's monster represents many things—but chief among them is the threat of romanticism in society, the havoc that could result if a philosophy of feeling is followed to its conclusion. In Shelley's novel, the monster justifies his crimes by saying that he has been cast out of human society—why should he now be asked to obey its rules? This is exactly the threat implied by emo— that of a whole generation of kids so alienated from society that they no longer believe in society at all, and no longer care what happens to it. This, I've realised, is why people looked at me funny when I started speechifying about 'Welcome to the Black Parade'. They were scared.

The relationship between My Chemical Romance and emo is complex, to say the least. The simplest way to put it would be to say that the band's fans are, but that the band itself is not. Gerard Way has repeatedly insisted that this is the case, and I tend to agree with him—for reasons I hope to make clear in this book. Emo is characterised by a hopelessness that is not compatible with Gerard Way's ambition. He is not content—as most emo bands are—to stir powerful emotions in his audience. He wants, as he has stated many times, to make a difference. He's taken it upon himself to defend the rights of his community—more than that, to lead them in a pitched battle against the world that has rejected their ideals. My Chemical Romance's nineteenth-century military jackets are not just for show. They've taken the romantics' obsession with Napoleon to its logical conclusion, by forming a liberating army in the name of emotion, dreams and solitude, and fighting for your right to be alone at the party. 'The Black Parade' represents romanticism on the march.

3.

The fate of Gerard Way's quest to liberate the broken, the beaten and the damned forms one narrative that runs through the book, along with other strands following the adventures of Bowie, The Cure, and Weezer—whose career is crucial to the history of emo, and in many ways represents the polar opposite of My Chemical Romance's. But through it all, I've done my best to tell the story of the romantic movement in a fairly linear fashion—beginning with the last days of the Enlightenment and the formalism of Alexander Pope, moving through Rousseau, Goethe and Wordsworth and on to Byron, Keats, and Mary Shelley, then the Victorians—Matthew Arnold, the Pre-Raphaelites, and the late romanticism of Wagner, then Dostoyevsky, and finally, Nietzsche. I've then gone on to demonstrate how romantic ideas—Nietzsche's in particular—played themselves out in the early twentieth century, in Expressionist music, art and theatre.

I've made no attempt to be definitive, but I have sought to bring history to life and, hopefully, to build a bridge (or several) between the history of the romantic movement and history of rock and roll. In the process I've learned new ways to love my record collection, thanks to (who knew?) poetry and philosophy. Having returned from my travels in the nineteenth century I've found (as travellers always do) that the world I thought I knew looks slightly different—and mostly better. I've heard new ideas and relationships jumping out of the speakers, a new sense of the history that informs a song like 'Heroes' or 'Born to Run' or 'Bohemian Rhapsody', a new sense of excitement at the demands being made in an album like *Faith*, *The Queen Is Dead*, *Violator* or *Siamese Dream*. I've discovered why I was so moved by the song I heard on the radio that day—it is, in a sense, a song two hundred years in the making, and I was feeling the full force of those two centuries. I've realised that my irrational, unreasonable devotion to 'Welcome to the Black Parade' was an entirely reasonable response; given that the song is a demand for the unreasonable and the irrational. In the following pages, I've tried to explain why the singer's demands deserve our attention—in as reasonable and rational a manner as my subject matter will allow.

Gerard Way: 'Feel something!'

Emotional People

BECAUSE THEY'RE YOUNG, American and wear a lot of black; because they play melodic punk rock with their hearts on their sleeves; and because they're fond of eyeliner and introspection, My Chemical Romance is, in the eyes of the world, an emo band. In fact, last year in the UK, they became *the* emo band—the only one people over the age of thirty would be able to identify in a line-up. Gerard Way's face, covered in make-up, screaming into a microphone, or just looking moody and mysterious, stared out from the cover of thousands of music weeklies and tabloid rags. His lyrics were the subject of urgent debate, the band's Black Parade tour was a news story. But this newfound notoriety did not please My Chemical Romance one little bit. The band's press coverage was up, but the quality of that coverage had plummeted out of all proportion. Way and the band rolled into town ready to talk redemption and rock and roll—what they got was a barrage of questions about things that, to them, had nothing to do with My Chemical Romance: things like Marilyn Manson, Mexican homophobia, teen suicide and—worst of all—emo.[1]

'Emo', Gerard Way says, 'is a pile of shit'.[2] He's not the only one who feels that way. Not only is the sentiment echoed by thousands of punks, goths, and indie-rock fans, it's a conviction shared by most of the bands people think of as emo—members of Panic at the Disco, Fall Out Boy, The Get Up Kids, Saves the Day, Weezer, and Jimmy Eat World have all, at one time or another, declared that they want nothing to do with it. It seems to be one of those genres that's only useful to music journalists and record store owners, along with other much maligned terms such as trip-hop, new rave and electroclash. Unlike these, however, emo has proved surprisingly durable—the history of the genre is long, and its fans are passionate about it. Whatever else it might be, emo—like punk—is important enough for people to keep arguing about it.

Meanwhile, the sheer diversity of the music demonstrates just how unstable emo is as a concept. Sunny Day Real Estate's *Diary* sounds nothing like Weezer's *Pinkerton*, but both are emo landmarks. This diversity is the very reason why many insist that the term is useless. In the beginning emo referred to a very specific handful of Washington DC hardcore bands, beginning with Rites of Spring, who traded political rage for emotional angst and were thus labelled 'emo-core'. Now it seems any band whose singer is pale and pretty looking (or not) and sings about his feelings, accompanied by loud guitars (or not) is emo. Emo can sound like mall-punk, synth-pop, goth, glam, country, classic rock, or Morrissey fronting a hardcore band.

So it's impossible to work out whether My Chemical Romance is emo or not based on the sound of their music. Nor is it possible to peg them on the basis of their lineage. My Chemical Romance does occupy one of the outer branches of the emo family tree—they were supported early on by Geoff Rickley from Thursday, they've recorded a cover of David Bowie and Queen's 'Under Pressure' with The Used, and they've been touring and writing with James DeWees of the Get Up Kids. But by that logic both The Mars Volta and The Foo Fighters would also be emo—and nobody would argue that they are.

Surely at this point, say the critics, it's time to either find a more precise definition for this thing, or forget about it entirely. In 2008 Tonie Joy, whose band Moss Icon was one of the first to be described as emo, had this to say:

> Over the years it's been diluted and shifted so much,
> it's pretty inaccurate compared to what the term was
> first pinned to. I think Ian MacKaye summed it up best
> when the term was first coined…He just thought it
> was stupid, saying that any music that's real is
> emotional, whatever the genre.[3]

William Goldsmith, formerly of Sunny Day Real Estate, agrees:

Emo means emotional, right? Human emotions have been the driving force of all art since the beginning of the beginning. To say that ... emotionally driven music is a new thing ... it just doesn't make sense to me.[4]

Here, these two veterans of the scene have hit the nail on the head. When all the musical and genealogical arguments have been worn out, the only grounds for finding that My Chemical Romance is emo is that they're emotional artists who write emotional music. This they will admit to. 'We're all very sincere, emotional people', Way once told *Spin* magazine.[5] Way's lyrics come from feelings, and his goal is to make you feel those feelings too. 'Feel something. That's what we've always been fighting for,' said the singer in 2007.[6] But if that's your definition of emo, does that mean Kurt Cobain, Ian Curtis, Robert Smith, David Bowie, Bruce Springsteen, Mick Jagger, Richard Wagner and Beethoven are all emo too?

For the term emo to exist, and for it to last as long as it has, implies that there is some kind of music which is less emotional, or not emotional at all. This is exactly how emo began, as an alternative to staunchly un-emotional music. In the late 1980s, American hardcore bands were singing about society and the world, and the kids at their shows, while enjoying the power of the music and the feeling of community it created, were virtually screaming, 'Sing about my feelings!' Over the next ten years, the history of emo would be written by the bands that answered this silent prayer. Rites of Spring, Mineral, Texas is the Reason, Sunny Day Real Estate and Drive Like Jehu turned the steely gaze of hardcore inward, the ruthless critique of the world became a ruthless critique of oneself and one's feelings. This rebellion against punk orthodoxy from within is as old as punk itself.

Buzzcocks

In 1977 Manchester band the Buzzcocks released their first EP, *Spiral Scratch*. In punk's year zero it was the punkest thing you ever saw—recorded in a couple of hours using mostly first takes and one overdub, and released on the band's own label, using money borrowed from guitarist Pete Shelley's dad. On 'Boredom', singer Howard Devoto spat out his lyrics in a fake cockney accent at breakneck speed, pausing only to make room for Shelley's two-note guitar solo—a snot-nosed act of defiance toward prog-wankers and school music teachers alike. Music, *Spiral Scratch* seemed to say to its audience, is easy. All you need is a feeling and the will to express it. Blag a couple of quid off the old man, and you're away.

But, coming as early in punk's history as it did, *Spiral Scratch* already contained an argument against punk—or against what it was becoming. The noise coming out of London, engineered in no small part by Sex Pistols impresario Malcolm McLaren and happily parroted by the music press and the papers, suggested a musical movement rising up from the streets; kids from council estates seizing the means of production and transforming everyday life. The Sex Pistols illustrated this with three singles that seemed to map out the road to revolution:

1. *Discredit and destroy the existing political system.*
2. *Discredit and destroy the head of state.*
3. *Discredit and destroy rock and roll.*

By 1977 punk had a recognisable uniform, a mandate to critique the conditions of everyday life, and the momentum of a mass movement. But there was nothing in its charter about the importance of self-expression. With the possible exception of righteous rage, emotions were considered a luxury the punk singer could not afford to indulge in. And *love*, as Jon Savage notes in *England's Dreaming*, was the one topic punk bands (and punk critics) considered totally out of bounds. Love songs were stupid songs, chart songs, product. Love confined rock and roll to the teenage bedroom and the school dance. The love song was mere escapism; an easy way out. Punk, as Savage puts it, was 'determinedly *in* the world'.[1] Punk saw myriad injustices and humiliations wreaked on the world by conservatives and capitalists—all of these needed to be exposed. Of course you like love songs, punk says, they let you off the hook. *They* want you to like love songs—as long as you're obsessing over your feelings, you won't notice what's really going on.

But no amount of Marxist rhetoric or agit-prop sloganeering could convince teenagers, then or now, that their feelings are not important. This is the key to the success—and the continuing importance of—the Buzzcocks. Pete Shelley's songs are as punk as you like—fast, unpretentious and full of bile and snot. There're no clichés, no grandiose gestures, and very little ornament—but there's also none of the pious preaching or undergraduate politicking that characterises the work of agit-punk heroes like Tom Robinson Band or Sham 69. Shelley wrote about what he knew, his voice was the bitter voice of teenage experience. 'I just want a lover like any other,' he yelps on 1978's 'What Do I Get?':

> *For you things seem to turn out right*
> *If it could only happen to me instead!*
> *What do I get?*[2]

'You didn't have to be a political rebel or riotous anarchist to relate to Buzzcocks' lyrics,' writes Annie Zaleski in *Alternative Press*, 'being a bored, disgruntled teenager or introverted social misfit was good enough'.[3] Seventeen-year-old Robert Smith of Crawley was a little of both.

Robert Smith: The melancholy man should make the best use of his moods.

The Cure

ROBERT SMITH WAS galvanised by the energy of punk in 1976. But in the sprawling suburbs south of London where he lived, the call to riot in the streets seemed oddly useless. 'Living in Crawley you really didn't have to go out of your way to get beaten up,' says Smith. 'I couldn't really see the point in putting a safety pin through my nose.'[1] The fury of the Sex Pistols was a much-needed shot in the arm, but in the Buzzcocks' nervy love songs for loners, Smith heard something of more lasting value, something he could use. The Buzzcocks had sent a signal out into the suburbs saying it was okay to be a punk and sing about your feelings, and Smith was about to take unprecedented liberties with this idea.

Smith formed The Cure in 1976. The band released their first single 'Killing an Arab' two years later, and a debut album, *Three Imaginary Boys*, in 1979. The accompanying single 'Boys Don't Cry' had all the nervous adrenalin charge of punk, but the lyric was introspective and confessional. 'Boys Don't Cry' made perfect and immediate sense in the musical climate of 1979, and The Cure were regarded as promising.

Then—as far as the critics were concerned—they blew it. From a band that seemed to have such a perfect grasp of the post-punk pop song, The Cure's next single, 'A Forest', was a baffling move. The song hardly seemed to be a song at all, more like a ghostly moan over three minutes of bleak Euro-disco. Smith's sense of humour and irony—the 'oh well, don't worry about me'—tone that had made 'Boys Don't Cry' so charming, had seemingly vanished along with the girl he was chasing in the gloomy lyric of 'A Forest'. And given that the song had no discernable hook or chorus, the only thing that seemed left was the singer's unhappiness. The faint twinge of despair that added spice to 'Boys Don't Cry' had become the entire musical world of 'A Forest'.

Sadly, for those who still held out some hope for The Cure as the future of New Wave, 'A Forest' proved to be a sign of things to come. The Cure's second album, *Seventeen Seconds* was—like its single—a ghostly, impenetrable affair. Amazingly, it reached the Top 20 in the UK charts—but neither this, nor the critics' griping had much of an effect on Smith. From this point on, Smith's main goal was not to have hits or get good reviews, but to describe emotions.

Over the course of three increasingly troubled records— *Seventeen Seconds*, *Faith* and *Pornography*—Smith would document his failing relationships and secret fears with unflinching honesty. These albums form one of the most important—and most misunderstood—bodies of work in the history of rock. They were hard to understand at the time of their release precisely because they were so personal, so singular, so much the product of one man's inner turmoil. There are musical reference points in early eighties Cure—Joy Division, Bowie, Eno, psychedelic rock—but in the end, Smith's most important influence seems to have been despair, of which he became an avid student. When Smith felt despair creeping up on him, he didn't do what the rest of us do— shrug it off, think positive thoughts, and try not to make too big a deal about it—instead he grabbed despair by the scruff of the neck and looked right into its pitch-black eyes. 'I was letting myself slip in order to write those songs,' he later recalled. 'I wasn't fighting it, whereas in everyday life you have to fight those feelings.'[2]

But the process of extracting and recording all this inner pain would take its toll, not just on Smith, but on the whole band. Recording an album like *Faith* was one thing, spending the next twelve months playing it in front of audiences was something else. Smith later admitted that *Faith* was the one record they shouldn't have toured with at that point.[3] But they did, and as a result, Smith's gloom became self-perpetuating. By the time The Cure came to record *Pornography*, the singer was in the grip of a deep depression, further exacerbated by drugs and lack of sleep. *Pornography* opens with Smith howling, 'It doesn't matter if we all die'. Then it gets worse.

Realising that he was driving the band into the ground and himself into an early grave, Smith called a halt in 1982, effectively declaring The Cure dead. He spent some time playing guitar on a Siouxsie and the Banshees tour. 'Fat Boy just does what he's told,' Siouxsie explained at the time.[4] This was fine with Fat Boy, who was enjoying the feeling of playing music in which he had no particular emotional investment. Learning from this experience he began, in 1982, to write songs again—but of a very different kind from the ones on *Pornography*. Instead of recording his inner turmoil, he tried writing songs around themes—as though he were setting himself an assignment rather than writing a confession. Previously he'd aimed for authenticity, emotional sincerity; now he was trying to write a song that worked. He came up with a tune, gave it a solid, catchy beat, and loaded up the chorus with slinky 'doo doo doo doo's. He had a feeling 'Let's Go to Bed' would get played on the radio, and it did. He wrote another one called 'The Walk', and his mum told him, for the first time ever, that she liked it.[5] Neither song had anything near the level of emotional honesty of those on *Faith* or *Pornography*. But Smith was done, for the time being, with ripping his guts out for his art. Form, not feeling, had become his goal.

Rivers Cuomo: No feeling, no emotion.

Weezer

WRITING ABOUT EMOTIONS is hard—it demands a level of self-absorption that even the most well-balanced individual would find it difficult to maintain. And of course, it's never the well-balanced individual who decides to pick up a guitar and pour the contents of his diary into a microphone—only a real lunatic would do that. So what's the alternative? Well, you could write about social life or politics or the state of your neighbourhood. But what if you don't care about any of that stuff? Is it possible to write a song that's just...a song?

In 1983, Robert Smith proved you could; and in 1997, Weezer singer Rivers Cuomo—similarly exhausted by the effort of emotional music—decided to give it a go. He'd always written songs about himself, now he decided to see if he couldn't write a song about something that had never happened to him. Cuomo assembled a set of tried-and-true mythological images and set about describing them with words and music. He wrote a song about catching his sweetheart 'out in the eve, deep in the shady glen' in the arms of another man. The results surprised him. He'd always assumed great songs came directly from strong feelings triggered by personal experiences. But even though he'd never been in or near a shady glen, and the things in the song were entirely made up, the song still sounded great.[1]

To have discovered a method of songwriting by which he revealed nothing of himself was a huge relief for Cuomo. Not long before this, Weezer had released its second album, *Pinkerton*, in which Cuomo laid his heart completely bare. He'd spared nothing of himself—all his insecurities, his childhood anxieties, his sexual fantasies and his darkest thoughts went down on the tape. It was an extraordinarily brave thing to do, and it earned him, for his trouble, a pile of scathing reviews and a place in *Rolling Stone*'s list of the Worst Albums of 1996.[2]

These days, *Pinkerton* is rightly seen as a classic—many believe it's Weezer's finest hour. But it's not impossible, listening to it today, to hear the reasons why it was so badly received in its day. Pinkerton is, in a word, embarrassing. It's embarrassing in the way that an unnecessarily maudlin twenty-first birthday speech can be, embarrassing in a reading-your-old-high-school-diary kind of way. It's the kind of embarrassment we feel for someone when they're over-sharing.

Cuomo himself was not blind to this possibility. He'd first begun to experiment with this type of confessional songwriting in 1992, inspired by the example of New Radicals frontman, Gregg Alexander. In February of that year, he'd set about recording a cover of one of Alexander's songs 'The World We Love so Much'. He didn't want the guys in his band to hear it—he didn't want *anyone* to hear it. He didn't even hit record until he'd covered the walls of the room he was subletting with acoustic foam—not to enhance the sound quality, but to make absolutely sure no-one could hear him while he was 'emoting'.[3]

But the events of the following year made Cuomo bolder. The success of Weezer's insanely catchy—but surprisingly personal—debut album had given him reason to believe that there might be some level of interest out there in his emotions. So he decided to give them more emotions. Lots more. As a songwriter, he went into confessional mode—and he had plenty to confess.

Cuomo was deeply uncomfortable with his newfound rock-star status. 'He hated himself for achieving it,' said music journalist Andy Greenwald, 'and he hated himself for loving it.'[4] Stardom only increased his isolation and magnified the problems in his life, problems which went right back to his childhood. Rivers and his brother, Leaves, were raised on an ashram, an experience which left them totally unprepared for the brutal world of high school in America. The Cuomo brothers got the crap beaten out of them. But worse than that, they were outcasts, unable to connect with all the nice normal kids with their nice normal lives. No wonder, he thinks, he turned out weird. No wonder he can't communicate with people, except in the highly controlled form of songs like the one he's singing now. In 'Across the Sea' Cuomo dumps the blame for all of this squarely at his mother's feet. Then, disgusted by his own self-pity, and the entire song itself up to this point, he exclaims, 'goddamn, this business is really lame!'.

This was more or less the mainstream music press's reaction to *Pinkerton*. *Rolling Stone* magazine, and the vast majority of the people who'd bought and loved the *Blue Album*, weren't ready for this kind of thing at all. Where were all the catchy little pop songs? Why is he screaming like that? The record-buying public stayed away in droves, reviewers were unkind, and Cuomo went into retreat.

After we put out the first record, it seemed like a lot of the fans were really interested in me and were encouraging me to expose myself more, so that's what I did on the second record, and everybody hated it. I was really embarrassed.[5]

Pinkerton wasn't a disaster—it was an acquired taste. Grown-up rock journals like *Rolling Stone* felt let down by Cuomo's failure to deliver on the promise of a bubblegum rock revival, and dismissed the album as morbid and self-indulgent. But younger fans loved it for exactly the same reasons. At this point, a parallel universe was created. In the world we know, grunge rose and fell, and rock-rap begat nu-metal. Meanwhile, in the other dimension, *Pinkerton*, not *Nevermind*, was the greatest album of the '90s, and emo began its crucial second phase.

While the cult of *Pinkerton* was getting underway, Cuomo had begun writing non-autobiographical songs like 'Lover in the Snow', and judging their success not on their emotional authenticity, but on their formal qualities. Like Robert Smith (and for similar reasons) he was moving decisively away from emo toward what can only be described as 'formo'. Toward the end of the '90s, he began a study of rock structure in the form of his 'Encyclopedia of Pop', a ring binder full of hand-drawn charts in which Cuomo recorded the characteristics of hit songs by Green Day, Nirvana, Oasis and many other bands in an attempt to pinpoint the traits they share in common. This list has provided him with a set of models for songwriting, which he has been implementing ever since. The songs on the *Green Album*, he proudly told *Rolling Stone*'s Chris Mundy in 2001, contain 'no feeling, no emotion', just music.[6] Cuomo was not being entirely honest—'Hash Pipe' and 'Island in the Sun' are emotional enough. But he was making the point that he would happily sacrifice feeling for form. This new direction irritated *Pinkerton* fans as surely as *Pinkerton* itself had annoyed the critics. One fan, writing as 'whatawierdo' on Songmeanings.com, said:

> I think Rivers has traded his personal touch of neurotic and clever songs for more standard, less emotional songs.[7]

Diehard fans gritted their teeth and put up with the 'horrible pop songs'[8], scouring the albums for the rare flashes of Cuomo's old confessional mode that still showed up here and there. By the time of 2005's *Make Believe*, those who'd been seduced by *Pinkerton*'s emotional authenticity had had enough of Cuomo's songs about nothin'. *Pitchfork*'s reviewer wrote:

> *Pinkerton triumphed by being an uncomfortably*
> *honest self-portrait of Cuomo. On* Make Believe, *his*
> *personality has vanished beneath layers of self-imposed*
> *universality, writing non-specific power ballads like he*
> *apprenticed with Diane Warren, and whoah-oh-ohing*
> *a whole lot in lieu of coming up with coherent or*
> *interesting thoughts.*[9]

Cuomo would probably have taken the Diane Warren comparison as a compliment. The author of dozens of monster middle-of-the-road hits in the '80s and '90s, Warren's CV includes Starship's 'Nothing's Gonna Stop Us Now' and Chicago's 'Look Away', as well as co-writing credits with Bon Jovi and Cuomo's beloved Cheap Trick. The 'universality' and 'non-specificity' the pitchfork reviewer complains about on *Make Believe* is the key to the success of Warren's mega-hits. They're songs that (in theory) always work for everyone, because their structure is tried and true. That's why Diane Warren is a hit-maker. Hit-makers don't sit around waiting for painful personal experiences to happen to them—they sit down at the word processor and write hits according to the rules of hit-writing.

By compiling his 'Encyclopedia of Pop' Rivers Cuomo was learning these rules for himself. Pretty soon, he was rhyming 'lady' with 'maybe' and telling his girl that 'you're the air that I breathe'. He sang this stuff on stage in front of a huge glowing 'W' and played solos like he was in Van Halen. He left emo in the dust, and embraced its opposite—classic rock. He'd proved it was possible to write powerful music whose goal was something other than the sharing of feelings. But in the process, he'd demonstrated that the modern indie rock singer does so at his peril.

The Classics

THE KILLERS' DEBUT album *Hot Fu*ss is full of lyrics about nothing. What is 'Somebody Told Me' about? Who cares? The important thing is that the chorus contains the words 'boyfriend' and 'girlfriend'. These are words that sound good in the choruses of new-wave rock songs, and Brandon Flowers has fifty years of pop history on his side as he yelps them out over the song's skipping beat and buzzing synths. What about 'All these things that I've done'? The glorious sing-along refrain, 'I've got soul but I'm just a soldier', works like a charm. But as comedian Bill Bailey has pointed out, Flowers might as well be singing, 'I've got ham but I'm not a hamster'. By the time it came to record the Killers' second album, Flowers was feeling guilty about having got away with these powerful, but un-emotional lyrics. He made amends by getting his diary out and writing an album about his childhood.

Formalism in rock makes us uncomfortable. We're just as suspicious of Rivers Cuomo reducing rock to a series of lists and graphs as we are with the idea of songs being made-to-order by Diane Warren, or with Brandon Flowers writing lyrics by choosing words that sound good over music. Robert Smith was faintly disgusted with *himself* after he wrote 'Let's Go to Bed'. The song did the trick, but Smith felt like he'd got away with something, not like he'd made a great work of art. That's because in rock and roll, especially indie rock and roll, artists, critics and fans alike place an enormous premium on emotional authenticity. When an album is good, we say it's 'inspired', 'sincere', 'unflinchingly honest' or 'deeply personal'. If it misses the mark, it's 'formulaic', 'soulless' or 'unoriginal'.

The idea of art or music as a form of self-expression is virtually taken for granted today. It's the artist's ultimate authority—'I wrote it that way because that's how I felt,' says the artist. And this is no less than we expect of the artist—

authentic self-expression, in defiance of fashion, sensible advice or the dictates of the marketplace. We accept the idea that music might have other goals—social commentary, political protest, making you dance, getting the singer laid. But in every case, what we're mostly interested in is the artist's feeling for these things. Emo is just an extreme and uncompromising variation on a theme which is universally accepted. From the rarefied air of *The Wire* magazine (where an almost unlistenable album will be lauded for the artist's refusal to compromise his vision), to the set of *American Idol* (where week in, week out, the judges advise the contestants to 'be yourself'), the mantra is the same. Authentic self-expression = good art. What we look for in music is passion, because passion, we feel, makes good poetry.

This wasn't always the case. In eighteenth-century London, for example, nobody took much of an interest in poets' feelings, or how sincerely they were expressed. Back then, nobody would have cared very much about Robert Smith's depression, Gerard Way's rage, Rivers Cuomo's angst or Brandon Flowers' diary. In fact, most of the artists whose lyric sheets we pore over today would have been chased out of the coffee house for having too *many* feelings, for devoting too many stanzas to their emotions while forgetting all about the things that *really* make for quality poetry—a sense of balance and symmetry, a sound grasp of metrical composition, and the advancement of a useful moral theme or accurate social observation. Not to understand these things was, in eighteenth-century literary circles, as disastrous for one's career as to be seen about town in a poorly powdered wig.

In the pursuit of this ideal, the poet's emotions could be of no particular use—in fact they were most likely to get in the way. What was needed to write great poetry was not passion, but careful study of the classics. Alexander Pope was a master in this regard—he studied Horace to the point where he could imitate his style perfectly. He became famous, and it became the ambition of all young poets to imitate Pope's imitation.[1] And this was not impossible, since Pope took care to set out the rules of poetry he'd derived (and refined) from Horace in his *Essay on Criticism*. He even made them rhyme. Here, a poet could learn, if not how to write a great poem, at least how to avoid writing a bad one. These rules were more discussed than actually followed. 'No great writer,' literary historian Richard Barnard points out, 'allowed himself to be imprisoned in neo-classical theory.'[2] And yet the fact that this theory existed and was seriously discussed offers a glimpse of an artistic climate completely different to our own, one where order and stability were the qualities most admired in a work of art, and originality—far from being the poet's goal—was something best avoided, since it meant you were more likely to screw things up.

The good thing about formalism is that it usually works, but often that's about the nicest thing you can say about it. 'The classic,' wrote Walter Pater in his *Essay on Style*, 'comes to us out of the cool quiet of other times: as the measure of what a long experience has shown us will at least never displease us'.[3] In certain periods of history, Pater says, the classics assert themselves—and this is what happened in Europe in the eighteenth century. But eventually, there will be—there has to be—a reaction to this insistence on order and symmetry. A demand for the wild, the quaint, the passionate, and the unreasonable will make itself felt. The pendulum will swing back. Rules will be broken, books thrown aside.

Troublemaker

THE UN-EMOTIONAL, CLASSICAL phase that Rivers Cuomo had entered with 'Lover in the Snow' began winding down during the recording of 2005's *Make Believe*. But the real change came with the release of a compilation of his home demo recordings three years later. In collecting the material for this album, Cuomo went through tapes dating back to the very earliest days of Weezer. He listened, mesmerised, to the Rivers of fifteen years ago emoting in his carefully soundproofed isolation on 'The World We Love so Much'. He heard again the painful whimpering at the start of 'Crazy One', and the demo tapes of his wildly ambitious—and ultimately abandoned—space opera, 'The Black Hole'. He began to speak approvingly of *Pinkerton* for the first time since its traumatic birth.[1] When Weezer finally released their new album later that same year, it quickly became apparent that something had been fundamentally altered in the singer's approach to his art. *The Red Album*'s opening song, 'Troublemaker', is a manifesto for this new direction, in which Cuomo finally throws out the 'Encyclopedia of Pop', and asserts the value of originality and sincere personal expression. The singer insists that he is an original man with original thoughts. So instead of looking at books, he's looking inside himself:

Who needs stupid books?
They are for petty crooks
I will learn by studying the lessons of my dreams [2]

Dreams crop up again on *The Red Album*, on a song Cuomo describes as 'a big symphonic art-type number', 'Dreamin''. The tug of war between emo and formo in Rivers' soul meant the song very nearly didn't make it onto the album. He wrote it, and then somehow lost his nerve. He scrapped it, and started working on a reassuringly classic-sounding verse-chorus-verse type song that became 'This is the Way', which the band, and the record company loved immediately. But by the time Weezer started recording the album, Cuomo was feeling adventurous again. He argued passionately for 'Dreamin'' to be included and 'This is the Way' to be left on the shelf.[3]

'Dreamin'' is an ambitious ode to imagination and reverie, in which Cuomo expands on the idea contained in those lines from 'Troublemaker'. All his life, the singer explains, people have been trying to tell him there are rules. You have to go to school, you have to get a job, you have to learn to be responsible. And all his life, the singer has known in some profound way that this is a crock. How does he know? He just knows. 'Normal' life—school, job, etc, terrifies him to his soul. But when he's absorbed in his own imagination, he feels at home:

Dreamin' in the morning
Dreamin' all through the night
and when I'm dreamin' I know that it's all right[4]

The song moves through several different movements that illustrate the dreamer's different moods. At the beginning, when he's just staring out the window, the backing has a dreamy '50s' teen-pop feel to it. When the singer starts asserting his right to do what he likes and stops doing his homework, the guitars crank up a notch and the music takes a more defiant stance. Then, in the middle section, the city and its suburbs, the school, the freeways, disappear entirely. Cuomo leaps through a slightly hilarious *Sound of Music* soundscape, with choirs of angels echoing over the hills and taped birdsong twittering in the background. Here, the world of custom and convention seems far away—there are no teachers, no grown-ups, no cops and no record companies. As his voice rings out over the landscape, he starts to wonder if the natural world isn't somehow connected with the source of his own creativity. He feels cramped and constrained by human society, with its rules and regulations. People are always telling him to 'get with the program'. Out here, it quickly becomes obvious that there is no program, and the singer's imagination finally has space to roam. He throws away his schoolbooks and his 'Encyclopedia of Pop', and starts listening to the birds and the bees.

Wordsworth: Books! 'Tis dull and endless strife!

Wordsworth

THE SWING AWAY from classicism in eighteenth-century England began during Pope's lifetime, as the classical poetry of the day was supplemented by a growing interest in popular ballads of the Middle Ages. The authors of these unruly old poems were mostly unknown, and the verses themselves had changed many times over the centuries as different singers picked them up and adapted them to their purposes. They were rarely written down, mostly because they were considered too rough and bawdy to be proper literature—ballads were not for polite company, and they found no place in the eighteenth-century salons. The ballad's humble birth and lusty swagger landed it on the wrong side of the line dividing the Classical from its uncouth opposite, the Romantic. This made it the perfect vehicle for the poet who would knock the wig-wearers off their perch in the nineteenth century—a man who had no time for classicists or cafes. He announced his arrival in 1798 with a book of Ballads.

In William Wordsworth's 'Expostulation and Reply', we find the poet by the side of the road, sitting on a rock, staring into space. A wandering classicist stops to lecture him: shouldn't he be re-reading Horace or refining his couplets?

'Why, William, on that old grey stone,
Thus for the length of half a day,
Why, William, sit you thus alone,
And dream your time away?

'Where are your books? that light bequeath'd
To beings else forlorn and blind!
Up! Up! and drink the spirit breath'd
From dead men to their kind.'[1]

The man with the walking-stick wants Wordsworth to stop rambling about the countryside and get back to work. But what he doesn't realise is that Wordsworth *is* at work—the forest is his office and the lake is his library. He doesn't need the 'spirit breath'd from dead men to their kind', because he's chosen to learn from the living. In the poem's sequel, 'The Tables Turned,' he puts forward his case:

Books! 'tis dull and endless strife,
Come, here the woodland linnet,
How sweet his music; on my life
There's more of wisdom in it.
And hark! how blithe the throstle sings!
And he is no mean preacher;
Come forth into the light of things,
Let Nature be your teacher.[2]

These two poems first appeared in a book called the *Lyrical Ballads*, published as a joint venture with Wordsworth's friend Samuel Taylor Coleridge in 1798. This little book would change English poetry forever, and the after-effects of its discoveries would be felt all over the English-speaking world. But the poet's original intentions were humble enough. The previous year, Wordsworth and his sister, Dorothy, had moved to Alfoxden, overlooking the Bristol Channel. Here,

Dorothy had begun to keep a journal describing the sights and sounds of the countryside, and Wordsworth began some poems with the intention of doing the same thing in verse.

As he worked on these, it became increasingly clear to Wordsworth that the eighteenth-century's rules for good poetry would be of no use to him whatsoever. Imitating Pope imitating Horace might help you make a big splash at the coffee house but out in the countryside, miles away from London and its whirlwind social life, different standards prevailed. It made no sense to describe the lives of tramps and cottage girls in the language of Pope and Dryden—who talks like that? Not the tramps and the little girls, that's for sure. But classicism was equally useless for the task of describing Wordsworth's impressions of nature, the ecstatic sense he had of a great spirit moving through all creation. How could he take a feeling like that and chop it up into pieces to make it fit some prefab idea of classical proportion?

So while all the other poets of the day were knocking themselves out trying to nail their poetic diction and get their heroic couplets down pat, Wordsworth was working just as hard to remove every trace of eighteenth-century classicism from his work. That's why he spent all his time sitting on a rock and not at the library. All he would learn from books is how to write like poets who came before him, and Wordsworth had decided that their language, as good as it had been in its day, was of no use to him. He was determined, as he says in 'The Tables Turned', to learn from nature.

Civilisation

WORDSWORTH'S REJECTION OF culture in favour of nature doesn't seem that remarkable today. But in the century he was born into, it would have been considered deeply weird. In the eighteenth century, it was taken for granted that modern civilisation had improved and refined nature in every way. The spirit of the age was extraordinarily optimistic. On the 3 July 1750 Louis XVI's minister Jacques Turgot had told his audience at the Sorbonne that the world was getting better, and that if things seemed less than perfect now, it was simply because human civilisation had some growing up to do:

> ... the whole human species, looked at from its origins, appears to the philosopher as an immense whole, which, like an individual, has its infancy and its progress... The totality of humanity, fluctuating between calm and agitation, between good times and bad, moves steadily though slowly towards a greater perfection.[1]

Turgot's theme was a popular one during the eighteenth century, a period of time referred to by historians as The Age of Reason or the Enlightenment. The era was dominated by an enthusiasm for the discoveries of science and a belief that the power of rational thought would transform every area of human life. The thinkers of the Enlightenment didn't claim to know everything. But they maintained, by and large, that everything could be known. Whatever problems mankind faced now, they reasoned, would be solved in the future by fearless rational investigation. At least, that was the idea.

In 1749, philosopher and writer Jean-Jacques Rousseau, a native of the city of Geneva, read a notice in the *Mercure de France*, announcing an essay-writing competition on the topic: 'Has the restoration of the arts and sciences had a purifying effect on morals'. Rousseau pondered this, and soon found that his head was swimming with a thousand ideas. He felt faint. When he'd collected himself, he sat down and wrote twelve thousand words to the effect that, No, the restoration of the arts and sciences had not had a purifying effect on morals. Progress, Rousseau argued, was not improving society—it was making things worse.

Rousseau began his essay by pointing out that if the arts and sciences were improving morals, then France, which was supposed to have the best art and the cleverest scientists in the world at that point, ought to be the most moral place on the face of the earth. This, Rousseau insisted, despite appearances, was not the case:

> *There prevails in modern manners a servile and*
> *deceptive conformity ... politeness requires this thing;*
> *decorum that; ceremony has its forms, and fashion its*
> *laws, and these we must always follow, never the*
> *promptings of our own nature.*[2]

In the pages that followed, Rousseau offered a scathing critique of his supposedly 'improving' century. Where others saw the peak of civilisation and refinement, Rousseau saw only phoney manners held up to disguise a disturbing lack of real human feeling. But Rousseau also hinted, as in the passage above, at a 'true' human nature which had somehow been left behind or forgotten. He took up this theme in his next crack at the Dijon Academy's essay-writing prize; this time the given topic was 'What is the origin of inequality among men, and is it authorised by natural law?'. In this, his *Second Discourse*, Rousseau sized up the eighteenth-century man and tried to figure out what, in all his behaviour, is most 'natural'. This, he admitted, was tricky. Human beings had by this point been so altered by the societies they had evolved, that they barely resembled their ancestors. But Rousseau believed that he had discovered, lurking beneath the surface of these modern people, two 'natural' inclinations. These were not arrived at by reason, like our tacked-on modern philosophies, but came as standard with the human soul, part of our original design. One is an interest in our own welfare, the other is the feeling of repugnance at the sight of another's suffering.

But on top of this original design, Rousseau says, we have acquired a caked-on crust of false standards, all of which have their basis in our need to acquire privilege and distinction. This is in turn a result of the fact that human beings have, over the centuries, been coming together in greater numbers and living in closer proximity to one another. Now, instead of living naturally, the social man lives 'for others'. This is the case, not only for those on the lower rungs of society—who have to make their way in the world under systems designed for the benefit of the rich and powerful—but also for the privileged few, who judge their worth purely in terms of the power they command over others. From this artificial way of life has come all our law, and the hierarchies of our society. None of it, Rousseau concludes, has any basis in natural law.

Here was a resounding 'no' to the essay question posed—and something more. The *Second Discourse* contains Rousseau's most convincing, and most dangerous idea: that the furniture of eighteenth-century life—royalty, serfdom and myriad class distinctions in between—were not fixed, but moveable. Rousseau died in 1778. Eleven years later, the furniture of France would be thrown out the window.

The French Revolution

IN HIS INTOXICATING account of the French Revolution, historian Thomas Carlyle conjures a vivid picture of the forging of France's new constitution, 'amid glitter of illuminated streets and Champs-Elysees, and crackle of fireworks and glad deray'. Carlyle describes:

Twelve Hundred human individuals, with the Gospel of Jean-Jacques Rousseau in their pocket, congregating

in the name of Twenty-five Millions, with full assurance
of faith, to 'make the Constitution': such sight, the
acme and main product of the Eighteenth Century, our
World can witness once only. For Time is rich in
wonders, in monstrosities most rich; and is observed
never to repeat himself, or any of his Gospels:—surely
least of all, this Gospel according to Jean-Jacques.[1]

All sorts of factors were at work in the years leading up to 1789, and in any accurate account of the Revolution's causes, Rousseau's books would have to get in line behind such heavyweights as France's escalating financial crisis, the simmering resentment of the peasantry, the War of Independence in America, and a series of mini-revolutions in other parts of Europe. But there can be no doubt that Rousseau's name was associated with the Revolution from the moment it took place. Whether the actions of the revolutionaries themselves were inspired by his (very popular) books is almost beside the point. The Revolution seemed to put his ideas into practice—right from the start, hereditary privilege and serfdom were abolished, freedom and equality were the slogans. The new constitution's first clause, 'Men are born, and always continue, free and equal in respect of their rights', echoed Rousseau's famous statement in *The Social Contract*, 'Man is born free; and everywhere he is in chains'.[2]

The Revolution, as Victorian critic Matthew Arnold has observed, 'seemed to ask of a thing, "is it rational?"'.[3] In other words it was heralded as the culmination of all the hopes of the Enlightenment. For over a hundred years, philosophers and other thinkers had been talking about a society built on rational principles—now, it seemed, this society was being born. It's impossible to overestimate the optimism with which this was greeted among freedom-loving artists and intellectuals.

Bliss was it in that dawn to be alive,
But to be young was very heaven...

wrote Wordsworth, thinking back on the Revolution's early days, when anything seemed possible. The poet was in Paris for the first anniversary of the storming of the Bastille. He saw, at first hand, the 'fireworks and glad deray' Carlyle described. Then, two years later, in the winter of 1791, he was back. This time, he fell in love—twice—once with a girl named Annette Vallon, and once with the Republican cause. His political enthusiasm, as his biographer, Roger Sharrock, points out, was mingled in his mind with the natural beauty of the landscape he'd seen on his first visit. For Wordsworth the grandeur of nature seemed to point toward the dignity of man in his natural state. The essential rightness of democracy was indicated by the very ground he was standing on and the sky above his head.[4]

All of this was brought to a premature halt when Wordsworth's money ran out in 1792, and he was forced to return to England. There, he soon found that his deeply felt republican sympathies had made him a traitor to his own country, as the Pitt government declared war on France in February of the following year. Wordsworth cheered when he heard that English troops had been massacred by the French— and hated himself for it.

There were further shocks in store for the lover of freedom and democracy. By this time, France's monarchy had been abolished, and the king himself had been executed. Democracy it seemed was within sight. But the newly reborn nation was in a state of chaos, at war with almost every country in Europe while simultaneously being torn apart by civil strife, hunger and confusion. 'There was no room', as Rupert Christiansen puts it in his book *Romantic Affinities*, 'for the democracy that allows dissent.'[5] France's future was effectively placed in the hands of Maximilien de Robespierre, the most influential member of The Committee of Public Safety, and a staunch follower of the gospel according to Jean-Jacques. Robespierre had learned from Rousseau's *The Social Contract* that power came not from kings or governments, but from the will of the people. This, as philosopher and historian Bertrand Russell points out, is a much-misunderstood idea in Rousseau. In practice, it tends to mean that power-hungry individuals, or those with an axe to grind, can claim—by some mystic association—to 'represent' this will of the people, without having to go through all the fuss and bother of ballots and elections.

Robespierre was certainly one of these. The people, he maintained, were virtuous, but their virtuous new republic was under threat from aristocrats and royalists—leftovers from the bad old days. Robespierre prescribed a Reign of Terror—a necessary stage in which these counter-revolutionaries, and anyone else who stood in the way of freedom, would be rounded up and disposed of so that France could get on with the business of creating a new society. Robespierre's courts and police were kept very busy. The guillotines worked overtime, and seventeen thousand enemies of freedom were executed in the space of fourteen months.[6]

Persecution and mass-killings were nothing new in Europe—but this was something else. Crusades, witch-hunts, pogroms and inquisitions had always been carried out in the name of religion, or authorised by despotic kings; here was slaughter carried out in the name of natural virtue, the will of the people made manifest. Rousseau had always seemed to say (though this is not exactly what he meant) that if you made people free, they would be good and just. But this, it now seemed, was untrue. For many, the brightest hopes of the Enlightenment, the dream of freedom, equality and brotherhood, died sometime in 1793.

William Wordsworth, for one, was deeply confused. For him, as for all those who 'had fed their childhood upon dreams', the Revolution had promised nothing less than heaven on earth:

> *... O times,*
> *in which the meagre, stale, forbidding ways*
> *of custom, law and statute took at once*
> *the attraction of a country in Romance;*
> *when reason seemed the most to assert her rights ...* [7]

Now his faith in this vision was being sorely tested. For a while he clung to the idea that the Terror was simply a necessary means to an end, that true freedom and democracy could only be achieved after a difficult, but necessary, clampdown on freedom and democracy. When he realised how untenable this position was, he turned to the political philosophy of William Godwin, who advocated Universal Reason as mankind's brightest hope. In his much-read and discussed 'Enquiry Concerning Political Justice', Godwin argued that reason should be given priority over all other considerations in life, including law, social convention and family ties. What this meant in practice was, as Godwin illustrated in a famous example, that if you could save only your mother or the world's greatest philosopher from a burning building, you really ought to save the philosopher—reason says he will be of more use to the human race in the long run. Despite his initial enthusiasm, Wordsworth soon found he was incapable of being a good Godwinian. He just couldn't quite let go of his emotions—though it wasn't for lack of trying:

> *Thus strangely did I war against myself;*
> *A bigot to a new idolatry*
> *Did like a monk who hath forsworn the world*
> *Zealously labour to cut off my heart*
> *From all the sources of her former strength;* [8]

In his autobiographical poem, *The Prelude*, Wordsworth explains that the story of his life up to this point had been—

like that of the century he was born into—a story about things getting better:

> This history, my friend, hath chiefly told
> Of intellectual power, from stage to stage
> Advancing, hand in hand with love and joy,
> And of imagination teaching truth.⁹

But the Revolution and the Terror had knocked him badly off course. He'd found his youthful idealism diverted toward a cause that made him an apologist for murder. Then, searching for an alternative, he'd embraced a philosophy that required of him that he cut out his heart. This he knew he could not do. Irrational though it might be, the young poet had a feeling his heart would come in useful later on—and he was right.

Conor Oberst: 'A special moment governed more by intuition than intellect'.

The Story is in the Soil

Lifted or The Story is in the Soil, Keep Your Ear to the Ground is plainly too long for the name of an album—but Bright Eyes' Conor Oberst will always happily sacrifice tidy form to the expression of powerful feelings. In the album's first song, 'The Big Picture', we find the singer riding in the back of the tour van while the driver and the guy in the passenger seat argue jokingly about where this place they're looking for is supposed to be. Something about this conversation gives the singer an idea. He pulls out his guitar and starts picking out some chords, letting the words come as the music builds up a head of steam. It doesn't rhyme properly in places, and some of the words are crammed a little awkwardly into the metre—but the feeling is real, and it's the feeling, not some pre-conceived idea of 'good songwriting' that Oberst follows in bringing this tune to completion. 'The Big Picture' goes on for another six and a half minutes— bringing the whole to a total of eight minutes and forty-seven seconds. Too long, you might say, for a melancholy dirge banged out in the back of the tour bus. But to Oberst in 2004 criticism of this kind meant nothing. 'There's a point where they feel complete, and that's where I stop', he said of his songs. 'Maybe for some listeners they felt complete four minutes ago—they can fade it out.'[1]

Oberst is a student of nature, so he's not interested in rules or traditions. He might sound philosophical in 2005's 'I Believe in Symmetry', but really he's expressing a wish to be rid once and for all of philosophy—and all the other stuff they teach you at school. Has any of it, Oberst asks himself, made me happier?

An argument for consciousness
The instinct of the blind insect
Who makes love to a flower bed
And dies in the first freeze

'I want to know such simple things,' says the singer, 'no politics, no history.'[2] But ridding yourself of five centuries of tradition is not as easy as all that—politics is everywhere, and history keeps screaming in his ear. In 'Road to Joy', recorded the same year, Oberst decides to scream back. The song is a portrait of a young man with a sensitive heart and a head full of noise trying to get his thoughts down before it's too late:

So now I'm drinking, breathing, writing, singing.
Every day I'm on the clock.
My mind races with all my longings.
But I can't keep up with what I got.[3]

What he's got is a feeling, not just for himself, but for the whole country, the whole human race. Now, politics has become personal for the singer, and he's turned into a sort of emotional news anchor, reporting on the state of his world as it relates to President Bush's War on Terror. Everything is involved—his parents, his girlfriend, the flowers in the driveway, the dead bodies in the cemetery, everything hums to the tune of his anxious ballad. Oberst has what Wordsworth would call 'a heart that watches and receives', and hearts like this can't help but pick up the world's static. He gives his feeling words, and fits the words to a tune—not one of his own, this time, but one that was written to give voice to a similar mood of turmoil and hope almost two centuries before Conor Oberst was born.

In 1785 Friedrich Schiller had just gotten over his last girlfriend, and spring was coming to his village near Leipzig. He was overcome with an incredible surge of happiness and goodwill for the human race, and sat down to write an 'Ode to Joy':

Joy, brilliant spark of the gods,
daughter of Elysium, heavenly being,
we enter, drunk with fire,
your holy sanctuary.
Your magic reunites
what was split by convention,
and all men become brothers
where your gentle wings are spread.
Be embraced, you millions!
This kiss for all the world!

Brothers, above the starry canopy
must surely dwell a loving father.[4]

Schiller's lines expressed the highest ideals of his century—the hope that the clearing away of dogma and outmoded institutions would, in time, heal the rifts in modern society and bring an end to war and misery. They also hinted at something new (or something very old, which seemed new); a wish to take leave of one's senses—to dance, to sing, to lose oneself in a happy throng. Five years after he wrote it, young German poets were running through a meadow near the seminary at Tubingen shouting Schiller's poem into the night air, and pausing between stanzas to take swigs from a bottle of wine.[5]

Schiller, like Wordsworth, was deeply sympathetic to the Revolution; and like the English poet, he found his convictions impossible to maintain after the Reign of Terror. But if the Revolution shattered his faith in the ideals of the Enlightenment, it convinced him more than ever of the importance of art and poetry:

If man is ever to solve the problem of politics in
practice he will have to approach it through the
aesthetic, because it is only through beauty that man
makes his way to freedom.[6]

Even after world events had conspired to make Schiller's optimism seem naïve, it was impossible to dismiss out of hand the vision he had presented in 'Ode to Joy'. In fact, as the bright hopes of 1789 receded into the distance, the question of how to make people happy seemed more pressing than ever. Ludwig van Beethoven decided to tackle the problem himself in 1802, announcing his intention to set Schiller's 'Ode' to music. It would be another twenty-two years before he would write to his publisher with good news on this front:

Vienna, March 10, 1824.
…These are all I can at present give you for publication.
I must, alas! now speak of myself, and say that this, the
greatest work I have ever written, is well worth 1000
florins C.M. It is a new grand symphony, with a finale
and voice parts introduced, solo and choruses, the words
being those of Schiller's immortal 'Ode to Joy', in the
style of my pianoforte Choral Fantasia, only of much
greater breadth.[7]

At the asking price of 600 florins, the publisher had got himself a bargain. The Choral Symphony wedded Schiller's verses to one of Beethoven's most powerful pieces of music. The poem appears in the final movement, which begins with the ugliest blast of discordant noise that had been heard in a concert hall up to that time—which, for Beethoven, symbolised nothing less than all the misery in the world condensed into one gigantic, impossible chord. Then, as the smoke clears and the dust settles, a lone voice pipes up in the darkness, 'Oh friends! No more of these tones! Let us sing something full of gladness!'.

A chorus appears out of nowhere and joins the singer as he belts out Schiller's 'Ode' and the whole thing is carried by a magnificent, soaring melody—the same melody, in fact, that Conor Oberst rides in 'Road to Joy'. Beethoven, conducting this final section at the piece's premiere in 1824, got completely carried away—he was still furiously waving his arms in the air long after the orchestra had stopped playing. And Oberst seems to be swept up in the same feeling of wild abandon as his own song comes to its conclusion. 'Let's fuck it up boys!' he tells his band, 'make some noise!'

But where Beethoven had his cacophony redeemed by a dream of universal brotherhood, Oberst ends his song with the end of the world. Oberst had always tried to write hope into his sadder songs. But you can hear his optimism fading in the last verses, as he looks around at the world and what we've made of it. The same suspicion with which he regards Western civilisation in 'I Believe in Symmetry' here reaches fever pitch. He sneers bitterly:

> *I hope I don't sound too ungrateful,*
> *What history gave modern men.*
> *A telephone to talk to strangers,*
> *A machine gun and a camera lens* [8]

None of these are any consolation for the still missing-in-action dream of universal human brotherhood. It's over two centuries since Schiller wrote his poem, one hundred and eighty years since Beethoven set it to music, and three decades years since that music was adopted as the official anthem of the European Community. But the dream it represents seems further away than ever.

The cracked howl and burst of noise at the end of 'Road to Joy' signalled a shift in Bright Eyes' music. Oberst had already thrown himself into political activism, performing onstage with his hero, Bruce Springsteen, on the 2004 Vote for Change tour. Later, in May 2005, he released a download-only protest song called 'When the President Talks to God'—a direct critique of the Bush Administration. Then, at the beginning of 2008, he fell back—feeling, as he later described it, 'corrupted and corroded'—and turned his gaze inward again.[9] But the album he recorded—the first to be released since his very early days under his own name—was very different to *Lifted* or earlier efforts like *Letting off the Happiness*. Where Oberst used to look inside himself and see a world of trouble, here, on songs like 'Sausalito,' he seemed to have found a measure of self-reliance, even peace.

The source of this new strength, it turned out, was nature. In 'Sausalito', the singer describes a camping trip with his girlfriend—they drive out into the desert so as to have the stars all to themselves. Here, Oberst's experience of the landscape becomes almost religious; he has a sense of a spirit moving through creation, a 'sound too soft to hear'. This mysterious 'something' accounts for the new feeling of calm in the songs on his self-titled album, which was recorded in a small cabin in rural Mexico. The music, as Oberst explained to triple j's Zan Rowe, sprang from the landscape itself and the feelings it stirred in him. 'I believe places have an energy to them,' he said. 'I felt at peace, but also inspired.'[10]

A Motion and a Spirit

IN JULY 1798 Wordsworth and Dorothy travelled to Bristol to see *Lyrical Ballads* through the presses. They made their way up the Wye River and stopped at a place called Tintern, not far from the ruins of an old gothic abbey. Wordsworth was overwhelmed by conflicting emotions. On his last visit to Tintern five years previously, his state of mind had been desperate, to say the least. He'd had his heart broken by a woman he had to leave, and by a cause he could no longer believe in. He'd found himself a traitor to his own country, an apologist for tyranny, and an apostate to a faith he'd only recently converted to. He was, in other words, a wreck. Back then, he'd raced around this landscape:

> *Wherever nature led: more like a man*
> *Flying from something that he dreads than one*
> *Who sought the thing he loved...*[1]

But since then, much had changed in Wordsworth's life. In 1798 he could look back at the Wordsworth of five years previously with not a little admiration for his hot-headed romantic passion. But he knew he wouldn't trade that for what he'd found since:

A presence that disturbs me with the joy
Of elevated thoughts; a sense sublime
Of something far more deeply interfused,
Whose dwelling is the light of setting suns,
And the round ocean and the living air,
And the blue sky and in the mind of man:
A motion and a spirit, that impels
All thinking things, all objects of all thought,
And rolls through all things.[2]

Here, in 'Tintern Abbey', Wordsworth is describing the almost mystical faith in nature that would sustain him for the rest of his life. This feeling runs through even the plainest of the *Lyrical Ballads*, and it's the key to his admonishment to poets in 'The Tables Turned' to put down the books and go for a walk. Wordsworth's faith, and his ability to write poetry, had been restored by his year in the country. It seemed to him as though the source of life and the source of his creative power were one and the same. But this realisation had not come easily to him—to reach it he had, in a sense, found it necessary to jettison almost four hundred years worth of European history; four centuries in which man's ability to reason was prized above all else, and the kind of simple faith Wordsworth was longing for was thought to be a relic of a (thankfully) long-gone era. Wordsworth's new philosophy turned this attitude on its head.

For the second edition of the *Lyrical Ballads*, Wordsworth wrote a preface explaining his new ideas as they related to poetry. He warned his readers that they were about to enter a poetic universe in which the laws laid down by Pope and the coffee-house classicists did not apply. He had powerful feelings to communicate, feelings which had come to him in the presence of nature; feelings which could not be made to abide by a set of rules any more than nature itself could be made to fit the harsh geometry of an eighteenth-century garden.

'All good Poetry,' Wordsworth insisted in his now-famous preface, 'is the spontaneous overflow of powerful feelings.' But Wordsworth was careful to add a disclaimer to this, saying that poets should make sure they don't get too carried away with their emotions:

> *The end of Poetry is to produce excitement in*
> *coexistence with an overbalance of pleasure…But if*
> *the words by which this excitement is produced are in*
> *themselves powerful, or the images and feelings have*
> *an undue proportion of pain connected with them,*
> *there is some danger that the excitement may be*
> *carried beyond its proper bounds.[3]*

Here, Wordsworth is insisting on one hand that poetry must come from feeling, while warning on the other that the poet must temper this feeling with a mood of calm repose such as the one in which he wrote 'Tintern Abbey'. Over the coming century, generations of younger poets happily embraced the first part of his formula while completely disregarding the second. This, in a sense, was entirely fair. Wordsworth had revealed that the rules of poetry were a sham, and that the only authority the poet ought to respect was the poet's own feeling for truth. It was a bit late now to start talking about 'proper bounds'.

Romantic

WHEN CONOR OBERST said, back in 2002, that people who thought his songs were too long could just fade them down, it's almost as if he was saying, 'I don't care if you listen—these are *my* feelings'. This is the kind of thing Wordsworth warned about in his preface—the poet's 'excitement carried beyond its proper bounds' perfectly describes Bright Eyes' early music.

The singer has rejected formalism, and replaced it with nothing. As a result, Oberst sings too long, confesses too much, cries too easily, and screams too loud.

These days Oberst's position is closer to the Wordsworth of 'Tintern Abbey'; his music still comes from feeling, but that feeling is tempered by a sense of spiritual calm. He's even made some concessions to form—although the forms he uses are much more likely to come from the street-level tradition of popular balladry than from any encyclopedia of pop. And yet it's no less personal—everything comes from feeling and the artist's inner life, and he shares it with us because it moved *him*. No other reason is required. When he starts screaming and hollering in 'I don't wanna die in the hospital' or over-sharing about his sex life in 'Sausalito', the old Conor Oberst is not too far away. Is it a bit much for you? he seems to be asking. Go on, fade it down—see if I care.

He can afford to say this because he knows we won't—not all of us anyway. For every hundred souls who fade him down and fade up the new *Maroon 5* album, there's at least one or two who stay the distance, and those special few are hooked for life. Music writer Brian Howe has said that being a Bright Eyes' fan is about having 'a sense of being a part of a special moment governed more by intuition than intellect'.[1] Conor Oberst's music is about feelings, not rules; and to love him is to choose the sound of gut-wrenching sadness over polished perfection, to prefer soul-baring excess to cool refinement.

To like these things in 2005 made you emo; in 1798 it made you *romantic*. Romanticism is often seen as a reaction to the Enlightenment—a rejection of the philosophical and literary ideals of the eighteenth century. Its earliest stirrings can be found in the very midst of the Enlightenment itself. Rousseau was, in many ways, a typical Enlightenment philosopher, since he sought to improve life by discrediting assumptions. But because he preferred nature to society and strong passion to rational thought, he was also the first of the romantics.

After Rousseau came the Germans, who took things an important step further. Rousseau, as Isiah Berlin has shown in *Against the Current*, may have rejected the culture of science, but he never abandoned the idea that the world made sense.[2] The Germans of the late eighteenth and early nineteenth century—Haman, Goethe, Schiller, Heine, Hegel, Fichte and Schopenhauer—would not be so squeamish. These writers would replace the Enlightenment's clockwork universe with a world of flux and chaos, and this change was mirrored in the art and literature they produced and championed—classicism was replaced by folklore; refined elegance by untamed nature; good sense by intense emotion.

Meanwhile, in England, the achievements of Wordsworth, Coleridge and Southey were followed in the early nineteenth century by stronger stuff from Byron, Shelley and Keats. These poets looked to Wordsworth sometimes as an elder statesman, sometimes as an embarrassing old uncle. They were generally less cautious in their methods and more extreme in temperament than Wordsworth—and they augmented his idea of poetry as a description of the poet's inner life with an interest in darkness, despair, madness and other altered states. This was the legacy of another Counter-Enlightenment tendency—the gothic revival, which had been gaining momentum for almost half a century before the *Lyrical Ballads* was published.

By the time Byron's *Childe Harold's Pilgrimage* became a surprise smash hit in 1812, romanticism was a craze, and by 1830 any adherents to the school of Pope would be feeling— as literary historian Robert Barnard puts it—'very lonely indeed'.[3] Romanticism would, in various forms, dominate the artistic and philosophical world of the nineteenth century. By 1900 it had given the world Wordsworth's 'Tintern Abbey', Beethoven's *Choral Symphony*, Mary Shelley's *Frankenstein*, Keats's 'La Belle Dame Sans Merci', Goethe's *Faust*, Schopenhauer's *The World as Will and Idea*, Victor Hugo's

Les Miserables, Eugene Delacroix's *Liberty Leading the People*, Wagner's *Tristan und Isolde*, Nietzsche's *Also Sprach Zarathustra*, Bram Stoker's *Dracula*, Puccini's *La Boheme* and Oscar Wilde's *The Picture of Dorian Grey*.

If we could somehow get the authors of all these great works together in a room, we'd have a tough time getting them to agree on anything—and no hope at all of discovering a single artistic principle they all share in common. Romanticism is hard to define, partly for the same reason emo is; it's entirely predicated on the idea that the artist is a unique and special individual, and there's nothing unique and special individuals hate more than the implication that they are somehow one of a 'type'. But even if the artists' objections are ignored, the historian will have a tough time coming up with a definition of 'romantic' that holds true in every case. Romanticism seems to dissolve as it's subjected to scrutiny—a metaphor the romantics, with their suspicion of reason and science, would appreciate:

Sweet is the lore which nature brings;
Our meddling intellect
Misshapes the beauteous forms of things;
—We murder to dissect.[4]

In fact if one thing could be said to connect the movement's most famous voices—to provide a link between the careers of such singular and unclassifiable personalities as Shelley, Beethoven, Nietzsche, Puccini, Hugo, Friedrich and Keats—it's the idea Wordsworth speaks of here in 'The Tables Turned':

Enough of science and of art;
Close up these barren leaves;
Come forth, and bring with you a heart
That watches and receives.[5]

Nature is greater than science, emotion more important than reason. The romantic artist favours passion over good sense. He prefers the sound of lusty old ballads to well-observed satires, and he certainly prefers the sight of mountains to neatly trimmed hedges. Wordsworth was by no means the first to express this preference, but in art, timing is everything, and Wordsworth's timing was impeccable. *Lyrical Ballads* appeared in the midst of one of the greatest upheavals in European history, a period of time in which almost every aspect of life—politics, religion, philosophy and the arts—was fundamentally altered. The crisis of faith Wordsworth had been through in his twenties, when his head led him badly astray and his heart put him back on track, seemed to play out, in microcosm, the crisis of a whole generation.

Gerard Way: A world that sends you reeling.

Disenchanted

MY CHEMICAL ROMANCE front man, Gerard Way, has only just turned thirty, but we get the feeling he's already seen more of the world and what it can do than he'd care to, as he steps up to the microphone to introduce the next number. 'This is a song about dreams', he tells the audience. 'It's called "Disenchanted".'[1]

The occasion is a sold-out concert at Mexico's Palacio de los Deportes on 7 October 2007. My Chemical Romance has been on the road for over a year, playing to hundreds of thousands of fans all over the world. During that time, the band's most recent album, *The Black Parade*, has never stopped selling—gathering rave reviews and topping readers' polls as it goes. Before the inevitable world tour had even hit the road, Gerard Way was well on the way to the upper echelons of rockstardom. Now, he treads the stage as though he's never been anything less than a glam-rock superhero. He dips a shoulder, and thousands of girls scream. He shares his pain and millions of kids adore him for it. All of which begs the question: what does Gerard Way have to be disenchanted about? All his dreams would appear to have come true—and then some. So what exactly is the problem? A closer listen to *The Black Parade* uncovers the malaise at the heart of Gerard Way's emotional world, and—more importantly—reveals the means by which he hopes to transcend it. The album is a loosely structured rock opera in the vein of Bowie's *Ziggy Stardust*, and the star of the show is a little guy called 'the patient'—a shell of a human being, eaten away from the inside by disease, connected by wires and tubes to obscure machinery, counting out his last days staring at the blank walls of a hospital ward. The album's centrepiece is a song called 'Welcome to the Black Parade', in which death finally comes for our hero, in the shape of an undead marching band. Death, Way insists, arrives in the form of our most treasured childhood memory. For the patient, this was the day his father took him into town to see a parade. On that day, he recalls— as he lies in his hospital bed and the machines count out what's left of his life in metrical beeps—his father said something to him that would stay with him forever:

He said son when you grow up
Would you be
The saviour of the broken
The beaten and the damned [2]

The song starts out reflectively, as the patient describes the day he spent with his father all those years ago, and the promise he made. Then he starts to think about the world as it revealed itself to him in his teens and twenties, those years when, one by one, we are systematically disavowed of the simple dreams of our childhood. The singer's not reflecting anymore—he's snapping and snarling about decimated dreams and bodies in the streets. But this bitter mood is not the one he closes his song with. For the final section of their rock epic, My Chemical Romance shift gears from breakneck punk to anthemic glory. The last sixty seconds of 'Welcome to the Black Parade' are pitched somewhere between the epic grandeur of 'We Are the Champions' and Phil Spector's Wall of Sound as played by the E Street Band on 'Born To Run', and the singer's tone is doomed but defiant. He realises that through it all, no matter how much misery and pain life threw at him, there was one thing that he never let go of—his dream.

'Welcome to the Black Parade' is a story about a vision, glimpsed during the singer's childhood, of a better world. It's a story about how that vision was then betrayed by the failure of the real world to live up to the singer's hopes. And it ends with the singer realising that he couldn't care less what the real world does or says or will or won't let him do. He discovers, at the end of the song, that all he needs is himself:

> *Take a look at me*
> *'cause I could not care at all*
> *do or die*
> *you'll never make me*
> *because the world*
> *will never take my heart* [3]

Gerard Way has found that society, the real world, adult life—whatever you want to call it—cannot provide him with happiness or satisfaction. So he's moved the search for happiness from outside to inside, and has found it, deep within himself, in his own dreams, his own imagination. This is what puts the romance in My Chemical Romance—the rejection of society in favour of the individual.

The philosophers call this solipsism—a system of thought that insists that the self is the only possible area of knowledge—and up until the nineteenth century it was regarded as mostly a bad thing. But the romantics, as Oxford professor Alex de Jonge notes in *Dostoyevsky and the Age of Intensity*, flipped the script:

> *Whereas most philosophies seek to avoid solipsism…*
> *the Romantics positively embraced it. They did so*
> *because they found themselves in a world in which the*
> *self alone seemed to offer a measure of certainty…*[4]

This was the world Wordsworth found himself living in. In the hundred years before he was born, the Enlightenment had systematically picked apart every mystery of life until it seemed there was nothing left to dismantle but the Enlightenment itself. This was somehow foreseen by Rousseau and achieved by the Revolution—but at a terrible cost. Post-revolutionary Europe now had to live every day with the awful knowledge that nothing—not even such previously rock-solid ideas as king and country, not even God himself, certainly not the widely discredited god of Reason—was a permanent fixture.

Wordsworth, having placed his faith in several of these phantoms only to have them melt away into the air, turned his gaze inward. In his rural retreat at Alfoxden, he found his thoughts drifting toward his childhood, which had also been spent in the country. In *The Prelude*, Wordsworth describes the vivid scenes that were recalled to his mind, a stormy day just before Christmas when he had run up to the top of a hill and sat by an old stone wall:

Upon my right hand was a single sheep,
A whistling hawthorn on my left, and there,
With those companions at my side, I watch'd,
Straining my eyes intensely, as the mist
Gave intermitting prospect of the wood[5]

Visions such as these restored his faith. Exclaims the poet:

Oh! Mystery of Man
From what a depth proceed thy honours! I am lost, but see
In simple childhood something of the base
On which thy greatness stands[6]

The Prelude, is a rejection of Empiricism, a popular philo-sophical doctrine of the eighteenth century which maintains that all knowledge is derived from experience, and that the mind is, at birth, a blank slate. Empiricism played a key role in the Enlightenment's belief in the perfectibility of human beings. It also influenced the criticism and teaching of art to an extraordinary degree. The president of London's Royal Academy, Sir Joshua Reynolds, taught that excellence in art could, and must be learned. 'Our minds,' he wrote, 'should be habituated to the contemplation of excellence.' But Wordsworth's contemporary, the poet and engraver William Blake, was having none of it. 'This man,' said Blake of Reynolds, 'was fired by Satan to depress art.'[7] In the margin of his copy of Reynolds' *Discourses*, next to the sentence just quoted, Blake scribbled furiously:

Reynolds thinks that Man Learns all that he knows. I
say on the Contrary that Man Brings All that he can
have Into the World with him.[8]

For Blake the poet or artist is not, and never was, a blank slate—his unique visions come from within, not from without.

Wordsworth, too, rejected Empiricism. Like Rousseau, he believed in a sort of original human soul, connected to nature, which has been corrupted and distorted—not improved—by society. That's why his epiphany took place in the countryside, which in turn stirred memories of his childhood—both were a way back to this original state. Having reacquainted himself with it, this original self would become his guide in the wilderness, the one fixed point in a chaotic and unfriendly world.

It's this same self-reliance that allows Gerard Way, in 'Welcome to the Black Parade', to look back at the rise and fall, the bodies in the streets, and the world that disappointed him at every turn, and say, as though he really means it, 'I, don't, CARE!' The source of the singer's faith, the one thing he could hang on to in an unstable world, turned out to be hiding somewhere in the depths of his original self. Here, he found dreams and ideals formed long before society, with its books and rules, taught him how to think—and how not to feel. The world can go on being the world—he has his heart—his unique feeling for what is true and right. It's this brave heart that he holds aloft during the final section of the song, as he falls in line with the black parade, and the rat-a-tat sound of their skeletal drum major disappears over the hill.

Paint It Black and Take It Back

To GERARD WAY, the black parade is many things. It's an alter-ego for his band, an image of death, a hope for salvation, and a way to describe his fans.[1] It's also a dream of society in reverse—a place where the broken, the beaten and the damned can be alone together. It's a parallel universe where sorrow is sublime and the good guys wear black.

It's fitting then, that the grand tableaux on the album's inner sleeve looks like the cover of The Beatles' *Sgt Pepper's*

Lonely Hearts Club Band printed in negative. In 1967, Peter Blake's iconic pop collage hinted at a bright new world of colour and imagination, with The Beatles playing the national anthem. Mexican fashion designer Manuel fitted the band out in technicolour military jackets which neatly caught the spirit of the times. The Sgt Pepper uniform suggested a historical revolution, but a bloodless one, fought with flowers and buckets of Pop-art colour—nostalgia blended with optimism.

For the black parade's uniforms, Gerard Way handed Hollywood costume designer Colleen Atwood a sketch for a Sgt Pepper outfit with all the colour drained out of it. With their fabric a uniform black and the gold details bleached bone white, the ribbing on the jackets had become *ribs*. The black parade uniform makes a clever visual pun on the cross-braids of a nineteenth-century military jacket by forcing them into a closer resemblance to the stripes of white corpse-paint worn on stage by Gerard Way's heroes The Misfits in the early 1980s. In the sleeve photo, the five band members, now wearing Atwood's creations, embody Gerard's idea of the black parade perfectly—soldiers who are dead before they've even started marching. Atwood—who honed her craft working with director Tim Burton on films like *Edward Scissorhands*—was clearly the right artist for the job.

This image of the band as the black parade was inescapable in 2007 and 2008, as their gigantic tour wound its way around the globe. Then, just as the tour came to a halt, and Gerard, Mikey, Bob, Ray and Frank hung their uniforms up backstage for the last time, their look was stolen by (of all bands) Coldplay. Their costumes were a tad brighter than My Chem's, and a little 'deconstructed' (although that could have been due to the fact that the band made them themselves and aren't very good at sewing)—but the similarity was striking. Chris Martin appeared on the cover of *Rolling Stone* dressed in his new duds, looking like a doomed young freedom fighter, staring into the distance, hand on his heart.

The look he was aiming for was 'Revolution'. With their new album, *Viva La Vida or Death and all his Friends*, Coldplay had wiped the slate clean—they'd thrown out the hit-making formula of the last two records, turned up their guitars, and were about to make what Martin called 'a slightly angry restart. Or not angry, just passionate.'[2] As part of this mini-revolution, the band selected a very telling image for the cover of *Viva La Vida*—Eugène Delacroix's *Liberty Leading the People*.

Delacroix's painting is one of the most famous images of France in revolt—it's very likely the first thing that comes into most people's heads when they hear the words 'French Revolution'. The painting shows an armed rabble surging toward the viewer out of a haze of gun smoke; a ragtag mob, students fighting alongside workers, a street kid waving pistols. At their head is Liberty herself—boldly stepping forward with a bayonet in one hand and the tricolour in the other. A popular ode of the nineteenth century described Liberty as 'This strong woman with powerful breasts, rough voice and robust charm'.[3] And this is exactly the figure Delacroix painted—liberty made flesh.

This is not the Revolution of 1789, it's the Revolution of 1830. In July of that year, King Charles X had issued an unpopular decree that wound back a number of the hard-won freedoms of 1789—including the freedom of the press. Several newspapers protested, police were sent in to subdue the rabblerousers, and outraged Parisians banded together to fight them off. 'Paris streets,' writes Tom Prideaux, 'took on the look of the Revolution all over again.'[4] Less than a week later, Charles had abdicated. Delacroix began working up his canvas as the smoke was still clearing and the new 'Citizen-King', Louis Philippe, was being installed. He wrote to his brother:

I have undertaken a modern subject, a barricade ... and if I have not conquered for my country, at least I will paint for her.[5]

Delacroix's painting—like Delacroix himself, was not especially political. The artist was bored by politics, but the uprising of 1830 had just enough sex and violence to appeal to the painter of kinky masterpieces like *The Death of Sardanapalus*. The finished painting, however, proved to have a little too much of both for his critics. They complained that the rabble was too dirty looking and that Liberty made flesh was a bit too ... fleshy. Liberty, they felt, was all very well—but couldn't she put her top back on?

Nevertheless, the new government bought Delacroix's painting, with the idea that it would be hung in Louis-Philippe's throne room 'as a reminder to the new king of how he came to be sitting there'.[6] But the king eventually decided that while he approved of the 'people' in principle, he would rather not look at armed workers and revolting peasants all day long. The painting was taken down, and Delacroix sent it to his Aunt Félicité's for safekeeping. Now it hangs in the Louvre—or did, until Coldplay marched in with their spray cans and wrote 'Viva La Vida' all over it.

'From very early on,' says Coldplay's Guy Berryman, 'we had this painting in mind to show a slightly badly organised revolution—with everything a bit homemade and scrappy.'[7] The painting, in turn, matches their homemade scrappy outfits; and the whole package combines to give the feeling of a passionate struggle for (artistic) freedom, and a new world about to be born.

In July 2008 the band presented their new music and new jackets for the first time in a live TV performance. MTV's Buzzworthy, while noting that they seemed to have raided Gerard Way's wardrobe, described their new look as 'Napoleon meets American Apparel'.[8] This was most likely the first time that any of the members of Britain's nicest band had been compared to a would-be conqueror of the world. But it would probably have pleased them in a way that a comparison to, say, Hitler or Genghis Khan would not.

Napoleon: Always alone among people ...

Napoleon

THE YEARS BETWEEN France's first two revolutions were dominated, not only in that country, but across the whole of Europe, by the extraordinary figure of Napoleon Bonaparte. He first came to France from the island of Corsica in order to complete his military education. Having been made a general by the Revolution at the age of twenty-four, he then helped to put down the Royalist Uprising of 1795, was promoted to commander of the army of Italy in 1796, and became—in all but name—the dictator of France in 1799. Over the next fourteen years, his armies poured across Europe. By the time he was defeated and exiled in 1814, the map of the continent was completely redrawn, and thousands of Europeans had, as historian Norman Davies puts it, 'a taste for something entirely different'.[1]

While the crowned heads of Europe were—justifiably— scared stiff by the seemingly unstoppable Corsican, many of their subjects eagerly anticipated his arrival—for exactly the same reasons. Napoleon came in the name of Liberty, bringing French-style freedom and democracy with him: oppressive monarchies would be toppled, serfdom abolished. He was, in Holland, for instance, exactly the sort of foreign invader you'd want to be conquered by.

He was also, as British historian Eric Hobsbawm puts it, Europe's first secular myth.[2] In 1804 Antoine-Jean Gros painted a large canvas recording Napoleon's Egyptian campaign. In 1798, Napoleon had been trying to establish a foothold for France in the Middle East when a large number of his soldiers were infected with plague. Partly as an act of mercy, and partly so as not to be held up, he ordered the stricken soldiers to be poisoned—but the mission proved to be a failure in any case. This less-than-glamorous story is not, however, the one Gros portrays in his 'Bonaparte Visiting the Plague Victims of Jaffa'. Gros shows a resolute but compassionate Napoleon reaching out his hand to touch one of the plague victims in a symbolic gesture of healing. Gros's painting, in which Napoleon has become a Christ-like figure, was dubious as history, but enormously seductive as propaganda. It was this image of Napoleon as part military genius, part supernatural redeemer that captured the popular imagination.

Ludwig van Beethoven was, at first, convinced that Napoleon was the real deal, the living embodiment of democracy and freedom. Having heard of the First Consul's expedition to Egypt, he began dreaming up a symphonic tribute to the great man, which he sat down to compose in 1803. His friend Ferdinand Ries visited him around this time and saw, sitting on his work-table, the completed score for a new work with the word 'Buonaparte' written on the title page. But Ries had some bad news for the composer, which he did not take at all well:

I was the first person who brought him the news that [Napoleon] had declared himself Emperor. Thereupon, he flew into a rage and cried out, "He too is nothing but an ordinary man! Now he will trample underfoot

all the Rights of Man and only indulge his ambition: he
will now set himself on high, like all the others, and
become a tyrant!" Beethoven went to the table, seized
the title-page from the top, tore it up completely and
threw it on the floor.[3]

Napoleon was, at this time, a highly contentious figure for
the romantics. Blake and Wordsworth were opposed to him
for much the same reasons as Beethoven, while others—like
Delacroix, or the German philosopher Hegel, whose native
Prussia had been completely crushed by Napoleon's army at
the Battle of Jena in 1806—admired him.[4] But after his
defeat and exile in 1814, Napoleon became one of the
quintessential heroes of the second wave of the romantic
movement. For artists of Wordsworth's generation, who had
lived through the Revolution, he was too problematic. But
for those who came of age in the first decades of the new
century, the exiled emperor seemed to embody the
Revolution itself, with all its yet-to-be-fulfilled promise; 'a
semi-mythical phoenix and liberator', as Eric Hobsbawm
writes.[5] To Lord Byron, born one year before the storming
of the Bastille, Napoleon was a hero. When he heard of the
emperor's defeat at Waterloo, he said, 'I'm damned sorry
for it'.[6]

Napoleon's defeat led to the restoration of France's
monarchy, and a slow but inevitable winding back of the
Revolution's reforms, which would eventually lead to the
uprising of 1830. During this time a stifling conservatism
overtook public life, not just in France, but across the whole
of Europe. The feeling was that disaster had been only
narrowly averted, and that peace and stability could only be
maintained by a rigid adherence to the status quo.

But for the romantics, this mood of dull conservatism only
made the image of Napoleon's reign blaze all the more
brightly by contrast. New heroes started to appear in the

literature and art of this period. Eric Hobsbawm describes them as:

> *Dashing young men in guards or hussar uniforms*
> *leaving operas, soirees, assignments with duchesses or*
> *highly ritualised lodge-meetings to make a military*
> *coup or place themselves at the head of a struggling*
> *nation...* [7]

The hussars were a cavalry force in the Napoleonic wars—the armies of France, Austria and Prussia all included hussar regiments. They were notorious for their reckless behaviour, and instantly recognisable for their jackets—double-breasted affairs with horizontal stripes of gold braid across the front, inspired by Hungarian fashions of the late eighteenth century. Napoleon himself was known to wear them—some accounts of his last farewell before being exiled have him wearing a hussar guard's jacket as he made his way down the marble staircase and bid his officers *adieu*.

If Napoleon was often intentionally confused with Christ by his mythographers, then this departure scene, as Norman Davies has observed, was his Last Supper. It came to symbolise the end of an era, and did much to popularise the idea of Napoleon as a martyr—an idea the emperor himself had already succumbed to by the time he wrote this letter to his first wife, Josephine, on the weekend before he sailed for Elba:

> *They've betrayed me one and all...adieu, ma bonne*
> *Josephine. Learn resignation as I have learned it, and*
> *never banish from your memory the one who has never*
> *forgotten you, and will never forget you.* [8]

Napoleon was always seen to be a different kind of military hero. The poets and artists who admired him during his reign 'did not depict him as a victor', as art historian William Vaughn observes:

> *But as a man of emotion, anxious in mid-battle, compassionately visiting the plague-stricken, or expressing horror at the consequences of war.*[9]

And despite the exaggerated nature of some of these portrayals, Napoleon, as his letters show, *was* an emotional man—as a young man, especially so. In 1785 the seventeen-year-old army recruit confided thoughts of loneliness to his journal:

> *Always alone among people, I return home to dream by myself, and submit to the liveliness of my own melancholy.*[10]

In these moments, when the teenaged Napoleon felt most isolated from his fellow human beings, he found solace in a small book called *The Sorrows of Young Werther*. He wasn't the only one—*Werther* had, since its publication in 1774, become a runaway bestseller. Its readership was mostly made up of moody young men, and the key to its appeal lay in the fact that the book's protagonist, the young Werther of the title, was, like them, solitary, introspective and over-emotional. The book purports to be a series of letters written by this sensitive young man to a close friend, telling the story of his unhappy love affair, his descent into despair, and his eventual decision to end his life. The preface explains that the author's purpose in presenting these letters is to provide consolation for those similarly afflicted:

> *And thou, good soul, who sufferest the same distress as he endured once, draw comfort from his sorrows; and let this little book be thy friend, if, owing to fortune or*

through thine own fault, thou canst not find a dearer companion.[11]

Napoleon read it seven times.

Twenty years later, no longer just a lonely young man, but a lonely young master of the Continent, Napoleon finally got to meet the author, J W von Goethe. In fact, he'd just invaded and conquered Goethe's country, so there was not much chance of the writer refusing the invitation. On 2 October 1808 Goethe and the emperor met over a large round table while the latter was eating his breakfast. Napoleon told the fifty-seven-year-old author that he looked young for his age.

Having got the small talk out of the way, the Emperor owned up to how many times he'd read Goethe's novella. Werther being a tragedy, the talk then moved on to tragedy in general, which, in Thomas Carlyle's account, Napoleon told Goethe, 'ought to be the school of kings and peoples'.[12] He declared that there was no greater subject for a tragedy than the death of Caesar, and complained that Voltaire had not really done the story justice. 'A great poet', Napoleon insisted, 'would have given prominence to Caesar's plans for the regeneration of the world, and shown what a loss mankind had suffered by his murder.'[13]

That Goethe and Napoleon should have started out discussing the story of an emotional young artist who commits suicide on account of a hopeless love (Werther) and ended up talking about the assassination of one of the most powerful men in history (Caesar) might seem incongruous. But Caesar, Werther and—as he seems to have known himself—Napoleon are all, in the romantic imagination, tragic heroes. They have earned their place in the pantheon—alongside Hamlet, Don Giovanni and Lord Byron—because they are all, as Eric Hobsbawm puts it, 'trespassers beyond the limits of ordinary life'.[14]

The romantic hero is solitary. He retreats into himself because the world has failed to satisfy him, to live up to his dreams. A 'weak' romantic figure like Werther dies through inaction, because he can no longer cope with the divide between himself and the world. A 'strong' romantic hero like Caesar goes out into the world and tries to reshape it according to his vision, but he, too, is inevitably crushed by reality. This conflict between the individual and society, as Napoleon correctly guessed, was to be the basis of tragedy in this new century. Because no matter how hard the hero fights, and no matter how brave his heart is, in any contest between the self and the world, the self will come off second best. The romantic hero is always doomed, because his adversary is reality itself.

This Tragic Affair

IN THE VIDEO for 'Welcome to the Black Parade', the patient lies dying in a hospital bed. His life has been full of struggle and heartbreak, yet he clings to it as though it might still have something to offer him. Suddenly he looks up and sees the salvation he's been waiting for. If this were a religious painting from the Middle Ages, an angel would be hovering over his deathbed. But this is America in the twenty-first century, so the light beaming down on him from above comes from a TV. On the screen, the patient sees Gerard Way in his black parade uniform, singing the story of his life. He reaches up to touch the vision, the real world disappears, and he finds himself on a frozen road, with the black parade marching toward him.

The Black Parade contains a dangerous idea. It suggests that life might be a struggle for which there is no reward, a bad joke at best. In this world, where dreams are made to be broken, and the promise of happiness is an illusion, our only possible salvation lies in death. Which is not the same thing as writing a song that says; kill yourself. *The Black Parade* is, as Gerard and the band have pointed out many times, a very life-affirming record. It accepts that living is impossible, but insists that we must be brave enough to do it anyway. On the album's final song, 'Famous Last Words', Gerard recoils from 'a life that's so demanding', but refuses to give up the fight—which of course is the old romantic stand-off between the solitary hero and the cruel, cruel world:

> *I am not afraid to keep on living*
> *I am not afraid to walk this world alone*[1]

The Black Parade is a complex work, full of contradictions. Like any great work of art, it refuses to lie still and play the part of an illustration for a single idea. But the mass media has a way of flattening out the subtleties in art so it can be more easily squeezed into the grid of the six o'clock news bulletin. Sometime in 2007, having been put through this process, My Chemical Romance became a band who dressed like zombies, wrote songs about death and played them for a fan base primarily made up of *your children*. They also became, much to their dismay, an emo band—which in the UK was already tabloid code for 'suicide cult'. When thirteen-year-old My Chem fan Hannah Bond took her own life early in 2008, the band, and their album, had no hope of a fair trial. *The Black Parade*'s complex array of meanings was reduced to a series of wildly inaccurate sound bites—it was, according to one journalist, 'the place where emos believe they go when they die'.[2] Fans organised a day of action, holding up banners displaying the lyrics from 'Famous Last Words' and testifying to the power of the band's music to save lives. But it was too late. In the eyes of the British public, Gerard Way was a cult leader, a glamouriser of death, and a very bad influence on the youth of today.

In 1774, Johann Wolfgang von Goethe found himself in a similar position to Gerard Way. Goethe's novella, *The Sorrows of Young Werther,* was a runaway bestseller—Germany's first, in fact. More than that, it was a novel that seemed to speak for its age, to articulate the feelings of confusion and hopelessness that lurked beneath the surface of eighteenth-century life. It was the kind of book, as Goethe himself had predicted with his short introductory note, that people took to heart—young people especially. It gave rise to new behaviours—the emotional, death-obsessed youths who loved it became more emotional and more obsessed with death. They were easy to spot—Werther fans had *Werther faces*—they were dreamy, gloomy, cut off from the world, in love with their own misery. But Wertherism wasn't just a lifestyle—if taken to its logical conclusion it became a death-style. Werther, it was said, triggered a kind of suicide epidemic in the late 1770s. Of these, the most disturbing for Goethe was the case of a woman who drowned herself in a river not far from where he lived. When her body was dragged out of the water, she was found to have a copy of *The Sorrows of Young Werther* in her pocket.[3]

Even after this initial panic died down *Werther* continued to generate trouble for its author. Goethe was pestered on and off for the rest of his life about this little book—partly because of its shocking content, and partly because its story was rumoured to have come directly from Goethe's own life. This was true. In 1772 the author, then still a student, had moved from Frankfurt to a country town named Wetzlar. Here he pursued his legal studies by sitting in on sessions of the Court of Justice. He also became involved in the social life of the students and court administrators, and it was in this company that the young Goethe fell deeply in love for the second time.

Goethe met Lotte Buff, the twenty-year-old daughter of a court official and surrogate mother to her many brothers and sisters, at a ball at Wolpertshausen. They danced, she gave him flowers, and the two stared into each others eyes on the carriage ride back to town. Goethe was convinced that Lotte was the love of his life, and his subsequent discovery that she was more or less engaged to a secretary in the Hanoverian Legation did not deter him in the slightest. Even when Lotte's fiancé, Kestner, returned from his posting abroad, the smitten young poet continued to hang around the house—even going so far as to strike up a close friendship with Kestner. This arrangement worked out for a little while but eventually the situation became intolerable for Goethe—and as a result of his increasingly hysterical behaviour, he began to frighten Lotte and alienate himself from Kestner. Seeing no way out of the impasse, Goethe left the house for good on 10 September.

Back at home, and in a truly disturbed state of mind, he heard news of a fellow student of his from the University of Leipzig:

Of a moody temperament, disheartened by failure in his profession, and soured by a hopeless passion for the wife of another, he had borrowed a pair of pistols under pretense of a journey, and had shot himself on the night of October 29.[4]

The news of this young man's lonely suicide had an electrifying effect on Goethe—for obvious reasons. He soon wedded the story of his unhappy affair with Lotte to the grim tale of his acquaintance from Leipzig, and within four weeks, *The Sorrows of Young Werther* was complete. Goethe had become Werther, (an artist now, not a poet), Lotte had become Charlotte, and Kestner had become Albert, but in most other respects the story of the romantic young man and his impossible love affair was the same.

Young Werther, like Rousseau, Wordsworth, and Goethe himself, is a student of nature:

> *She alone is inexhaustible, and capable of forming the greatest masters. Much may be alleged in favour of rules, as much may be likewise advanced in favour of the laws of society: an artist formed upon them will never produce anything absolutely bad or disgusting; as a man who observes the laws, and obeys decorum, can never be an absolutely intolerable neighbour, nor a decided villain: but yet, say what you will of rules, they destroy the genuine feeling of nature, as well as its true expression.[5]*

At the start of the book, nature is for Werther a source of sublime joy. He longs to disappear into the tranquil scenes before his eyes, and, like Conor Oberst, he finds himself dreaming dreams of insect bliss:

> *Every tree, every bush, is full of flowers; and one might wish himself transformed into a butterfly, to float about in this ocean of perfume, and find his whole existence in it.[6]*

The next day, he floats further into raptures. Walking through the valley at sunset, he flings himself to the ground and presses his ear to the soil:

> *…as I lie close to the earth, a thousand unknown plants are noticed by me: when I hear the buzz of the little world among the stalks, and grow familiar with the countless indescribable forms of the insects and flies, then I feel the presence of the*

Almighty, who formed us in his own image, and
the breath of that universal love which bears and
sustains us, as it floats around us in an eternity of
bliss... [7]

Werther has a hard time getting all this down on paper. He has 'a heart that watches and receives' but it has no filter, no way of limiting or controlling the sensations that come his way. He feels overwhelmed, and finds it difficult to draw:

Oh, would I could describe these conceptions, could
impress upon paper all that is living so full and warm
within me, that it might be the mirror of my soul, as my
soul is the mirror of the infinite God! O my friend—but
it is too much for my strength—I sink under the weight
of the splendour of these visions! [8]

And this is the carefree, *happy* Werther! Clearly he's an excitable young man. His problem, as he admits to his penfriend, is that he is too sensitive. 'I treat my heart like a sick child,' he writes, 'and indulge its every whim.' Later, staring at another scene of birds, beetles and rolling green hills, Werther is completely overcome, and begins to hallucinate:

Stupendous mountains encompassed me, abysses
yawned at my feet, and cataracts fell headlong down
before me; impetuous rivers rolled through the
plain, and rocks and mountains resounded from
afar...Everything around is alive with an infinite
number of forms; while mankind fly for security to
their petty houses, from the shelter of which they rule
in their imaginations over the wide-extended universe.
Poor fool! [9]

By this point, as you might have guessed from the apocalyptic tone he's adopted, Werther's heart has begun to break. It's become perfectly clear to him that Charlotte will never leave Albert for him, and that his love is hopeless. And because everything—from the Homer he reads in the garden to the garden itself—is a big deal to Werther, this is a *really* big deal. As he sinks into despair, his relationship to the natural world undergoes a remarkable change. He's just as alive with sensitivity to the life of nature as he ever was; only now, if he steps on an ant, he immediately spirals into thoughts of cosmic despair, and begins to see nature as 'a monster, devouring her own offspring'. Universal love has become universal chaos.

Werther still sees the landscape as a mirror for his soul. It's just that now Werther's soul is clouded over with misery, and he's begun to find that rolling green hills and pretty butterflies just don't do it for him anymore. He doesn't go out early in the morning or at sunset anymore—he waits until it's dark—and if the weather has turned bad, so much the better to suit his foul mood. Here Werther is in luck, as the book moves to its grim conclusion the leaves begin to fall from the trees and autumn gives way to winter.

> *It is even so! As nature puts on her autumn tints it becomes autumn with me and around me.*[10]

Then in mid-December there comes an unexpected thaw, and the river bursts its banks. The town is plunged into chaos, and Werther, on the stroke of midnight, sets out into the freezing dark to survey the devastation.

> *And when the moon shone forth, and tinged the black clouds with silver, and the impetuous torrent at my feet foamed and resounded with awful and grand impetuosity, I was overcome by a mingled sensation of*

apprehension and delight. With extended arms I looked
down into the yawning abyss, and cried, 'Plunge!' For a
moment my senses forsook me, in the intense delight of
ending my sorrows and my sufferings by a plunge into
that gulf![11]

It's around this time that Werther becomes convinced that the only course of action left open to him is to 'quit his prison' once and for all. 'Yes, I feel certain, Wilhelm,' he writes, 'and every day I become more certain, that the existence of any being whatever is of very little consequence.'[12]

As he hangs around Charlotte's household moping and pining, he contemplates all sorts of crazy ideas. He wonders what would happen if he just swept Charlotte off her feet and kissed her; he wonders if he might have to kill Albert; he wonders, in his darkest moments, if he might have to kill Charlotte. But somehow he can't bring himself to do any of these things. He just wants to disappear.

I am ill; and yet I am well—I wish for nothing—I have
no desires—it were better I were gone.[13]

Young Werther is not very old, but he's already seen enough of life to know what's in store: more pain, more misery, and above all, more disappointment.

What is the destiny of man, but to fill up the measure of
his sufferings, and to drink his allotted cup of
bitterness?[14]

Charlotte implores Werther to be more reasonable—his love is hopeless—why wallow in misery? Werther *agrees* that his love is hopeless, but rejects Charlotte's conclusions—he refuses to get over it because this implies a walling off from feeling, a denial of his emotions, that he cannot accept.

Instead, he has chosen to see his love to its grim conclusion—he has begun to see that he must die. Frustrated at every turn, Charlotte feels there is nothing more she can offer Werther but her pity—but he already knows there is one more thing she can do for him. He wants her, in short, to finish him off. After his final confrontation with Charlotte, he has his servant visit her house with a request to borrow Albert's hunting-pistols 'for a journey':

> The arrival of Werther's servant occasioned her the greatest embarrassment. He gave Albert a note, which the latter coldly handed to his wife, saying, at the same time, 'Give him the pistols. I wish him a pleasant journey,' he added, turning to the servant. These words fell upon Charlotte like a thunderstroke: she rose from her seat half-fainting, and unconscious of what she did. She walked mechanically toward the wall, took down the pistols with a trembling hand, slowly wiped the dust from them, and would have delayed longer, had not Albert hastened her movements by an impatient look. She then delivered the fatal weapons to the servant, without being able to utter a word.[15]

Werther, upon receiving this final gift, falls into raptures:

> 'They have been in your hands you wiped the dust from them. I kiss them a thousand times—you have touched them. Yes, Heaven favours my design, and you, Charlotte, provide me with the fatal instruments. It was my desire to receive my death from your hands, and my wish is gratified…'[16]

The stage is set for Goethe's tragic hero to have his final showdown with the world that broke his heart.

Goethe: 'It is impossible to describe one's feelings save in the flash and fire of the moment'.

Passion Incapable of Being Converted into Action

EIGHTEENTH-CENTURY EUROPE HAD been dominated, politically and culturally, by the French—the rationalism of the *Philosophes* was the intellectual fashion. *Werther* was a book about feelings, told from the point of view of a character who is ruled by his emotions to an unprecedented degree. It was a revolt against French ideas, and the founding work of the German romantic movement.

German critics August Wilhelm von Schlegel and Friedrich Schlegel were among the first to reclaim the word 'romantic' as a positive term. To Sir Joshua Reynolds, it would have meant, as art historian William Vaughn puts it, 'those emotive extremes that lay beyond the proper sphere of the artist to depict'. For the Schlegels, emotive extremes would characterise the art and literature of the new century. They seized on the romantic as being closer to the spirit of the age than the watered-down classicism that had been in vogue for so long.[1]

In his *Vorlesungen über dramatische Kunst und Literatur* (1809), August Schlegel praised Goethe for jettisoning the tired rules of neoclassicism in favour of 'organic form'.[2]

Thanks to Schlegel's promotion, and the fact that his work was so widely translated, Goethe's name soon became indelibly connected with the romantic movement in England, Italy, Spain and—most surprising of all—France. Goethe's reputation was consolidated by Madame de Staël's appreciation of his work in her *De l'Allemagne*, which, as Martin Swales points out, virtually inverted the supremacy of France over Germany in the world of letters in one fell swoop.[3] By 1826 Goethe was being praised by French critics for having revived that country's literature by replacing the old classical insistence on learning and imitation with a new approach that drew on personal confession, 'finding the subject matter within oneself'.[4]

For the young Goethe, there was simply no other way to write. As Barker Fairley has shown in his study of the author, Goethe was fiercely anti-intellectual as a youth. At the age of eighteen, he had already realised that books had nothing to teach him, and that everything he had to offer the world could be found by plumbing the depths of his own soul. He was extraordinarily creative—but the idea of editing or refining his work, let alone ordering it or subjecting it to intellectual scrutiny, was absolutely abhorrent to him. 'It is impossible to describe one's feelings save in the flash and fire of the moment,' he wrote in 1775.[5]

By the time he died, Goethe was seen, in most European countries, as the father of German romanticism. The irony in this is that Goethe enjoyed being called 'romantic' about as much as Gerard Way likes being called 'emo'. He very quickly tried to distance himself from *Werther*'s emotional excess, maintaining that it was a crazy book written at a crazy time in his life. The older Goethe never read from *Werther* in public, and admitted once or twice that he was almost scared to open the thing, in case the terrible mood that had inspired it was somehow trapped between its pages, and might overtake him again.

Thomas Carlyle would have agreed that *Werther* was better left on the shelf. Not that Carlyle didn't admire Goethe, in fact, he did more for the cause of Goethe in Britain than anyone, including Madame de Staël. De Staël had unintentionally done Goethe a disservice by presenting to her English readers a version of his *Faust* that played up the work's 'satanic' overtones at the expense of its more important ideas. This merely confirmed Wordsworth and Coleridge's suspicions that there was something offensively immoral in Goethe. Carlyle's translations and essays improved Goethe's reputation in Britain a great deal. But Carlyle was not unbiased in his appreciation. 'Carlyle', writes Swales, 'saw in Goethe's career a reflection of his own spiritual development that led from gloomy despair to the recognition of community service.'[6] In other words, Carlyle saw *Werther* as a phase that Goethe had grown out of, and that the literary world had—or ought to have—as well.

In England *Werther* had been a smash hit. It had run to fourteen editions and been turned into a popular play. It was, for a while, inescapable: like something in the air, you could catch it just by walking around and breathing— although young men with good educations and nothing to do seemed more susceptible than most. Lord Byron didn't even have to *read* the book to understand its importance— he couldn't have, in any case, since he'd never learned to do anything other than swear in German. But Byron instinctively picked up on the mood of gloomy introspection in Goethe's novella, and rode the same unhappy bandwagon all the way to the bank, which in turn led to another wave of tortured poetry by young men with lots of feelings—all of them bad. Years later Carlyle, fed up with all the sobbing and moping *Werther* had inspired, made an example of Byron as an English 'sentimentalist'—hopefully, he said, the last:

For what good is it to 'whine, put finger i' the eye, and
sob,' in such a case? Still more, to snarl and snap in
malignant wise, 'like dog distract, or monkey sick?' Why
should we quarrel with our existence, here as it lies
before us, our field and inheritance...[7]

Carlyle is effectively telling the sentimentalists, the Werther faces and the Byronic brooders to grow up and get over it. And this is almost exactly what Charlotte, when she can no longer take his hysterics, says to Werther. In life, as in art, Werther follows his heart exclusively, and refuses to be bound by manners, good taste or commonsense—all of which he sees as every bit as deadening to life and love as they are to art. But by refusing to see reason and indulging his feelings to the exclusion of all else, Werther drives everybody crazy—in the real world, it seems, being emotional is not okay. Charlotte, who at first finds that her kind heart will not permit her to turn Werther completely away, eventually runs out of patience:

> *'Oh! why were you born with that excessive, that*
> *ungovernable passion for everything that is dear to*
> *you?' Then, taking his hand, she said, 'I entreat of you*
> *to be more calm: your talents, your understanding,*
> *your genius, will furnish you with a thousand*
> *resources. Be a man, and conquer an unhappy*
> *attachment toward a creature who can do nothing but*
> *pity you.'* [8]

Charlotte, in other words, sees that Werther needs to take control of his life. She wants him to stop standing around emoting and *do* something—anything. But Werther is paralysed by feeling. This, as Carlyle himself admitted, is why *Werther* is an important book. *Werther*, Carlyle insisted, *attempted the more accurate delineation of a class of feelings deeply important to modern minds, but for which our elder poetry offered no exponent, and perhaps could offer none, because they are feelings that arise from Passion incapable of being converted into Action.*[9]

The hero's 'quarrel with existence' is not one that can be resolved by practical means, because his revolt is a revolt against the practical world—he demands the right to be unreasonable in the Age of Reason.

Sentimentalists

ROMANTIC LOVE, SAYS Rupert Christiansen, began sometime between 1763 and 1774. The love we know from blockbuster movies, perfume commercials and daytime soaps—all passion beyond reason and waves of feeling bursting the banks of everyday life—was totally unknown in the early eighteenth century. Love, in the literature of Pope and Johnson's time, was a contract in the parties' mutual interest, in which the occasional bawdy romp was part of the give-and-take.[1]

But Rousseau's novel *Julie* and—fast on its heels—Goethe's *The Sorrows of Young Werther*, changed all this for good. In these books, love is not a part of the normal fabric of social relations, it's something so powerful and irrational that society can barely accommodate it. And where an earlier age might have used these eruptions of emotion to teach the reader a lesson about the wages of sin, here the moral universe of Christianity was reversed. Rousseau taught that feeling was more important than reason, and implied that the sensitive individual who feels more deeply than others is privy to a deeper, truer moral wisdom. Werther took this idea to extremes. Werther's emotionalism made him a hero—a martyr even. 'In Werther,' writes historian Walter Benjamin, 'the bourgeoisie finds the demigod who sacrifices his life for them.'[2] Reasonable people told him to get over it and do something useful with his life—but Werther would rather die of feeling than not feel anything. For this reason, *Werther* became the founding work of a late eighteenth-century cult of the emotions called sentimentalism.

In his book *Romantic Affinities*, Christiansen presents a fascinating document of the sentimentalist mindset—a collection of love letters written in 1777. Mary Hays and John Eccles fall in love but soon find that their perfect love is threatened by the dull world, which considers them too young and too poor to marry. Ignoring the advice of her friends and family, who urge her to calm down and get over it, Mary goes half-hysterical with frustrated passion. Of course, she knows they're right—that she could, if she chose, set her sights on finding a husband with better prospects, settle down, raise a family, and leave all this sentimental nonsense behind. But Mary would rather live in sorrow for the rest of her life than suppress her true feelings for even a day.

Half the world have no souls. I envy them not their dull insipid calmness—rather would I suffer all those heart-rending, exquisite distresses, which too often flow from sensibility. [3]

It is, as Christiansen admits, enough to make you gag. From this small piece of evidence, Carlyle's objections to sentimentalism are easy enough to understand. At the heart of the sentimentalist's philosophy is the trendy Rousseauistic idea that human beings are naturally good, but have been corrupted by society. Rousseau's novels, as Norman Davies points out, made unprecedented links in the public imagination between nature, feeling and virtue. Emotions are natural, society is artificial. Therefore, to the sentimentalist, feelings are sacred, and nobody can tell him otherwise. But this is a selfish philosophy which in the end leads to a profound estrangement, not only from society and its problems, but from other people. This is exactly what happens to Werther.

> *I could tear open my bosom with vexation to think how little we are capable of influencing the feelings of each other. No one can communicate to me those sensations of love, joy, rapture, and delight which I do not naturally possess; and, though my heart may glow with the most lively affection, I cannot make the happiness of one in whom the same warmth is not inherent.[4]*

Werther is full of feeling, but he doesn't treat people very well—because they're not him, and they don't understand how he feels. As Martin Swales notes, this 'dreadful solipsism' of Werther's ruins his relationship with Lotte before it's even begun.[5] Again and again he cries to heaven; Why, how can she not feel how *I* feel? For all his ability to empathise with her, she might as well not exist.

Across the Sea

RIVERS CUOMO'S SENTIMENTALIST phase reached its logical end point with *Pinkerton*. Here, the exploration of his emotional world that he'd begun in the privacy of his bedroom some years earlier bore its bitter fruit. Cuomo's over-sensitivity to feeling, combined with his estrangement from the world, resulted in songs like 'Across the Sea', where the hero despairs of ever being able to connect with another human being,

Why are you so far away from me?
I need help and you're way across the sea.[1]

But as he admits on the album's last song, a beautiful acoustic lament called 'Butterfly', it's mostly his fault. He spins an allegory about going out into the garden with a mason jar to catch a butterfly. He snares one—a real beauty. But after a couple of days, it's dead. This kind of thing, the singer tells us, happens to him all the time, 'Everytime I pin down what I think I want it slips away.'[2]

It always *feels* like he's doing the right thing. 'I did what my body told me to', he reflects. He acts naturally, according to his emotions, but it doesn't make him happier. 'Butterfly' contains an important insight—that a philosophy based on feelings almost inevitably leads to romantic despair—and with *Pinkerton*, Cuomo had ridden the snake all the way to the bottom of the board. It's little wonder that, after he'd recovered his strength again a couple of years later, he had no desire to go back down there. Like Goethe, he must have had a slightly superstitious feeling that he'd simply stuffed the nightmare into those songs and shoved a cork in the top—why risk letting it out again? 'The most painful thing in my life these days,' he told *Rolling Stone* magazine in 2001, 'is the cult around *Pinkerton*.'

> *It's just a sick album, sick in a diseased sort of way. It's such a source of anxiety because all the fans we have right now have stuck around because of that album. But, honestly, I never want to play those songs again; I never want to hear them again.*[3]

'It's so weird being at total loggerheads with your fans,' he said of the *Pinkerton* obsessives who were so frustrated by his new unemotional music.

*I don't know how to deal with it. I don't want to
say anything that would sound condescending, but
those fans are probably younger and they probably
just want to hear that extreme emotion from
moment to moment. They need to hear that
excess.*[4]

Any definition of emo, as music writer Andy Greenwald has
discovered, has to begin with the fans. This is the only thing
that could be said to connect the hundreds of bands who have
found themselves described as such. What do My Chemical
Romance, Weezer, Sunny Day Real Estate and Dashboard
Confessional have in common? Almost nothing. But their fans
all want the same thing—feelings.

In *Nothing Feels Good: Punk rock, teenagers, and emo*,
Greenwald meets four young friends from Plainview, Long
Island, united by their love of Dashboard Confessional and
their belief in the importance of emotion. While all the other
kids are drinking beer and watching football, Ian, Howie,
Anthony and Justin sit around playing acoustic guitars,
writing poetry and…feeling stuff. The girls at their high
school, sick and tired of pretending to be interested in sports,
start to look their way more often. Justin is not surprised.
'They'd never seen real people that are emotional,' he
explains.[5]

Elsewhere, fifteen-year-old Tracy drives the point home—
emotional people are *real* people—everyone else is fake.

*I don't care what anyone else thinks anymore—I'm not
gonna be fake. I'm gonna be real. I made all new
friends because I didn't want to have fake friends, and
all of them are themselves too.*[6]

In 1973 theatre critic John Weightman noted that the world is
full of people who subscribe to a basically Rousseauistic

philosophy without ever having heard of him.[7] He was thinking of hippies, but emo is, in many ways, even closer to the mark. Emo fans share a strikingly similar language to that of the sentimentalists, and an almost identical set of priorities. Greenwald quotes an online review of Sunny Day Real Estate's Diary, which insists that the album:

> Strikes at the heart of all that makes us human,
> begging us to profess our deepest sympathies and
> dearest sensibilities.[8]

Two hundred years ago they were saying the same thing about Rousseau's *Julie*. Emo fans, like their sentimentalist forebears, have evolved a system of values in which powerful feelings automatically have moral superiority, because they're seen as authentically human. This is why emo culture is inherently terrifying to parents, and an irresistible target for news organisations who profit from their secret fears.

> Emo is a very specific sort of teenage longing,
> a romantic and ultimately self-centered need to
> understand the bigness of the world in relation
> to you.[9]

To the kid who feels that her emotions are the most important thing in the world, the singer says: it's true. 'What has AFI taught you?' asks a thread on the goth-punk band's website. 'The main thing for me,' says kXa, 'was I don't need to live up to anyone's standards. I don't have to put on a fake smile and go through my day.' 'They've taught me that being emotional is okay,' says edenforever, 'and to express myself any way possible.'[10]

Davey Havok: As nature puts on her autumn tints, it becomes autumn with me and around me.

Love Like Winter

LIKE MY CHEMICAL Romance, AFI is not a band anyone would have thought to call emo ten years ago. But then, ten years ago, AFI was a very different band. As music writer Neil Strauss has observed, the AFI of today barely resembles the group that recorded 'I Wanna Get a Mohawk (But Mom Won't Let Me Get One)' in 1997.[1] Since 1999, Havok's steady diet of mostly English bands—The Cure, The Cult, Bowie and Morrissey—has pushed AFI's music in a completely different direction from its scrappy punk roots. These days, AFI is larger than life, mythic. Like Gerard Way, Havok is a proper glam-rock superhero. His look is an ultra-stylised synthesis of kinky goth-wear, punk ink and Misfits-style Halloween corn. His band, likewise, eschews the snot-nosed pop-punk typical of recent emo bands for a much more eclectic sound. 2006's *Decemberunderground* was their most ambitious effort to date, sounding by turns like The Cure, Depeche Mode, Bowie and Bon Jovi—with even a hint of Timbaland-style stadium R&B in the album's intro.

Like his hero Robert Smith, Havok is not really interested—from an artistic point of view—in the outside world or its problems, his subject matter comes entirely from his turbulent inner life. The letters that make up the band's name stand for

A Fire Inside, and it's this fire—and never the candidate on TV or the war in Iraq—that their songs attempt to describe. From inside, outside can just fall apart. Here is where AFI finds its common ground with emo.

Davey Havok's estrangement from twenty-first century society, from the world as it is, has driven him to the bleakest extremities of nineteenth-century thought. 'It is against a sense of a hostile, alien and valueless reality that romanticism mounts its various strategies of escape,' writes Alex de Jonge. 'It is the reality of the romantic age that inspires some of the richest and most ambitious attempts to deny reality that the west has known.'[2] Two centuries later, reality is still a big problem, and the poet's attempts to escape its grip are no less ambitious. *The Black Parade* is one such attempt, AFI's *Decemberunderground* is another. Where, or when, is this 'Decemberunderground'? On the band's website, Havok explains:

> *It is where the cold can huddle together in darkness and isolation. It is a community of those detached and disillusioned who flee to love, like winter, in the recesses below the rest of the world.*[3]

Who are these detached and disillusioned? They are those, like young Werther, who are cursed with an excess of feeling and an inability to make compromises. Real people, emotional people. *Decemberunderground*, Havok told *Rolling Stone*, describes 'a sort of exclusive, unique type of feeling that certain people have'. These lucky few, he says, know a special love: '… it's that strange love, it's that dark love, it's that cold love, it's the outlook that it's completely different than what most people perceive as something maybe even positive.'[4]

What most people perceive as positive, if the images on TV are anything to go by, is equilibrium, a sense of stability. They want money in the bank, a good school for their kids, a holiday once a year, white teeth and a tan. To the romantic, such people are a mystery. Mary Hays, in 1777, did not envy their quiet uneventful lives. She preferred misery to calmness—because at least when you're miserable you're feeling something. She would much rather suffer the 'exquisite distresses' that result from her attachment to feeling than lead a normal life.

Davey Havok's lyrics are full of these exquisite distresses—intensely pleasurable feelings derived from a surrender to sadness. He's a connoisseur of misery. Like his hero Robert Smith, he's found that not only does he not fight it anymore, he actually looks forward to it. He admits in 'The Interview' that he's always 'waiting for disaster'. Later we find him,

> *Swimming, bathing*
> *Drowning in sorrow.*[5]

Here is that 'cold love' Havok described earlier. The idea gets a further workout in the first single from *December-underground*, 'Love like Winter'. 'Warn your warmth to turn away,' he sings, 'here it's December everyday.'[6] In the song's big-budget video, Havok is seen dressed in his customary black, his face the usual whiter shade of pale, wandering through a snow-bound forest in the depths of winter. Like Young Werther, he seems quite at home in this frozen landscape—if nothing else, it suits his mood. Life has turned cold for the storm-singer, and his feeling for nature can now only be satisfied by scenes of decay and desolation. The nu-folksingers can have their sandy beaches—he's only at home where it's dark and cold.

As the snow whirls around him and the storm clouds brood overhead, our singer starts to hallucinate—he sees, as though in a dream, a beautiful woman walking toward him, dressed in a hooded cloak. They share a moment together, an unspoken understanding. Could it be that he's found true happiness at last? Has he finally found a way out of his dreadful solipsism? Has he realised that impossible romantic dream, an actual connection with another human soul, someone with whom he can be alone—together?

Well, yes and no. The beautiful woman pulls back her hood—she has removed the last of her defences, the way has been cleared for a pure union of souls. And in that very instant, when the singer's happiness seems assured, catastrophe strikes. The ice gives way beneath his feet, he sinks into the freezing darkness. And as he struggles, his exquisite distress is made more exquisite by the reappearance of the beautiful woman, holding him down under the water. She smiles, and holds him in a tender, but deadly embrace.

In real life, the woman is a model from the Ukraine. In an interview for a making-of special, the video's director refers to her as 'the ice-bitch'.[7] But to Davey Havok, she is nothing less than 'the beautiful physical embodiment of hopelessness'.

Alone and Palely Loitering

IN 1816 SEVENTEEN-YEAR-OLD Thomas Keats began receiving letters from a mysterious French girl named Amena Bellafila. She claimed to have met him—though he didn't remember meeting her—through a mutual acquaintance, Thomas's school friend Charles Wells. The letters were written in a curiously old-fashioned idiom, like Elizabethan sonnets— Amena told Tom that he was her knight in armour, that he would rescue her, and that she, in turn, would soothe him. Tom travelled over France trying to find her, but never could.

Two years later, Tom was dying. The doctors said he had tuberculosis, but he fancied he knew better. In October

1818 he told his brother John the truth—he was sick because his heart was broken. He was in love with Amena Bellafila, but Amena had disappeared. He was dying of unrequited love.

John Keats was twenty-three and a promising poet. He was utterly devoted to his younger brother and never left his side during these final days—but something about this 'Amena Bellafila' made him uneasy, and he took time to make some investigations regarding Tom's disappearing French girl. The results confirmed his worst suspicions: there never was an 'Amena'. The letters were fabrications, written by Charles Wells in exaggeratedly feminine handwriting, and composed in the mock-Elizabethan language of his and Tom's schooldays. After Tom's death, Keats finally got to see the letters for himself. 'It is a wretched business,' he wrote to his other brother, George. 'It was no thoughtless hoax—but a cruel deception.'[1]

A few days later Keats wrote to George again. If he was still preoccupied with the cruel trick played on his dead brother, there was little sign of it. Keats described the review he'd just written of a new parody of Wordsworth's *Peter Bell, A Tale*, and shared his thoughts on a diorama of the North Pole he'd recently seen. Then, in the middle of all this casual chat, he copied the stanzas of a poem he'd just written called 'La Belle Dame sans Merci'. It was a ballad, told in a style that showed the influence of Wordsworth (who was probably on Keats's mind because of the review), as well as another of Keats's heroes, the Elizabethan poet Edmund Spenser.[2] The poem's action is set in the depths of winter—the leaves have fallen off the trees, the birds are silent. In the midst of this desolate scene, the narrator meets a knight-at-arms 'alone and palely loitering', who tells the tale of how he came to haunt this particular patch of frozen ground:

IV
I met a lady in the meads,
Full beautiful—a faery's child,
Her hair was long, her foot was light,
And her eyes were wild.[3]

The knight tells of a forest idyll—he made the lady a garland of flowers and set her on his 'pacing steed'. She said, 'I love thee true.'

IX
And there she lullèd me asleep
And there I dream'd—ah! Woe betide!
The latest dream I ever dream'd
On the cold hill side

X
I saw pale kings and princes too,
Pale warriors, death-pale were they all;
They cried—'La Belle Dame sans Merci
Thee hath in thrall!'

XI
I saw their starved lips in the gloam,
With horrid warning gapèd wide,
And I awoke and found me here,
On the cold hill's side.

XII
And this is why I sojourn here,
Alone and palely loitering,
Though the sedge is withered from the lake,
And no birds sing.[4]

'La Belle Dame' condenses a number of Keats's fears and preoccupations. Much like a dream, it seems to give form to anxieties even the poet himself was not consciously aware of at the time—though some of the motifs are more easily recognisable than others. The knight-at-arms is most likely a version of Tom, dressed up to suit the conceit of the 'Amena' letters, 'haggard and so woe-begone' from a long illness exacerbated by a broken heart.[5]

It follows, then, that the 'Belle Dame' is Amena Bellafila. She certainly fits the part—a vision of perfect love which turns out, as soon as the knight falls asleep, to be a trick. The knight's terrifying dream expresses the full extent of Keats's horror at his brother's death. Tom had died broken-hearted, feeling that the happiness he'd sought had been denied him. But the worst of it was that this happiness had never really existed. In the end, as Keats's biographer Robert Gittings points out, the lady in the meads is no simple allegorical figure representing Tom's disappearing girl.

> *She is, when all literary hints from other sources, when all the accidental events of Keats's day-to-day life are exhausted, the symbol of the eternal fusion between love and death.*[6]

A Forest

THE JOURNEY INTO despair that Robert Smith made between 1980–82 began with a walk in a forest. The first single from *Seventeen Seconds* was already a fairly gloomy proposition, and not the follow up to *Boys Don't Cry* that most critics were hoping for. Julie Burchill, writing for the *NME*, accused Smith of 'trying to stretch a sketchy living out of moaning more meaningfully than any man has moaned before'.[1]

Burchill was right on two counts—'A Forest' is full of moaning *and* full of meaning. The song describes a dream in which the singer hears a woman's voice calling his name. He follows the sound into the trees, and the band takes up the theme, conjuring the feeling of a headlong rush into a dark world. Electronic whooshes zip past like drifts of fog. But as Smith searches for his mysterious lover in the forest, a terrible thought occurs to him:

Suddenly I stop
But I know it's too late
I'm lost in the forest
All alone
The girl was never there
It's always the same
I'm running towards nothing
Again and again and again and AGAIN![2]

'A Forest' illustrates an important idea in romantic thought. Many of the romantics—Rousseau and Wordsworth being the clearest examples—idealised nature as a symbol of all that is good, pure and true in *human* nature, and a standard by which our behaviour can be measured. But there is a flip-side to this, in which the romantic individual, having rejected society, runs out into nature and finds that he is not really at home there, either. Since he is now out of options, his philosophy becomes one in which reality itself is hostile. His goals—happiness and love—exist somewhere outside of the world.

All of this makes love complicated for the romantics—and makes it more likely that they will end up confusing love with death and despair, as Keats, Robert Smith and Davey Havok have all done. Love, in the romantic imagination, is pure and natural, part of the mysterious world of feeling and the human heart, which society cannot touch. But to think this is to overburden love with a weight of unrealistic expectations. Ideal love, like nature, becomes one of the romantics' escape destinations—existing outside of the cares of the world, or as Davey Havok would have it, in the cold regions below. But this, like all the romantics' attempts to escape reality, is doomed to fail, since there is no real escape from the world other than death. As a consequence, love becomes an illusion, forever out of reach—

> *The girl was never there*
> *It's always the same*
> *I'm running towards nothing*[3]

—or fatal, pulling the poet toward oblivion. The singer finds his perfect love, the ice cracks, the poet and his fatal lover sink into darkness.

John Keats: Fallen lemons in my path.

Lemonade

AMONG THE STRANGE brew of ingredients that went into the writing of 'La Belle Dame sans Merci' was a copy of Robert Burton's *Anatomy of Melancholy*—one of the most popular and most talked-about books of the seventeenth century. Keats's copy was heavily marked up, 'almost as if with a personal application to himself' as his biographer Robert

Gittings puts it.[1] It was Burton's book, according to Gittings, that gave Keats the image of the sorrowful knight 'alone and palely loitering'. It also provided him with the subject matter and imagery of another of his great odes—'Ode on Melancholy'. As this poem begins, Keats dismisses some of Burton's medicinal cures for sadness. His argument is a little like some of the current debates about anti-depressants—wolf's-bane and the like might leave him in a state of happy forgetfulness, but they would also 'drown the wakeful anguish of the soul'. What does he need *that* for? Keats's answer is simple: poetry.

> *But when the melancholy fit shall fall*
> *Sudden from heaven like a weeping cloud,*
> *That fosters the droop-headed flowers all,*
> *And hides the green hill in an April shroud;*
> *Then glut thy sorrow on a morning rose,*
> *Or on the rainbow of the salt sand-wave,*
> *Or on the wealth of globed peonies;*
> *Or if thy mistress some rich anger shows,*
> *Emprison her soft hand and let her rave,*
> *And feed deep, deep upon her peerless eyes.*[2]

In 'Ode on Melancholy', Keats advises the reader not to drown his sorrows with wine, but to put them to work. This is exactly what Weezer's Rivers Cuomo did in the mid '90s—though he got the idea not from Robert Burton or John Keats, but from his mum. When Rivers was having a rough time growing up (which he frequently did), his mother would cheer him up with a little homespun philosophy: 'If life gives you lemons, make lemonade'.[3] One day in 1992 she said it again, and Cuomo turned his mother's saying into a song. Back when he was younger, he reflects in 'Lemonade,' he used to just let his rage and frustration rot where it fell:

Till the day I couldn't pass
Fallen lemons in my path
So with my mom I now agree
And use the lemons life gives me[4]

Cuomo had begun to understand that 'making lemonade' was exactly what he'd been doing with his recent songs, the songs that would soon appear on Weezer's debut. With 'Buddy Holly', 'In the Garage' and 'Say It Ain't So', Cuomo was turning bitter experience into sweet treats; great pain into little songs (or as he would later call them 'angst muffins').[5]

Weezer's second single, 'Buddy Holly' is lemonade of a fine vintage, drawn partly from Cuomo's high school days (where he and his brother Leaves 'got the crap beaten out of them'), but mostly from an incident that took place during his time at Santa Monica College. Already in Weezer, Cuomo also enrolled in the college choir where he made friends with a girl named Kyung He.[6] The song recalls a day when the Weezer guys were making fun of Kyung He's accent.

Your tongue is twisted
Your eyes are slit
You need a guardian[7]

Cuomo, furious at his band mates and feeling protective toward his friend, wrote a lyric which said, in the plainest terms possible, 'it's okay to be different—we can make it together'. It was deceptively simple powerful stuff, set to an irresistible tune. Pain had been turned into poetry—more than that—a huge hit which finally made all of Rivers Cuomo's rock-star dreams come true.

The lesson was not lost on the singer. Even after he'd abandoned the confessional mode of *Pinkerton* for the classicism of the *Green Album*, Cuomo continued to recognise the importance of melancholy as a songwriting resource. In

2002 he assured the readers of *Spin* magazine (in an obvious bit of emo-baiting) that he still had feelings 'like everybody else', but had carefully compartmentalised them. 'I like to exploit them and use them for my own purposes,' he explained.[8] A couple of years later, when producer Rick Rubin suggested to Cuomo that he try transcendental meditation as a way of focusing his mind on the recording process, Cuomo was horrified.

'I sent him a very anxious page, saying, "Rick, no. I cannot get into meditation because it will rob me of the angst that's necessary to being an artist."'[9]

Cuomo's reasoning was sound—after all, you can't make angst muffins without angst. But the idea, taken too far, can turn ugly. If great songs come from unhappiness, is it now the songwriter's job to remain unhappy? Most Weezer fans, after the *Green Album*, would have answered in the affirmative. They hated the new classical Rivers, with his well-constructed hits. They wanted more suffering and emotional excess, like on *Pinkerton*, the album he wrote in the mid '90s when he was incredibly miserable. One fan, lavishing praise on *Pinkerton* while writing off Weezer's current output as 'horrible pop songs', remarked, 'depressed people sure do write good music'.[10]

There is, it has to be said, something ghoulish about this. Cuomo's fans didn't care in the least about his wellbeing, they wanted him to suffer so that their appetite for intense emotion could be satisfied. This Cuomo steadfastly refused to do.

Weezer could have cashed in on the cult of *Pinkerton* many times over—they could have, at the very least, included the occasional *Pinkerton* song in their shows to keep the fans happy. But as Pete Wentz from Fall Out Boy recently admitted to *Rolling Stone*, 'it's really a fine line between being an inspiration to your fans, and creating an industry out of misery.'[11] Wentz, being a bass player in an emo band, would know all about it.

Billy Corgan: Misery Industry.

Anatomy of Mellon Collie

THIS 'MISERY INDUSTRY' is a tough gig. Entertainers have it easy with their pantomime of emotion. All they have to do is turn it on at the start of the show, then turn it off when they get backstage. For them, it's just a job. But for the romantic poets, with their commitment to emotional truth, the pain has got to be real, the tragedy drawn straight up from the well of their unique sensibility, their ability to feel.

Smashing Pumpkins' Billy Corgan is one of these fearless explorers of inner space. Like Keats, Corgan learned to make use of his moods—but in a more dramatic fashion that seems closer to German poet Heinrich Heine's secret formula for *sturm und drang* poetry;

> *Aus meinen groszen Schmerzen*
> *Mach' ich die kleinen Lieder.*
> *[From my great pain*
> *I make little songs.][1]*

Corgan would accept no other method for his art—every song came from real emotional experience. But not just any old emotional experience. 'A good song, a smiling face, a true feeling, doesn't do it.' He said in 1994, 'People want to see things smashed to bits. They want to see you rip your heart out'.[2] Corgan had just done more or less exactly that with the Smashing Pumpkins 'Disarm'. The song is an aching ode to childhood innocence. Corgan surveys the wreckage of his teens and twenties, and wonders how everything went so wrong. 'I used to be a little boy,' he screams. Of course, his parents and teachers couldn't let him stay that way, they 'cut that little child' out in order to prepare him for the so-called real world.[3] But something went wrong with Corgan's de-programming. He's like one of those science fiction secret agents whose memory was supposed to have been erased, and who then finds he starts remembering things—things responsible grown-ups aren't supposed to remember. A world of sunlight, ice-cream and daydreams; a world where it was okay to be emotional. He knows too much, and this knowledge has made him lonely; and prolonged exposure to loneliness has made him angry and vengeful. But because he's a poet, Corgan, instead of taking up arms against his oppressors, took up his diary and wrote a song. And as the song took shape, Corgan realised he had to turn bitterness into beauty. Later, he said:

> The reason I wrote "Disarm" was because I didn't have the guts to kill my parents, so I thought I'd get back at them through song. And rather than have an angry, angry, angry, violent song I thought I'd write something beautiful and make them realise what tender feelings I have inside my heart.[4]

This kind of bold personal confession, Corgan felt, was the future of music. Speaking to Richard Kingsmill in 1998, he insisted that extreme personal emotion was 'the only place left to go in rock and roll'.[5] But this had already taken its toll on the singer. Remember, Heine says that from great pain you only get little songs, and Smashing Pumpkins' fans wanted to hear little songs like 'Disarm' over and over again, which, for Corgan, meant several emotional apocalypses a night for a six-month stretch. The singer found that, while his sadness was infinite, his ability to keep exploiting it was not. At 1994's Lollapalooza festival, Corgan found himself confronted with an impossible choice—to keep giving his audience the 'real thing' and risk bleeding himself dry; or to 'fake it' for the sake of his sanity. Unfortunately, this second option was something his romantic commitment to emotional truth would never allow. 'I do feel a responsibility to best articulate what I feel,' he said.[6] So, he couldn't just walk away or do the show on autopilot, he saw it as his job to express suffering, and the suffering had to be real.

He was furious at finding himself trapped like this, and decided to channel the rage into his performance. But what good does that do? He can snap and snarl all he wants on stage, but in the end he's just a performing bear—worse, a rat in a cage, running hopelessly on his little wheel so as to satisfy his audience's taste for extreme emotion. Hey, rat in a cage, that's pretty good. He explores this image and the angry, bitter feelings associated with it, and pretty soon he has…another song—that people like! That his fans want him to perform onstage every night of the week for the rest of the year! When, he wonders, will his torment end?

On one level, Smashing Pumpkins' 'Bullet with Butterfly Wings' reflects fairly standard rock-star anxieties about Corgan's relationship with his audience and the music industry that pushes him in front of them. 'Secret destroyers,' he sings, 'hold you up to the flames.' But here, already, the imagery has become somewhat biblical, and when Corgan screams that he cannot be saved and starts comparing himself to an Old Testament prophet, it becomes clear there is more at stake than just the perils of show business. 'Bullet with Butterfly Wings' was, as Corgan later admitted, written about his experience at

Lollapalooza. Nirvana was meant to headline the festival, but when lead singer Kurt Cobain, similarly trapped between his own anxieties and his audience's expectations, took his own life, Smashing Pumpkins was invited to fill the void. The grisly implications of this were not lost on Billy Corgan. When, in 'Bullet with Butterfly Wings,' he accused the whole world of trying to kill him, and then made a simile between himself and Jesus, it's because he was all too aware of the way Cobain had become a martyr to his audience's expectations, and had a terrible feeling he might be next.[7]

In the early '80s Corgan's hero Robert Smith had felt himself being pushed toward the edge of a similar precipice. He too had become a pressure valve for his audience's anxieties by writing with unflinching honesty about the horrors of life. But writing about horror meant living with horror while you recorded it, and then touring the horror for another twelve months. Smith began to wonder just how much horror he could take. And looming over it all was the spectre of Joy Division's Ian Curtis, who'd hanged himself in 1980. Curtis had collapsed under the same pressure Smith was now feeling. In fact, Smith had a feeling he'd only arrived at this point because Curtis was gone, and that he was next in line. Later he said:

> I hate the idea that you'd die for your audience, but I was rapidly becoming enmeshed in that around the time of Pornography; the idea that Ian Curtis had gone first and I was soon to follow.[8]

With the news of Kurt Cobain's death still fresh in his mind, Corgan couldn't help feeling that history was repeating itself. The story of Billy Corgan and the Smashing Pumpkins was starting to take on the characteristics of a modern tragedy, in which he, as the hero, must perish. This might seem absurd—after all, they're just songs, and he's just a singer, right?

Wrong! For Corgan, his life was his art and his art was his life. To an eighteenth-century spectator, the idea that a singer would die for his audience *would* be absurd. But in a post-romantic world, it's entirely plausible.

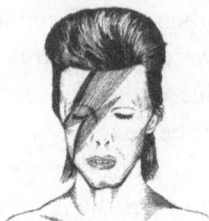

Ziggy Stardust: The rake's reward.

Rock and Roll Suicide

IN 1971 DAVID Bowie was dreaming of re-inventing musical theatre with a story about an alien rock star. But time got away from him, and before he got the chance to write the story out properly, his rock musical had become a rock album. 'There was no time to wait,' he later told *Mojo*'s Paul du Noyer. 'I couldn't afford to sit around for six months and write a proper stage piece, I was too impatient.'[1]

Still, as Bowie admits, the resulting album, *The Rise and Fall of Ziggy Stardust and the Spiders from Mars,* does retain a rough dramatic structure. The first act deals with the arrival of a man from the stars who picks up a guitar and decides to become a star of the more worldly variety. As the album plays on we watch as Ziggy ascends to the heights of fame, and enjoys all the rarefied pleasures it has to offer. Everybody loves him, everybody wants him—and all of this is going to Ziggy's head. So by the time the third act rolls around, and we hear that he's been 'making love with his ego', we know our hero is headed for a fall. He dies, spectacularly, at the end of his theme song 'Ziggy Stardust'. 'He took it all too far,' Bowie reminds us.[2]

To an eighteenth-century audience the tale of Ziggy Stardust, despite confusing references to twentieth-century phenomena like radios, ray guns and vaseline, would be instantly familiar. Ziggy is clearly a gross libertine, who indulges his every appetite. His exploits are disgraceful, but since the story advances a useful moral theme, these can be overlooked (and not-so-secretly enjoyed). The useful moral theme is this: that a dissolute rake like Ziggy will eventually get his just desserts.

On 29 October 1787 Wolfgang Amadeus Mozart conducted at the premiere of a new opera—whose premise was exactly the one described above—at The National Theatre in the old city of Prague. The title on the program that evening was '*Il dissoluto punito*', or 'The Rake's Reward', but the opera later came to be known by the name of its protagonist— the rake of the title—Don Giovanni. The opera was a hit, but that was virtually a foregone conclusion, since Don Giovanni was a retelling of a story that had been playing to packed houses in Europe for almost two hundred years—the seventeenth-century legend of the great seducer, Don Juan.

Mozart's opera begins with a scene where Don Giovanni sneaks into the apartments of Donna Anna, the daughter of the Commandant of Seville. He means to make her the latest of his many conquests, but she screams, and her father comes to her rescue. A fight breaks out between Don Giovanni and the furious *Commendatore*, and the older man is killed. Don Giovanni escapes, his thoughts already turning to his next seduction. A little later, we learn the full extent of Don Giovanni's debauchery in a scene where his servant, Leporello, recites the history of his amorous adventures in front of a horrified Donna Elvira—six hundred and forty in Italy, two hundred and thirty-one in Germany, *a thousand and three* in Spain...

Then, in the second act, after yet another narrow escape, Don Giovanni and Leporello rendezvous in a churchyard near a stone statue erected in the memory of the dead *Commendatore*. Incredibly, the statue comes to life, and informs Don Giovanni that he will be dead before the sun comes up. Leporello sees that under the statue is written the inscription: 'Here I await vengeance upon a vile assassin'. Now, the *Commendatore*'s long wait is over. But Don Giovanni treats this warning the way he treats everything else—as a laugh. His response to the threat of eternal damnation is to invite the statue round for dinner.

To Leporello's horror, the statue proves to be as good as his word. Hearing some commotion, he goes outside to investigate, and comes back to his master with terrifying news—he's so frightened he can barely speak. 'The stone…man…all white,' he stammers. The statue pounds on the door, and since Leporello is too scared out of his wits to answer it, Don Giovanni does it himself, while his servant hides under the table. Don Giovanni, still maintaining the light-hearted and cynical attitude that has carried him through life thus far, offers the stone man a seat. But the ghost is not here for dinner: 'A graver purpose than this, another mission has brought me hither.' He tells Don Giovanni that he must come with him, and extends his hand. 'Will you in turn come and sup with me?' asks the stone guest. Don Giovanni, not one to be called chicken, accepts. As his hand touches the statue's, he becomes locked in a vice-like grip. 'Tis colder than the tomb!' he exclaims. The *Commendatore* demands three times that the wicked rake repent for his sins, and each time Don Giovanni answers with a defiant, 'No!'. 'Your time has come!' roars the ghost. Right on cue, a crack opens up in the floor, and Don Giovanni feels himself being pulled downward. It starts to get hot. 'Whence come these hideous bursts of flame?' he cries. From the unfathomable depths below the earth comes an answer:

> No doom is too great for your sins
> Worse torments await you below! [3]

Don Giovanni is dragged down to hell with a blood-curdling scream.

Mozart seals the villain's fate with a couple of conclusive chords—and this really sounds like the end of the opera. But it's not. With Don Giovanni's final terrified yell still ringing in our ears, Leporello, Donna Elvira, Donna Anna, Massetto and Zerlina come come back out on the stage to let us know what they're up to now that Don Giovanni is locked out of harm's way. Donna Elvira says she's off to enter a convent, Zerlina and Massetto are going home for a nice quiet dinner and Leporello tells us he's going to the pub. Why are they telling us all this stuff? Because they have a useful moral theme to deliver. Zerlina, Masetto and Leporello:

> *Let the scoundrel remain below*
> *with Proserpine and Pluto;*
> *and we, good people,*
> *will gaily sing*
> *the ancient moral.*

All:

> *This is the evil doer's end!*
> *The death of sinners*
> *will always match their life!*[4]

That's the end of Don Giovanni—or at least, it was when Mozart wrote it. But if you'd gone to see the opera in, say, 1816—you'd find this ending had vanished. For most of the nineteenth century, Don Giovanni concluded with the no-good rake being consumed by the flames of hell—Leporello, Zerlina, Masetto and their useful moral theme were nowhere to be seen.

In the twenty years since Don Giovanni made its debut in Prague, the world had changed dramatically, and popular taste had changed with it. Nineteenth-century music-lovers still wanted Don Giovanni—but they didn't want a moral enforcing the importance of moderation in all things. What they wanted was a story about a man who did whatever he liked, in defiance of society's rules, and died heroically as a result. The German writer E T A Hoffman (the 'A' stands for 'Amadeus') defined the role of this new Don Giovanni in his 1813 story *Don Juan*. Here, a concertgoer watching Mozart's opera is treated to a special director's commentary by the ghost of Donna Anna. She reveals that Don Giovanni was not a bad man who got his just desserts, but a hero. He lived a life of passion and inspiration while everyone else just went to work and paid their taxes. In this version of the tale, Don Giovanni is preferred to the society whose limits he refused to accept. As a result, he becomes the very definition of the tragic romantic hero—the inspired individual who picks a fight with society, a fight which he can't possibly win. The romantic hero is always outnumbered, because he is always alone.

Like Don Giovanni, Bowie's Ziggy Stardust comes with an epilogue. The hero takes it all too far and is destroyed—not by demons from hell, but by the mass of grabbing hands just below the stage. In his live shows, Bowie illustrated Ziggy's demise even more dramatically with a cover of the Velvet Underground's 'White Light/White Heat', in which the rock star hero is burned to a crisp by the sheer velocity of his lifestyle. But just when you think he's gone forever—his threat to the status quo safely locked away in the depths of the earth or burned away into space—he's back. He sits on the side of the stage, smoking a cigarette and snapping his fingers to the beat. He sings a song called 'Rock and Roll Suicide'. Ziggy didn't actually take his own life—but then he also knew (or should have known) what he was signing up for when he decided to become 'the special man', to live among humans while reserving the right to ignore all of their moral laws and social conventions As he tells his story, the song builds and builds—and then comes to a halt. He waits a beat, leans in to the audience, and delivers his message to the kids:

You're not alone!
Just turn on with me,
and you're not alone![5]

Here is a great paradox, but one that Bowie, and the artists he inspired—Robert Smith, Billy Corgan and Gerard Way— would attempt to resolve. The singer tells us that he was a solitary rebel who died tragically in his one-man war against society. But he didn't do it so he could end up as an illustration for a moral principle—he did it for everybody else who ever felt like they didn't fit in. He died for us, and for the idea that someday, some way, we might find a way to be alone— together. But in the meantime, Ziggy reminds the faithful, though the world is cruel and will rob the young romantic hell raiser of his dreams, one must carry on regardless.

This is the one part of Ziggy's story that would have been deeply confusing and disturbing to our imaginary eighteenth-century audience. In 'Ziggy Stardust', it's the libertine—and not the shopkeeper or the nun—who has the last laugh. This, to an eighteenth-century spectator, would seem shockingly immoral. But sometime around the first decade of the nineteenth century, things changed—permanently, it would seem. Because in 1973 David Bowie could virtually guarantee that everyone in his audience would be rooting for the dissolute rake in his story, and not for the society whose rules he refused to accept. He took it all too far—but the moral of 'Ziggy Stardust' is not 'pride comes before a fall' or 'fiery doom is the rake's reward'. After the curtain comes down on Bowie's low-budget rock opera, there's no little party of regular folk to deliver a lesson about the virtues of hard work, abstinence and commonsense. In rock and roll, this rarely happens—in glam rock (which Bowie more or less invented with 'Ziggy') it never does. The rock star is not a moral scarecrow—he's a hero in death, because his non-stop sinning is a protest against the limits of ordinary life.

In AFI's 'Miss Murder', the singer contemplates his own rock and roll suicide. The song weds the melody of Depeche Mode's 'Strangelove' to the sound and rhythm of Gary Glitter's glam classic, 'Rock and Roll Part 1'. Havok's lyrics tell the tale of a beautiful, otherworldly rock star. 'How they all adored him,' he sighs. As the chorus kicks in and the band 'whoah-ohs' like they're Bon Jovi, Havok poses the mother of all romantic dilemmas:

Hey, Miss Murder can I
make beauty stay if I
take my life?[6]

Two hundred years of the romantic tradition says: yes you can. It's not just about dying young and leaving a good-looking corpse. The existential dilemma of a Don Giovanni or a Ziggy Stardust comes from the fact that society wants him to be useful, whereas he respects only beauty. As both of these romantic ur-myths show, there is only one way out of this dilemma, but by taking it, the hero becomes a martyr to the principle by which he lived his life, which is the pursuit of strange beauty at all costs.

In 'Miss Murder', death, once again, takes female form. The full-length version of the song's video incorporates a prelude. We see, in a series of cuts, a beautiful woman seated at an ornate writing desk where she writes a letter, as Davey Havok stalks the marble floors of a cathedral. The singer has been betrayed—by the woman, by love, by the world in general—we don't know, but he's mad as hell, and as he walks, he sings a poisoned lullaby. He's decided to quit this world—but before he does, he has one more thing to ask of his beloved:

... you may forget me
I promise to depart just promise one thing
Kiss my eyes and lay me to sleep[7]

As the last notes of his lullaby die away, and the glam rock goose-step of 'Miss Murder' fills the cathedral, we see that the singer has been granted his wish. The 'Miss Murder' of the title, we now realise, is the woman sitting at the writing desk. She folds a piece of paper, swallows it—and it instantly appears in the singer's mouth. He pulls it out, unfolds it, and sees an image of three black rabbits arranged in a circle—a symbol of death in AFI lore.

Havok doesn't break down in tears at the news of his imminent demise, and he doesn't scream like Don Giovanni. He adopts an air of melancholy resignation, as though he knew, all along, that this is where his flaunting of society's rules would lead him (which of course he did). This is the 'tortured poet charisma', which Matt Diehl, in his book *My So-Called Punk*, insists is key to AFI's appeal.[8] Havok most likely copped the pose from careful study of the posters of Bowie, Morrissey and Robert Smith that line the walls of his vocal booth during recording sessions. But this 'tortured poet charisma', while being fairly familiar in the world of rock and roll, is something relatively new in the world of poetry. It would have been completely alien to the poetry-lover of the eighteenth century—in the days of Pope and Johnson, poets were not tortured. Poets were sharp-eyed observers of society, but they always knew they belonged in society—what could they have to be tortured about? Wordsworth undermined this assumption in 1798, but it was completely overturned in 1812 by a much younger poet—a man much admired by such literary heavyweights as Goethe and Nietzsche—but also by a large reading public, who enshrined him as the archetypal romantic hero of the eighteen-hundreds. Thanks to George Gordon Byron, 'tortured poet charisma' quickly became the only kind the nineteenth century cared about.

Screamin' Lord Byron

IN THE DECADE following the success of 'Ziggy Stardust', Bowie killed Ziggy off twice, reinvented himself as a blue-eyed soul singer, then a Teutonic robot, and then a tragic Pierrot. Finally, he transformed himself into the only thing that could really surprise his fans—an ordinary bloke. In Julian Temple's extended video for his 1984 single 'Blue Jean', Bowie plays Vic—an ordinary bloke—who, while working up a ladder one day, falls in love with a girl. Trouble is, she looks straight past him—right over the top of his scruffy head in fact—to the huge poster of exotic pop singer Screamin' Lord Byron across the street. So the resourceful Vic blags his way into a date with the girl by making up a cock-and-bull story about being a relative of Screamin's', and promises to use his influence to get some free tickets to the show. Because he's in no position to do any such thing, he eventually resorts to breaking into the club where Screamin' is doing his show. Vic crashes through the ceiling into the horrified singer's dressing room in a hail of plaster and a shower of dust.

Screamin' Lord Byron is the opposite of Vic in every way. The singer is not so much a human being as an assemblage of affectations and complications—heavily made-up, even more heavily medicated, terrified of human contact and absolutely scared stiff of Vic with his cheery cockney brusqueness. But this cringing mess is also a superhuman god. Later, we see him on stage at the Bosphorous Rooms where he holds the audience in thrall with his deep voice and hypnotic gestures. The rapt fans raise their hands up as if to worship him—he clicks his fingers to the beat and they all do the same, never taking their eyes off him for a moment.

They worship him, but he barely notices them. He leaves the stage without so much as a wink or a smile. He waits in his dressing room until almost everyone has left before venturing back into the room, where Vic and his date are waiting, hoping for an audience. Vic leaps to his feet on seeing Screamin'—but the singer doesn't see him at all. He goes straight for the girl, sweeps her off her feet, and stalks out of the club—leaving the furious Vic hurling insults at the star's flashy car as it disappears down the street. 'Your record sleeves are better than your songs!'[1]

The joke is that Screamin' Lord Byron is also played by David Bowie. This is a great bit of casting, because we all know that before he was a regular bloke, Bowie was a narcissistic, antisocial rock and roll superman. And just as the superman's name was a dream amalgam representing Bowie's rock and roll ideal—in which the glam fantasy of the Original Stardust Cowboy met the Dionysiac excess of Iggy and the Stooges—so 'Screamin' Lord Byron' weds the show-business flash of early British rock 'n' roll ('Screamin' Lord Sutch') to the name of the nineteenth-century poet who most resembles a rock star before the fact—Lord Byron.

Byron: 'melancholy and sullen detachment'.

Lord Byron

IN THE MONTHS before he wrote 'La Belle Dame sans Merci', John Keats had been in a terrible mood. His friend Benjamin Robert Haydon, the painter, remembers that around this time Keats became 'morbid and silent', though he was also prone to outbursts. When a family friend made a comment on

Keats's growing reputation, saying to Mrs Brawne, 'O, he is quite the little poet,' Keats angrily exclaimed, 'You see what it is to be under six foot and not a Lord!'[1]

Time has been kinder to Keats's poetry than Byron's. But in 1818 Keats had good reason to be jealous. It wasn't just that Byron was tall (he was not quite six foot in fact) or that he was of noble birth. The real reason why Keats was feeling so sensitive was that he'd just learned that Byron had sold over four thousand copies of the last canto of *Childe Harold's Pilgrimage*. This poem, the first two parts of which had been published six years earlier, had already made him incredibly famous.

Byron had written Childe Harold while travelling in Spain, Malta, Turkey and Greece between 1810 and 1812. While abroad he'd lived the life of a libertine: frolicking with olive-skinned youths on the beach, being courted by Turkish warlords and enjoying 'fooleries with the females of Athens', as Byron put it.[2] As he returned home to England to claim the estate that came with his title, with all the responsibilities that entailed, those two carefree years in the south started to seem more and more like the best years of his life. The future, on the other hand, was almost too grim for the twenty-three-year old Byron to contemplate. He felt done with life. He'd seen the world, and was now looking, he told a friend, for 'the most eligible way out of it'.[3] In this gloomy frame of mind he moved into his dilapidated gothic abbey at Newstead.

While travelling, Byron had been working on a poem. He'd recently changed the name of the protagonist from Childe Burun to Childe Harold, but there was no mistaking him for anyone but his creator—he stands to inherit a title and a 'venerable pile', and his travelogue, as described in the poem, is similar to Byron's.[4] This worried Robert Dallas—a family friend of Byron's who was arranging for the poem's publication. Dallas loved the poem, but was concerned about the state of its author's soul. If Byron had done half the things his literary alter ego claimed to have done, he was going straight to hell.

> *Ah me! In sooth he was a shameless wight,*
> *Sore given to revel and ungodly glee;*
> *Few earthly things found favour in his sight*
> *Save concubines and carnal company,*
> *And flaunting wassailers of high and low degree.*[5]

Byron told him he was right to be worried. 'My whole life has been at variance with propriety, not to say decency', he admitted, with melancholy resignation.[6] This last was the real trick up Byron's sleeve. The poet Samuel Rogers, who read the proofs of Childe Harold, predicted that it would be a flop because the hero was both an unrepentant sinner and a misery guts. Who would want to read about the doings of a man like that? But this double whammy of debauchery and despondency, as Colin Wilson insists in his book, *The Misfits*, is exactly what caught the public's imagination.[7] Childe Harold was not a 'cheerful voluptuary' in the mode of Mozart's Don Giovanni. He sinned, but he did so with an air of sorrow and detachment, as though there were some terrible sadness in his past that he could never quite escape. This drove the ladies wild. When Childe Harold was published on Saturday 7 March 1812 Byron was a nobody. By the following Monday, he was famous.[8] Childe Harold was well on the way to selling out its first print run, and its author was presented in his rooms with a salver full of visiting cards. 'Women,' as Wilson writes, 'begged for introductions.'[9]

Dallas had guessed that the close identification of Byron with Harold would increase the poem's appeal, and he was right. He was correct, too, in believing that the poem was something new under the sun. To Dallas, as Byron's biographer Peter Quennell writes, Childe Harold 'seem[ed] to catch and concentrate an unresolved element in the life of the period, something to which no novelist or versifier had yet been able to give a literary shape…'[10] This was probably the same 'unresolved element' that Goethe had isolated thirty-five years earlier—or at least a very similar one. But where the celebrity hunters would later look in vain for Werther in Goethe, they found Childe Harold in Byron. There was, as Goethe himself observed, an unconscious quality to Byron and his work, as though the one simply sprang fully formed from the other, unmediated by any normal artistic process. This makes his poetry a little unsatisfying when compared with Keats's or Wordsworth's. But neither of those two achieved, in their lifetime, anything like the fame and notoriety of Byron. Byron was a star, courted by society, endlessly propositioned by female admirers, and studiously imitated by young men.

In the London of 1812, the Werther face had been replaced by the Byronic limper. Byron had been born with a club foot that gave him a curious and distinctive dragging gait. That his young admirers should start imitating this, his least attractive physical feature, might seem strange. But Byron's deformity, his 'mark of Cain' as he called it, was actually the key to his whole 'look'—and much more besides. The club foot had been a source of endless torment for Byron in his childhood. Doctors had prescribed various cures involving braces and harnesses, all of which were physically painful and—much worse—socially crippling. His unlovable mother did nothing to help matters by calling him a 'lame brat'.[11] All of this left him with a desperate need for approval on the one hand, and a deep-seated conviction that he was doomed to be lonely and unhappy on the other. So it made no difference to him how famous he became, how many books he sold, how many times his portrait was painted, or how many girls—or boys—he slept with. He pursued all these things vigorously, but none of them, not fame, money or pleasure, could compensate for the blow he'd been dealt at birth. As Quennell writes, 'The admiration he might arouse while stationary must vanish, he felt sure, when he crossed the room.'[12] His solution to this was to stand still—and here was the origin of the famous Byronic look—the pose people still imagine when they hear the words 'romantic poet'. Peter Quennell describes it vividly in *Byron: The Years of Fame*:

As he leant on one elbow, his small white hand
clenched beneath his cheek, meditative, immobile ... in
the anteroom of some brilliant London party—
melancholy and sullen detachment pervaded his
attitude ...[13]

This stance communicated volumes. As Quennell points out, a young, healthy-looking man like Byron must, it would be assumed, have a good reason for standing still. But since there was nothing obviously wrong with him, his audience was forced to assume that he was paralysed by existential boredom—which was not too far from the truth. This pose, combined with his extremely pale complexion—a side-effect of his brutal skin care regime—created the impression that Byron was a creature from another world. In his heart of hearts, Byron longed to be *in* the world, to relate to others as an equal. But since he knew this would never happen (because of the terrible curse), he further entrenched himself as an outcast by creating mythologised versions of his suffering self in his poems. These reinforced the impression his insecurities had created until it was impossible to tell where the myth ended and the man began. Tortured poet charisma starts here.

There was in him a vital scorn of all:
As if the worst had fall'n which could befall,
He stood a stranger in this breathing world,
An erring spirit from another hurl'd;[14]

By portraying himself as a solitary, inspired individual, forever cut off from society, Byron was simply acting out the dilemma of all poets and artists since the revolution. But Byron, with his flair for publicity and his gift for self-mythologising, was the first to make this idea popular with a middle-class public.

> So much he soar'd beyond or sunk beneath,
> The men with whom he felt condemned to breathe,
> And long'd by good or ill to separate
> Himself from all who shared his mortal state;[15]

The source of his estrangement, as he explains in 'Lara', lay in his childhood. He was born with a double handicap—a deformed leg and an oversized heart.

> his early dreams of good outstripped the truth
> and troubled manhood followed baffled youth [16]

The world had already broken Byron's heart when he was only twenty-three. From there, things could only get worse, and sure enough, they did. His insatiable appetite for kicks conspired with his desperate need for attention to produce a series of scandals that culminated in an affair with his half-sister Augusta in 1814. After that, he went from society darling to social pariah in record time. He left England for the continent shortly after, and remained in exile for the rest of his life. This, of course, only confirmed his belief that he was a man apart.

Like Werther, Byron ascribed almost cosmic significance to his emotions, and the feelings stirred up by the Augusta affair led him to his most spectacular conclusion. He loved Augusta, and for that society denounced him as a sinner. Since his feelings couldn't be wrong, he must be a sinner, and since, as the philosopher Bertrand Russell says, 'he *must* be remarkable, he would be remarkable as a sinner, and would dare transgressions beyond the courage of the fashionable libertines whom he wished to despise'.[17] He would become a super-sinner. Byron had seen his way marked out for him even before a furious Madam de Staël told him he was *'un demon'*—he had already compared himself in verse to a fallen angel.[18] Like Don Giovanni, Byron was hell-bound. But unlike the light-hearted seventeenth-century rake, Byron knew in advance where he was headed, and would get there on his own terms.

For the hero of the modern tragedy, there's no question of survival—he's doomed before the lights go down. But he can decide how he wants to go out. Werther and the emo singers simply take the path of least resistance and let the world roll right over them. They're paralysed by the sheer pointlessness of everything, and by the world's refusal to live up to their expectations. So they wait until life has them boxed into a corner, and slip quietly into oblivion with a heavy sigh. Werther can barely bring himself to commit suicide; he prefers to think that he's allowed Charlotte to kill him. Byron started out this way: returning from his pilgrimage in 1812 he asked nothing more of the world than a way of walking out of it, and wondered if, somewhere in London, he might find someone who'd be willing to save him the trouble.[19]

But after the Augusta scandal his position had changed. He'd become a 'strong' romantic, the kind who sees that society cannot accommodate him, and so sets out to oppose everything that society stands for. If he's already doomed, he's going to do whatever he likes and make as much trouble as possible along the way. What's more, he'll have the last laugh. Life might be impossible for the romantic outsider, but he can still go out in a blaze of glory—or hellfire, as the case may be.

Give Them Blood

THERE IS A twist in the tragedy of Ziggy Stardust: when he finally goes down, he doesn't overdose on smack or choke on his own vomit. Even the threat of his jealous band mates turns out to be a red herring. In the end it's the kids—Ziggy's own fans—who finish him off. This is what Bowie means when he sings about Ziggy being 'a leper Messiah'. His fans, no longer satisfied with admiring his 'snow-white tan' from afar, took him up on the offer he seemed to be making of his body. They all wanted him, so they each grabbed a piece and ripped him apart.[1] And in 'Rock 'n' Roll Suicide' he explains that he gave himself willingly, gave up his body as a sacrament so that the fans might finally achieve the communion they craved.

Ziggy Stardust has endured as a rock and roll myth because it has its basis in something terrifyingly real. Bowie had already lived through the deaths of Jimi Hendrix and Jim Morrison, 'strong' romantic heroes who—quite self-consciously in Morrison's case—pushed at the limits of life and paid the price. He knew better than most that the message of these stories is not a moral one. And Ziggy is prophetic, too. When Bowie first unveiled the album in 1973, the world had yet to witness the likes of Ian Curtis and Kurt Cobain. These were singers who, in a very real sense, died because of their audience's emotional expectations. They expressed suffering on behalf of their fans, and their deaths came to be understood as the logical end point of that suffering. The moment of panic Billy Corgan experienced at Lollapalooza, as recorded in 'Bullet with Butterfly Wings' was a result of his realisation that he'd been cast as the lead in a Ziggy-like tragedy, in which his own fans demanded his head so that the show they'd come to see would have a proper ending.

Back in the days of the Ancient Greeks, the first tragedies were performed to accompany the ritual sacrifice of a goat.

The name itself comes from the word *tragodia*, meaning 'goat song'.[2] So when Gerard Way invites us along to witness a tragic affair in the opening moments of *The Black Parade*, two thousand years of tradition say that blood will have to be spilled. And by insisting that the suffering we are about to witness must be his own, the romantic artist has put himself forward as the most likely candidate. By the end of the album Way has come to understand this. Like Ziggy Stardust, *The Black Parade* ends with an amoral conclusion. After the smoke has cleared, the Patient is wheeled back onstage on his hospital gurney to perform a jaunty cabaret number called 'Blood':

> Blood, blood, gallons of the stuff,
> give them all that they can drink and it will never be
>   enough[3]

Earlier in the album, Gerard had promised blood—he just had no idea the kids would want so much of it. Here, the tragic hero resigns himself to his fate; his fans want blood, and he'll give it until his veins run dry. He is, he explains, their favourite dish. Billy Corgan felt the same way, and expressed the feeling in similar terms—though without Gerard's weary resignation. 'Bullet with Butterfly Wings' contains a dizzying mix of metaphors, which is part of its charm. The singer's terror and paranoia will not allow him the peace of mind needed to choose his images carefully—they tumble out of him in a great flood. When he compares himself with Jesus, he's evoking the image of the sacrament, the idea that he gave up his body and his blood so that his fans might mosh. But this is a thought that's grown out of an earlier one—the great statement Corgan delivers, a cappella, at the beginning of the song: 'The world is a vampire'.[4]

Corgan evokes the sexualised threat of the vampire to describe the way the music industry, the media, and even his own fans seem to be slowly draining him, body and soul. It's an image Gerard Way has returned to again and again. The horror hospital scenario of 'Blood' and the nocturnal cannibalism described in 'The Sharpest Lives' are the last drops of a great tide of vampire imagery that flowed through My Chemical Romance's early work. They became so well known for it, in fact, that Gerard swore no more for *The Black Parade*. But somehow, a couple of those pesky bloodsuckers crawled in there. They are, as Way explained in an online interview with X V Scott, almost unavoidable in his line of work:

> *...there's just something about the bloodsucking walking dead that can say so much to people. There are really so many people trying to get control over you on a daily basis and...take a part of you.*[5]

Count Dracula: 'He stood a stranger in this breathing world'.

The Vampyre

CONSIDERING HOW LITTLE time he had for romanticism of any stripe, it seems odd at first to learn that Goethe admired Lord Byron. This, after all, was the same Goethe who wrote off the flood of gloomy sentimental prose that appeared in the wake of *The Sorrows of Young Werther* as 'the literature of despair', and who blasted the French romantics of Delacroix's generation for perpetrating 'aesthetics of the grotesque'.[1] For Goethe 'romantic' usually meant 'deranged', if not merely 'badly done'. If he was so down on despair and derangement, what could he possibly find to admire in the author of *Childe Harold's Pilgrimage*?

Goethe, as Gerhart Hoffmeister has shown, did not renounce any of his convictions for Byron's sake—but he did make an exception for him.[2] To Goethe, Byron was a special case, for the simple reason that he was a natural genius, to whom no rule could apply. He belonged, not with other poets, but with Napoleon. Creatures such as these, Goethe believed, could not be judged by society's laws, because their very purpose in life is to break free of those laws—and any others they might find along the way—forever. It's this highly idealised Byron—spontaneous genius and rebel angel—that Goethe paid tribute to by including him as a character in the second book of his epic drama, *Faust*—completed just before Goethe died in 1832. Here, the poet Goethe claimed to love like a son has become Faust's son, Euphorion.

Euphorion: let me be springing,
Let me be leaping,
Pressing on, mounting,
Through the clouds sweeping,
Strong these desires
In my thoughts run
Faust: gently, ah gently,
Be not too daring,
Lest in disaster
All of us sharing...[3]

True to life, Euphorion does not do as he's told—he's a force of nature. When he dies, it's as a flaming ember shooting up to the stars. White light, white heat; Euphorion appears in *Faust* only briefly, but burns very brightly.

In 1819 Goethe got hold of a new prose work of Byron's called *The Vampyre*. The story, published in *The New Monthly Magazine*, had all the elements Byron's fans had come to love. Brooding, black-clad anti-hero of noble birth? Check. Secret sorrow? Check. But *The Vampyre* had a new twist, the gloomy protagonist was not just deathly pale in the approved Byronic mould, he was actually dead. Or rather, he was undead, a ghoulish parasite feeding on the blood of the living. Like Byron himself, *The Vampyre* seemed to present a distorted mirror image of ourselves—a creature loosed from moral restraints for whom the only good is what brings pleasure. And as always with Byron, the protagonist was scandalously identified with the author himself. It was a dead giveaway, really—the vampire's name, Lord Ruthven, was the same as the one given to the Byron character in Lady Caroline Lamb's *Glenarvon*. This, even for Byron, was daring stuff. Putting the story down, Goethe proclaimed it the poet's best work yet. But here Goethe was wrong on at least one count. *The Vampyre* wasn't Byron's. Well, not exactly.

After leaving England in 1816, Byron had paid a visit to the field of Waterloo before stopping in Switzerland at the Villa Diodati by the shores of Lake Geneva. Here, he'd settled in to write the last two cantos of *Childe Harold's Pilgrimage*. He later described his circumstances, with typical understatement, to the poet Tom Moore:

> *I was half mad during the time of its composition, between metaphysics, lakes, love unextinguishable, thoughts unutterable, and the nightmare of my own delinquencies. I should, many a good day, have blown my brains out, but for the recollection that it would have given pleasure to my mother-in-law ...*[4]

At Lake Geneva Byron was plagued by a horde of celebrity spotters, clamouring for a glimpse of the scandalous poet.

There was also the usual parade of not-so-secret admirers, including the highly resourceful Claire Clairmont, who'd enjoyed a fling with the poet in London and had now, it seemed, journeyed eight hundred miles to 'unphilosophize' him, as Byron put it.[5]

The good news in all of this was that Claire had come with her stepsister Mary Godwin (daughter of the philosopher William Godwin and the feminist Mary Wollstonecraft) and Mary's husband-to-be, the poet Percy Bysshe Shelley. Theirs was a whirlwind romance—only two weeks earlier the couple had been courting by Mary's mother's gravestone. Now, following a bizarre honeymoon in war-torn rural France, they were staying at a house at the base of the hill below Byron's villa. Byron, bored out of his skull by the company of his physician, John Polidori, welcomed the more stimulating conversation of the Shelleys.

Byron and Shelley took walks in the surrounding countryside visiting places they knew from Rousseau's books, and discussed Wordsworth's latest poem, 'The Excursion'. But the weather soon turned nasty, which not only kept the literary conversation indoors, but seemed to demand literature of a type better suited to thunderstorms. Byron suggested that the holiday-makers should each try their hand at writing a ghost story. But according to Mary, the great poet's enthusiasm for the project quickly ran out.[6] He wrote only a small fragment of a story about a vampire. In his biography of Byron, Frederic Raphael makes the interesting suggestion that, in producing a story in which the victim is 'drained of blood by battening predators', Byron may have been inspired by his own situation—besieged by celebrity spotters and groupies who all wanted a piece of him. Raphael wonders whether it was 'this aggrieved sense of being constantly drained', which led Byron 'to concoct a little fragment which added a fanged twist to the Gothick repertoire ...'[7]

Polidori's contribution to the contest—concerning a woman with a skull for a head, was by Mary's account, laughably bad. But he made up for it later. The temperamental doctor took up the idea Byron had laid aside and expanded it, over the next year or so, into a novella called *The Vampyre*—the very same one Goethe enjoyed so thoroughly. Goethe can be excused for his confusion over the story's authorship. The *New Monthly*, without Polidori's permission, published *The Vampyre* as a new work by Byron.[8]

Although he didn't write it, Byron's hand is all over *The Vampyre*—and not just because the original idea was his. Polidori's tale effectively updated the old folkloric version of the vampire for nineteenth-century tastes by 'Byronising' him. Polidori's Lord Ruthven is exceedingly pale, is burdened by a secret sorrow, and preys on society ladies and young girls. All of this gives him an irresistible allure—he's always being invited to parties 'in spite of the deadly hue of his face', and once he gets there he 'gaze[s] on the mirth around him as if he could not participate therein'. Ruthven is both a very thinly veiled portrait of Polidori's former master, and an attempt to capitalise on Byron's notoriety and the perceived threat of romanticism to the stability of bourgeois society. *The Vampyre* invites the reader to imagine the damage that could be done to a well-ordered world by a creature with an insatiable passion and no moral qualms to speak of.

Polidori's modifications to the vampire would survive intact in his most famous appearance, in Bram Stoker's 1897 *Dracula*. And since it's Dracula that's won over in the popular imagination as the definitive version of the monster, the Byronic traits that Polidori introduced to his character are now fixtures. For this, we have Hollywood to thank. F W Murnau's expressionist classic *Nosferatu* (1922) was an unofficial adaptation of Stoker's novel. But the real breakthrough for the Byronic vampire was Tod Browning's 1931 *Dracula*, starring Bela Lugosi. Lugosi's exotic, cape-wearing aristocrat defined the look and the manner of movie vampires for decades to come, and Browning's *Dracula* was to become the foundation stone of an entire vampire film industry, which flourishes to this day

In June 1983 a film by Tony Scott called *The Hunger* opened in cinemas, starring David Bowie as Blaylock—a pale, aloof, aristocratic vampire living in 1980s Manhattan. *The Hunger* received terrible reviews, ('incoherent and foolish,' said the *Observer*),[9] but it did contain a few striking set pieces, including the opening sequence set in a nightclub and cut to the rhythm of Bauhaus's 1979 single, 'Bela Lugosi's Dead'. The band appeared on screen, performing the song inside a cage under stark expressionist lighting, while singer Peter Murphy—frequently criticised for being a Bowie copyist—did nothing to shake off the comparison. The song, like the movie it appeared in, was brilliant nonsense. Over skittering rhythms and disorienting dub effects, Murphy paid tribute to the world's most famous movie vampire in a voice as deep as the hollows under his cheekbones. Meanwhile Bowie, as Blaylock, surveyed the club's clientele with a mixture of predatory lust and superior disdain.

Casting Bowie as Blaylock was an inspired choice. The vampire is an easy role for a rock singer to play, for the same reason that 'rock singer' makes a good disguise for a vampire. Both are a threat to society because of their voracious sexual appetites and their indifference to conventional morality. It would already have been assumed that Bowie—as a rock and roll star—came out at night, preyed on young women, and shrank in terror from crucifixes and holy water—all that was missing was the teeth and the cape (and Bowie wore a few of those in the '70s too). Peter Murphy, as the singer in a darkly glamorous post-punk band, would have been perceived in much the same way, and his pale skin and skull-like features only added to the 'creature of the night' effect. And of course, it went without saying that neither had any time for bourgeois morality. Bowie had spent the last decade demolishing taboos with the disdain of an alien aristocrat, and Bauhaus were already (much to their dismay) seen as standard bearers for a musical movement that dressed in black, came out only at night, and despised nothing so much as middle-class suburban conformity. Over the next ten years, the adherents of this new post-punk religion would turn *The Hunger* from a box-office turkey into an object of worship. The scene in the nightclub would be endlessly rewound and replayed in teenage bedrooms across Britain: 'undead, undead, undead…'

Goths

WHILE *The Hunger* was playing in cinemas, an unusual nightclub tour was making its way around Britain. The Batcave promised to bring unsavoury sounding entertainment from the likes of Alien Sex Fiend, Flesh for Lulu and Specimen to Sheffield, Birmingham, Manchester, and any other English town foolish enough not to have stocked up on garlic and crucifixes in advance. This Batcave had begun as a Wednesday night happening in a Soho club called, appropriately, The Gargoyle. The flyers promised something 'thoroughly nasty'[1] and guaranteed 'absolutely no funk'.[2] Not that there wasn't dancing—here, 'Bela Lugosi's Dead' had become a certified floor filler along with other nocturnal odes such as The Birthday Party's 'Release the Bats' and Siouxsie and the Banshees' 'Spellbound'. The regulars were described by David Johnson in *The Face* magazine as looking like 'Dracula meets the Muppets'.[3] The décor was Victorian romance gone to seed, with posters from classic 1930s horror movies on the walls. Very quickly, the denizens of the Batcave came to resemble their surroundings—here you could see make-up by the living dead, clothes by Count Dracula, and hair by the Bride of Frankenstein.

'You had to take a lift up to the top floor, which used to be a hostess club', recalled Soft Cell singer Marc Almond. 'There was a little theatre where stripteases used to take place and they used it to watch gothic movies, or bands would perform there, and you could see people like Robert Smith hanging out at the bar.'[4] In 1983 the makers of a BBC documentary on The Batcave lamented the lack of any proper celebrities to film—but they may have turned up on a bad night—or maybe it was just too dark. 'The usual tykes were spotted flaunting their disease-wracked bodies at the Batcave last Wednesday night', wrote a *Sounds* reporter in 1983, 'Including (yawn)...a fat Siouxsie Sioux, a dazed Nick Cave'.[5]

No-one will ever know exactly who first used the word 'Gothic' to describe the scene that moved into the Batcave and soon became synonymous with it. But the best story comes from The Cult's Ian Astbury. Long before he started fronting the resurrected Doors, Astbury was playing Jim Morrison to Peter Murphy's Bowie in the early goth scene with his first band, Southern Death Cult. Astbury remembers giving Andi from Sex Gang Children a nickname:

> I used to call him the Gothic Goblin because he was a little guy...and he lived in a building in Brixton called Visigoth Towers.[6]

This is an unusual name for a block of flats. The Visigoths were one of a number of Germanic tribes whose migrations across Europe led to the weakening and finally the collapse of the Roman Empire in the fifth century. Inspired by the success of the Ostrogoths at Hadrianopolis in 378, the Visigoth's king, Alaric, successfully sacked Athens in 396, and then Rome itself in 410. This, in turn, put a strain on the Empire's resources, making it easier for the Burgundians to push back the Romans and establish their own Kingdom in the Rhone valley. From here, occasional victories notwithstanding, the Roman Empire went into decline, and Europe as we know it began to take shape.[7]

The ensuing historical period—which lasted from the fall of the Roman Empire to the beginning of the Renaissance around the fourteenth century—was considered by most Enlightenment historians to be a sort of temporary interruption in the course of Western civilisation—a lapse into primitivism from which Europe had, thankfully, begun to recover. By the eighteenth century, it was far enough away to seem like a bad dream. Sanity had been restored, and the arts and sciences could begin to reconnect with the knowledge of the ancients, to pick up where the Romans had left off before their glorious civilisation had been overrun by Goths and the world had been plunged into darkness.

That's why in the Age of Reason the worst thing you could say about a building, a painting or a poem was that it was *Gothic*. This was, unsurprisingly, an Italian put-down, coined during the Renaissance to describe the spooky, mystical and (to the refined fifteenth-century mind) not very well-drawn art of the Middle Ages—as well as the suspiciously pagan-looking architecture of the period. The term has its origins in a misunderstanding, whereby the makers of these artefacts were assumed to be Goths. But the word stuck because, as art critic John Ruskin points out in *The Stones of Venice*, medieval building styles 'appeared like a perpetual reflection of the contrast between the Goth and the Roman in their first encounter'.[8] In other words, the Gothic style was an affront to civilisation. In the midst of the great triumph of science, reason and the classical ideal, Gothic buildings, by their very presence, made an unwelcome reproach—at best, they were like family members you'd rather forget you had but found yourself obliged to invite to Christmas dinner.

Toward the second half of the eighteenth century things began to change. Just as the reign of classicism in poetry was slowly but surely undermined by an interest in medieval ballads; in the world of architecture, it gradually became acceptable to admit that Gothic buildings had a sort of primitive appeal. The first significant stirring of this new feeling can be found in a letter written by Horace Walpole, the fourth Earl of Orford, to the Honorable H S Conway in June 1747. Walpole was writing to tell his friend that he'd just moved house:

> *You perceive by my date that I am got into a new camp, and have left my tub at Windsor. It is a little plaything-house that I got out of Mrs. Chenevix's shop, and is the prettiest bauble you ever saw. It is set in enamelled meadows, with filigree hedges ...*[9]

Walpole's 'bauble' was a country house near Twickenham on the outskirts of London. For several years after he wrote this letter, he continued to commute between Strawberry Hill and London, where he sat as a member of Parliament. But Walpole was never that interested in politics—his appearances in the House grew more and more sporadic and by 1768 he had stopped showing up for good. He had plenty of other, better ways to amuse himself—he entertained at the drop of a hat, played cards till two in the morning, and wrote stories and poems which he published with his own press. But the majority of Walpole's time was taken up with his two greatest passions: renovating and decorating, and it was Strawberry Hill itself that would become his life's work. When he wasn't supervising construction work or poring over sketches and architect's drawings, the future fourth Earl of Orford could be found hanging around the auction houses of the greater London area, looking for bargains. As to what it was exactly that he was looking for, his letters give us a pretty good idea. Writing to Horace Mann, he described the state of Strawberry Hill in 1753:

> *The bow-window below leads into a little parlour hung with a stone-colour Gothic paper and Jackson's Venetian*

prints... From hence, under two gloomy arches, you
come to the hall and staircase, which it is impossible to
describe to you, as it is the most particular and chief
beauty of the castle. Imagine the walls covered with (I
call it paper, but it is really paper painted in perspective
to represent) Gothic fretwork: the lightest Gothic
balustrade to the staircase, adorned with antelopes...[10]

Gothic, gothic, gothic. Walpole's passion for all things
medieval led him, over the next thirty years, to transform
Strawberry Hill, both inside and out, into a strange hybrid of
medieval castle and gothic cathedral. Its growth was entirely
improvised—Walpole would return from a walking tour of
the countryside or a trip to the Continent with a head full of
ideas, and would quickly have his architects and builders
incorporate what he'd seen into extensions for his rapidly
growing country mansion and its grounds. By the time its
owner died, Strawberry Hill had grown from its original five
acres to forty-six, and the house itself had become an eccentric,
ad-hoc tribute from a wealthy and slightly eccentric English
gent to what, in his lifetime had been an almost universally
reviled form of architecture. By 1763 it was a much-visited
and much-discussed tourist attraction.

What no-one could have suspected, was that even as
Walpole had been transforming Strawberry Hill, Strawberry
Hill had begun to transform its owner. One morning in June
1764 Walpole woke from a nightmare.

...I thought myself in an ancient castle (a very natural
dream for a head filled like mine with Gothic story)
and that on the uppermost banister of a great staircase
I saw a gigantic hand in armour.[11]

That night Walpole sat down at his desk to write, 'without
knowing in the least what I intended to say', and before he

knew it, a novel had appeared: a tale of medieval intrigue laced with family curses and underground passageways. *The Castle of Otranto* is generally regarded as the very first gothic horror novel, although in Walpole's day, that would not have been considered a compliment. Walpole knew as much when he wrote it. It was, as he explained to a friend, a book out of time. 'It was not written for this age, which wants nothing but cold reason.'[12]

Walpole, aware of the difficult proposition he had on his hands, decided to publish Otranto anonymously, and to further cover his tracks by not using his own press. He then concocted an intricate ruse to explain the appearance of this superstitious tale in his age of reason. In the book's preface Walpole introduces himself as the anonymous translator of a sixteenth-century text based on a story written during the crusades. This did the trick. As British literary historian Michael Gamer points out, Walpole's conceit allowed the eighteenth-century reader to swallow the impossible events in his story, because the reader could accept that people in medieval times *would* believe such things.[13] The *Monthly Review* praised it as an entirely worthy historical curiosity. Unfortunately, Walpole blew it by revealing himself as the true author in the preface to the book's second edition, after which the reviewers changed their tune entirely:

> *While we considered it as a translation, we could readily excuse its preposterous phenomena, and consider them as sacrifices to a gross and unenlightened age. But when, as in this edition,* The Castle of Otranto *is revealed to be a modern performance, that indulgence we afforded to the foibles of supposed antiquity we can by no means extend to the singularity of a false taste in a cultivated period of learning. It is, indeed, more than strange that an*

author of a refined and polished genius, should be an
advocate for re-establishing the barbarous superstitions
of Gothic devilism![14]

Walpole had the last laugh. In 1781 Otranto was adapted for the stage as *The Count of Narbonne*. Its run would last for the next two decades, during which time Otranto itself became a bestseller. Walpole's story inspired a whole new genre of literature, the gothic novel, whose popularity would last well into the next century.

Walpole's *The Castle of Otranto* exploited a chink in the armour of Enlightenment culture which would eventually bring the whole edifice crashing down. His story gently tricked his readers into admitting that there is beauty in terror and darkness, and that there are things in the universe that can never be explained. These tendencies—our desire to be frightened and our need to believe—are irrational, but undeniably human. The Age of Reason could not, for all its efforts, suppress them forever.

As historian Norman Davies has observed it seems deeply strange to us now that an entire culture could have been built around the veneration of a single human quality—reason—to the exclusion of all else.[15] But 'Enlightenment' can only be understood in terms of the 'darkness' it was meant to illuminate. The irrational was deeply troubling to Enlightenment thinkers because it was believed that mankind's surrender to the irrational—to superstition, belief in magic and dogma—had created the horrors of the Middle Ages. The reaction to Walpole's novel from critics was symptomatic of the widespread feeling that if the guard was let down even for a moment, the horror might return. Walpole snuck horror in by the backdoor in a way that allowed the eighteenth-century reader to feel virtuous (following the exploits of the hero) while secretly enjoying terror, mystery, blood lust, and a variety of other unreasonable feelings.

Rocky Horror

EVEN AFTER THE popularity of the original craze for gothic fiction died down, its conventions survived in other literary forms. William Beckford's *Vathek*, Mary Shelley's *Frankenstein*, and the historical romances of Walter Scott are all directly indebted to Otranto. But so, less directly, are Stoker's *Dracula* and Oscar Wilde's *The Picture of Dorian Gray*. And closer to our own time, *Alien*, *Raiders of the Lost Ark*, *The Shining*, *The Blair Witch Project* and the Harry Potter films still make use of the conventions Walpole established. The most crucial of these, as American academic Michael Gamer points out, is his re-imagining of the medieval castle, 'transformed in Walpole's handling from a locus of safety into a place of sexual transgression and supernatural visitation, of secret passageways and political intrigue...It is a place that harbours guilty secrets and unlawful desires'.[1]

If Gamer's description sounds a bit like a plot summary of *The Rocky Horror Show*, it's with good reason. The props of the gothic story—the dark and stormy night, the horror in the dungeon and, of course, the castle itself—were already clichés by the nineteenth century, which makes them perfect materials for satire. Unfortunately, somebody forgot to tell Brad and Janet. In blissful ignorance of the conventions of over two centuries of gothic fiction the squeaky-clean pair shows up at Frank-N-Furter's castle expecting a locus of safety. What they get is a whole lot of sexual transgression and supernatural visitation. The castle, as Gamer puts it, has become a fortress—not for keeping people out, but for keeping people in.[2] Not that we really want Brad and Janet to escape. In Frank-N-Furter's world, conventional morality has been turned on its head, and that's the way we like it. Outside it's the 1950s—a world of white picket fences, high-school hops and the missionary position. In the castle civilisation has disappeared, and Frank-N-Furter instigates a sort of pan-sexual freakout in which Brad and Janet blissfully surrender to the power of the irrational. The lyric Frank-N-Furter sings at this point, 'Don't dream it, be it', was actually used as an epigram for the NME's very first story on the rising Goth scene.[3] That line, as Little Nell (who played Columbia in the film) later recalled, 'hit a nerve' at the time. *Rocky Horror* tied up a number of ideas that were floating around in the '70s, linking the sexual transgression of glam rock to the androgynous threat of the vampire and other movie fiends. (Richard O'Brien's make up and costume for Riff Raff was modelled on stills of Max Schreck in *Nosferatu*.) The transsexual from Transylvania became—along with Alice Cooper and David Bowie—one of the spiritual forefathers of goth.

Rocky Horror still changes lives. Davey Havok remembers being fascinated 'at a very young age' by his mother's copy of the soundtrack album.[4] Sixteen-year-old Gerard Way first tried on his mother's lipstick after he got dumped by a girl, but he knew he *liked* it when he looked in the mirror and realised he looked like Frank-N-Furter. 'It definitely reminded me of *Rocky Horror* and I was definitely into it,' Gerard later recalled, 'and then, uh…then came the clothes, you know?'[5]

For both AFI and My Chemical Romance, horror—rocky or otherwise—is an important ingredient. Their undead aesthetic connects the dots from tortured romantic poet, to blood-sucking fiend, to darkly attractive rock star. This explains the appeal, for both Gerard Way and Davey Havok, of The Misfits—the legendary US punk band formed in New Jersey by Glenn Danzig and Jerry Only in 1977. After seeing The Damned play later that same year, Danzig and Only knew where their future lay—in the unholy union of punk rock and fake blood. Danzig let his love of old horror movies run riot over songs like 'Horror Business' and 'Night of the Living Dead'. By the following year, they looked like a punk band fronted by extras from a zombie movie—Only had hollowed his eyes out into black holes, Danzig had transformed himself into a living skeleton using nothing more than a black shirt and a bucket of white house paint. Videos of Misfits shows from around this time look like dispatches from the more forbidding regions of hell. Monsters lurch around on some sort of primitive altar, sending ear-splitting noises into the darkness, while an army of zombies lift their arms and their voices in worship. 'Muhs-fuhts! Muhs-fuhts!'[6] Watching over it all is the image of a horrible grinning skull. This is The Misfits 'Fiend' logo, which the band found on a poster for an old horror movie and had stencilled onto their gear and printed on T-shirts. These continue to outsell the band's records by a considerable margin.

My Chemical Romance has performed The Misfits' 'Astro Zombies', as well as paying the band the more significant tribute of adapting Danzig's 'Corpse Paint' for its Black Parade uniforms. For Gerard Way, The Misfits provided a crucial alternative to the political statements that dominated punk when he was growing up. While other punk bands were speaking up about injustice, oppression and social inequality, The Misfits were creating a world in which these things simply didn't exist.

The Misfits inhabited the reversed moral world of the gothic, a world where despair, torment, darkness and even death are sublime. The appeal of the gothic, for romantics, is part of the same impulse to escape the world as it is that sends them running out of the city into the forest. But where Wordsworth's or Rousseau's was largely a flight through space, for the lover of the gothic, it's a flight back in time—to a world that existed long before civilisation, and never fails to creep back in wherever reason lets its guard down. This, for the romantic, is where we find the things that really connect us all to one another—the sight of blood, the eye-sockets of a skull, the elemental power expressed in a dark and stormy night.

Vincent

Vincent Malloy is seven years old
He's always polite and does what he's told
For a boy his age he's considerate and nice
But he wants to be just like Vincent Price![1]

VINCENT MALLOY, WITH his sunken cheeks and shock of black hair, is the claymation star of director Tim Burton's first short film, made while he was working at Disney in 1979.

Young Vincent's imagination is steeped in horror movie imagery. When his aunt comes to visit, he smiles indulgently as she pats him on the head. But in his mind, he's Vincent Price slowly lowering her into a vat of hot wax. His mother sees him playing nicely with his dog, Abercrombie. How is she to know that in his imagination he's Dr Frankenstein hooking Abercrombie up to some infernal electrical machine? He throws the switch, and the dog is zombie-fied. Later:

He and his horrible zombie dog
Can go searching for victims in the London fog.[2]

No tale of gothic horror would be complete without the ghost of a dead lover and a scene in a graveyard at midnight. So Vincent, despite the fact that he is seven years old, convinces himself that he has a beautiful wife who has been buried alive, and promptly rushes out into the gloom with a shovel:

He dug up her grave to make sure she was dead
Unaware that her grave...was his mother's flower-bed.[3]

Vincent's mother is not so much upset about the flower-bed as by her son's insistence that he is cursed and alone, condemned—like some tiny Lord Byron—to 'wander dark hallways alone and tormented'. It's not like she's grounded him or locked him in the attic, in fact, she'd much rather he went out and kicked a ball around with the other kids. But young Vincent feels distant and aloof from other people. For this, he has sound philosophical reasons. Vincent, like Byron, has no time for the idea of human perfectibility. Staying indoors wrapped in morbid thoughts of doom and horror might seem unhealthy, but Vincent refuses to 'get better' because it implies that his inner torment can be affected, even extinguished by reason, whereas he knows it cannot.

Little Vincent strongly resembles his creator—and not just in the hair. As a kid, Burton spent a lot of time alone. 'I didn't have a lot of friends,' he recalled in 1994, 'but there's enough weird movies out there so you can go a long time without friends and see something every day that kind of speaks to you.'[4] He grew up physically close enough to Hollywood to be able to see at an early age where these weird movies came from. He took a tour of Universal Studios and saw the streets where they shot *Dracula* and *Frankenstein*. 'It was a powerful feeling,' he said.[5]

He wasn't much interested in school, in fact, one of his very first efforts behind a camera was a film made in response to an essay question on psychology. Burton handed in a montage of shots of schoolbooks shown to the accompaniment of Alice Cooper's 'Welcome to My Nightmare'. Art school wasn't much better. Here, Burton came to the same conclusions as Vincent on the subject of Empiricism, the same ones William Blake had reached as he'd angrily flipped through Joshua Reynolds's discourses on art education over two hundred years earlier. Man comes into the world with something unique, and society, with its rules and systems, does its best to rationalise that something out of existence.

> *I remember going through art school, and you've got to take life drawing, and it was a real struggle. Instead of encouraging you to express yourself and draw like you did when you were a child, they start going by the rules of society. They say, 'No. No. No. You can't draw like this.'*[6]

Growing up in the California town of Burbank, Burton made important links between the horror movies he loved watching, and the suburban conformity he saw all around him. As a kid, he dreamed of being the actor who played Godzilla so that he could enjoy the thrill of smashing the grown-up world beneath his scaly feet. He already felt that society needed to be destroyed, and nothing he learned as he grew older changed that feeling to any significant degree. That's why when he watched horror movies Tim Burton always sympathised with the monster. Of these, the one to make the biggest impression on him was James Whale's 1935 classic *Bride of Frankenstein*. Images from Whale's film have turned up in a number of Burton's, though he insists that the similarities are usually not so much a matter of homage as of his ideas and Whale's coming from the same place, meaning that they tend to be expressed in the same way. Burton instinctively connected the monster's rage with his own, and recognised his need to destroy as the necessary flip-side of his need to be loved.

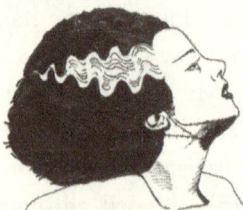

The Bride of Frankenstein: 'More capacity for love then earth / bestows on most of mortal mould and birth ...'

Frankenstein

Bride of Frankenstein begins, not with the Monster or his creator, but with a prologue set in a Swiss villa. It is, of course, a dark and stormy night. The actor Gavin Gordon stands by the window with his chin set at an impressive angle and tosses his curly locks about. He begins to poetise, in a fairly overripe English accent, about the raging storm outside. 'I should like to think that an irate Jehovah was pointing those arrows of lightning directly at my head—the unbowed head of George Gordon, Lord Byron—England's greatest sinner!'[1]

A young woman sits across from him, clearly bemused by Byron's posing. She refuses Byron's invitation to come to the window and watch the storm, and asks her fiancé, Shelley, to light another candle. Byron is tickled by this. 'Frightened of thunder! Fearful of the dark! And yet you have written a tale that has turned my blood to ice!'[2]

Mary Shelley smiles a secretive smile, as if to say, There's more where that came from. The tale Byron is referring to is *Frankenstein*—the dark horse of the story writing contest he'd instigated.

While the characters and the setting are based on fact, this little scene in the film is a fiction—Mary never imagined a sequel to her horror story. In fact, when the contest was first suggested, she'd despaired of being able to contribute anything at all. Byron had written his vampire fragment, and Polidori—when not flirting with Mary or challenging her pacifist fiancé to a duel—had written the tale of his skull-headed woman. But Mary's inspiration had deserted her. 'Have you thought of a story?' her friends would ask her when she came down for breakfast. 'Each morning,' she says, 'I was forced to reply with a mortifying negative.'[3]

One night, still furiously trying to think of something really scary, Mary half drifted off to sleep. As she floated in that strange zone between consciousness and unconsciousness, she saw, in her mind's eye, a series of terrifying visions—a dark shape bent over a corpse, an unnatural twitch, and a pair of watery yellow eyes in the darkness. Scared out of her wits, she sat up in bed and tried to compose herself. Well, she thought, *that* was terrifying. If only I could come up with something as scary as that, I'd be able to write the best ghost story ever...hang on!

The story Mary Shelley set down over the next few days—and eventually expanded into a novel—tells of a young doctor named Victor Frankenstein who sets out to break the ultimate scientific taboo: the creation of life itself. Frankenstein works in darkness and secrecy for two years to get it done. But as soon as his goal is accomplished and his creature begins to twitch with artificial life, he sees that he shouldn't have done it, never in a million years. Not only has he made a terrible mistake—he's made a mistake that walks, a mistake that creeps up to his bed in the dead of night, pulls back the curtain, and reaches a horrible greyish hand in his direction. Frankenstein flees his apartment at the university and spends a cold night on the street, hoping that the nightmare will simply evaporate in the morning. And at first, it seems as though it has—until his friends and family begin to die...

When the monster and his maker finally meet again, we are surprised, along with Frankenstein, at how eloquently he expresses himself. The monster learned the rudiments of conversation, it turns out, by eavesdropping on a rustic family as he hid in their barn. But his education was completed by a package of books he found by the roadside one day—that included Milton's *Paradise Lost*, Plutarch's *Lives* and Goethe's *The Sorrows of Young Werther*—which moved him deeply. 'I did not pretend to enter into the merits of the case,' said the monster of Werther's tale, 'yet I inclined towards the opinions of the hero, whose extinction I wept, without precisely understanding it.' The monster, it seems, sympathises in a very profound way with Werther's feelings of apartness and aloneness. He takes Goethe's advice in the book's preface—*The Sorrows of Young Werther* becomes a friend to the creature, who has no friends at all.[4]

It's fitting that Frankenstein's monster should identify with Goethe's angst-ridden young romantic, since young romantics have always found something to relate to in the monster. He is, as Bertrand Russell has observed, virtually the embodiment of romanticism, and the changes he undergoes in the novel demonstrate the trajectory of romantic philosophy in a startling way.[5] Byron's words in 'Lara':

his early dreams of good outstripped the truth
and troubled manhood followed baffled youth[6]

neatly sum up the monster's life up to the point when Frankenstein confronts him. He is barely human, but just human enough to want to be loved like everybody else. And because he was cursed at birth to be freakish and unlovable, humanity lets him down.

The monster tells his creator that, after fleeing Frankenstein's apartment, he made several attempts to befriend his fellow beings, all of which ended disastrously—the only exception being a blind man, who only loved him because he couldn't see how ugly he was—which only goes to show how shallow and judgemental human beings are! The whole human race turned away from him in horror, so the monster turned his back on humanity. He sought solace in nature—even the steely-grey sky above the alps seemed more welcoming to him than the people who lived beneath it. But being an artificial creature, he didn't feel at home in nature any more than he did in society. At this point, the monster's natural goodness began to collapse under the strain of his exile. 'The mildness of my nature had fled', he explains, 'and all within me was turned to gall and bitterness…I am malicious because I am miserable. Am I not shunned and hated by all mankind?'[7]

And yet even in his despair, the monster believed he could be redeemed, which is why he set out to find Frankenstein—whom he had grown to hate by this point—who held the keys to his happiness. Now, he implores his creator to recognise him and his needs, to create a female who will complete him. Frankenstein, horrified by the idea, rejects the monster's plea out of hand—and this proves to be the last straw. Now, having nothing to live for, the creature's rampage becomes unstoppable.

But Frankenstein's creature never becomes an unthinking killer—and he certainly never becomes an un*feeling* one. On the contrary, the inhuman monster is full of human feeling. As Bertrand Russell points out in his *History of Western Philosophy*, no matter how base his actions become, his sentiments are always noble.[8] After he commits the patricide he has been threatening for the entire book, he stands above Frankenstein's corpse and delivers a moving soliloquy.

> *Oh, Frankenstein! Generous and self-devoted being! What does it avail thee that I now ask thee to pardon me?*[9]

Walton, the ship's captain who observes this, boldly points out that it doesn't avail Frankenstein much at all that the monster is so full of remorse. If you'd listened to your conscience and not killed all those people, says Walton, none of this would have happened. The monster is outraged at this suggestion. Don't you understand, he asks Walton, how I *feel*?

> *'Do you think that I was then dead to agony and remorse? He,' he continued, pointing to the corpse, 'he suffered not in the consummation of the deed. Oh! Not the ten-thousandth portion of the anguish that was mine during the lingering detail of its execution... Think you that the groans of Clerval were music to my ears? My heart was fashioned to be susceptible of love and sympathy, and when wrenched by misery to vice and hatred, it did not endure the violence of the change without torture such as you cannot imagine.'*[10]

Here, romantic solipsism is taken to its most frightening conclusion. The monster's murders are justified by his feelings. No wonder he found so much to admire in Werther—Frankenstein's creature is in fact a super-Werther, whose physical strength gives him the power to act out his feelings in ways that Goethe's gloomy protagonist could only dream about.

In The Smashing Pumpkins' 'Disarm', Billy Corgan invents a fantasy version of this scenario, in which he hacks off his parents' limbs in order to teach them a lesson about what it's like to live your life as a lonely freak. But like Byron and Frankenstein's monster, he doesn't do harm because he's evil, but because he feels too much, and he can't contain his feelings any longer. The singer in 'Disarm' feels 'the bitterness of one who's left alone'[11]—all those years sitting by himself in the school cafeteria—because his heart is full of 'tender feelings'.[12] The way he sees it, his parents gave him the desire for love, and then made him unlovable, condemned to eternity in a lonely Tower of Doom. 'Ooh, the years burn', sighs Corgan.[13] How can they expect him to play nicely with the other children when he is, as Frankenstein's monster puts it, 'shunned and hated by all mankind'?[14] The extreme menace in 'Disarm' comes from the idea, never too far from the surface, that a killing spree has been only narrowly averted by cathartic song writing.

Edward Scissorhands

IN THE WINTER of 1989 Johnny Depp was sent a movie script called *Edward Scissorhands*. At that time the actor was stuck in the depths of TV hell, mouthing god-awful dialogue on the set of *21 Jump Street*. After reading this script, he believed he could be saved.

> *It was the story of a boy with scissors for hands—*
> *an innocent outcast in suburbia. I was so affected*

and moved by it that strong waves of images
flooded my brain—dogs I'd had as a kid, feeling
freakish and obtuse while growing up, the
unconditional love that only infants and dogs are
evolved enough to have.[1]

Soon, the nervous actor was meeting with the director, and after talking to him for an hour or so, he realised, 'this hypersensitive madman *is* Edward Scissorhands'.[2] Here Depp was right on the money. If the script had brought his awkward teenage years flooding back to him, it was because it was heavily inspired by the director's own painful adolescence—a period of time when, as Burton later described it, he felt like he had a big sign around his neck saying 'Leave me the fuck alone'.[3] The whole idea for the film came from a drawing Burton did when he was a teenager of 'a character who wants to touch but can't, who was both creative and destructive'.[4]

Depp also recognised in the script a feeling of profound sympathy for 'those who are not others'—just one of the many important lessons Burton learned from his steady diet of B-movies while growing up.

I always loved monsters and monster movies. I was
never terrified of them, I just loved them ... I felt most
monsters were basically misperceived, usually they had
much more heartfelt souls than the human characters
around them.[5]

After a short prologue, *Edward Scissorhands* begins with Avon lady Peg Boggs having a bad day. She drives around her pastel-coloured suburban town in her pastel-coloured car trying to sell make-up to bored housewives and surly teenagers, but to no avail. So, with nothing left to lose, she decides to try the one house in the neighbourhood she's never been to—the evil-looking gothic mansion at the top of the hill. She drives up the winding path and walks through the massive front doors. 'Avon calling,' she cries hopefully into the gloom, her words echoing through the castle's empty halls. Not quite empty as it turns out. Peg finds a strange creature hiding in the shadows—deathly-pale, encased in black from head to foot, with giant scissors where his hands should be. Her heart breaks:

Peg: *What happened to you?*
Edward: *I'm not finished.*[6]

Edward, like Frankenstein's monster, is an experiment abandoned by his creator in a half-formed state. His inventor father (played by Vincent Price), died before he was finished, so instead of real hands, Edward is stuck with scissors. His freakish appearance has kept him confined to his crumbling castle, where he lives in a world of imagination and memory, cutting the hedges in the garden into giant pairs of human hands—topiary as dream-wish fulfilment.

Peg takes him home and cleans him up, and for a little while it looks like he might have finally broken back into the lovely world below, redeemed himself by being accepted and loved. But eventually the regular folk turn on the monster in their midst—and who can blame them? Those scissor-hands he uses to cut the townspeople's hedges and barbecue their shish kebabs are terrifying weapons. Not that sensitive Edward would ever intentionally harm anyone. But he's pushed and pushed by these shallow greedy people until he can't help it. And then, in the moments where he's most human, when he reaches out to touch or protect someone he loves, he hurts them.

As his story unfolds, it becomes increasingly clear that he just doesn't belong with other people, that he has to be alone. Like little Vincent Malloy, he goes back to his tower of doom, where he spends the rest of his days poring over his painful memories. The sculptures he makes in his garden are suffused with all the longing he feels to be a part of human life—to be loved, to be accepted.

Of all the director's films, *Edward Scissorhands* is probably the purest distillation of Tim Burton's worldview. In a telling moment near the start of the film, just as Peg is about to give up on her door-to-door sales and head home for the day, she adjusts her side-view mirror. We see from Peg's point of view out the car window and into the street, where neat pastel-coloured houses roll out as far as the eye can see. Then, in the mirror, we catch a glimpse, as she does, of Edward's spooky, dilapidated home on the hill. Edward's world is the reverse of Peg's—but only the one in the mirror is real for Burton.

'People ask me when I'm going to make a film with real people,'[7] Burton once remarked. Of course, for him, monsters like Edward are real people, the only people worth knowing. All his heroes are freaks or outcasts of some description: Edward is a half-finished science project, Ed Wood is a toothless cross-dresser who makes terrible movies about grave robbers from outer space, and Burton's Batman is a sociophobe with a fetish for latex. In *Beetlejuice*, Betelgeuse the bio-exorcist is a disgusting undead ghoul, the young couple he agrees to help are ghosts who distort their faces into monstrous masks or rot away before our eyes, and Lydia, the teenage girl who befriends them, can only see the strange and unusual beings haunting her parents' house because she is, herself, strange and unusual.

Lydia is an original '80's goth—her decision to wear black and obsess about death is an intentional affront to her shallow, materialistic, style-obsessed mother. Her dad doesn't really understand her either—but he does at least try to keep with her interests. He makes an attempt to cheer her up by promising to build her a darkroom in the attic so she can develop her photos. But Lydia will not be consoled—'My whole life is a dark room. One. Big. Dark. Room.'[8]

One of the film's funniest moments comes when Lydia sneaks into the attic where the ghosts have taken up residence. The ghosts aren't in—but Betelgeuse has made himself at home—Lydia finds the miniaturised ghoul lounging obscenely on a tiny deckchair. At the sight of Lydia, with her funereal get-up and deathly complexion, Betelgeuse perks up. 'Hey,' he says, 'you look like someone I could relate to!'[9] Like Frankenstein's monster reading Werther, the bio-exorcist senses an important connection between himself—a horrible monster shunned by humanity—and the miserable teenage girl in front of him. Betelgeuse hopes to enlist Lydia in his efforts to get out of the underworld and into the game. Lydia wishes they could trade places. 'I wanna be in there!' she says, pointing to the miniature diorama that represents the spirit world in the film's peculiar mythology. Betelgeuse is mystified by this. 'Why?' he asks. 'Well', he goes on, 'I'm sure you have your reasons.'[10]

She does. Like Vincent Malloy, Lydia has been banished to the tower of doom. But not by her parents—they want her to get out, get involved in social life, have some fun. No, Lydia has banished *herself* to the tower of doom, locked the door from the inside, and swallowed the key. She knows she'll never be like all the other kids, so she rejects the possibility of joining their world and moves permanently into her own. Here, she thinks, in darkness and isolation, is where I belong. Lydia shares the fate of all Tim Burton's oddball heroes. She has been kicked out of the garden—and has come to understand that what everyone else calls happiness is not for her.

Lydia: Am I not shunned and hated by all mankind?

The Dark Side of
Human Things

THE TENOR OF Mary Shelley's *Frankenstein* is profoundly religious. Victor Frankenstein is clearly shown to be a sinner— plunging himself into death and filth in order to create life. His account of his midnight expeditions in search of corpses for his experiments, is permeated by a deep sense of shame. In fact, his whole tale is a confessional. We hear the story through the device of Frankenstein unburdening himself to the captain of the ship which will take him to his final encounter with the monster (and this will become a convention of horror stories for decades to come—My tale is almost too horrible to relate, yet I must confide in you before it is too late …). And to hear Frankenstein tell it, he knew, even at the time, that what he was doing was deeply unnatural and wrong, but he imagined that in his perversion of nature the scientific ends might justify the means, and that he would in the end be rewarded. But he sees now that he could not have been more wrong—his only reward is death—for himself and for those he loves. Frankenstein's monster is the punishment for his sin—which turns out to be one of the oldest—the sin of wanting to know too much.

Of course, all of this stuff about sin and punishment is very medieval, part of a way of thinking that was supposed to have vanished long before 1819. But the Shelleys had grown up in an age that had already stretched the eighteenth-century ideal of reason and enlightenment to breaking point. Prior to arriving at Lake Geneva, the couple had seen up close the havoc and destruction that the Revolutionary wars had visited on the people of rural France. The romantics of Wordsworth's generation had already processed the effects of this, watching as the carefully maintained equilibrium of the eighteenth century was destroyed, giving voice to the crisis in their poetry, and finally finding a third position outside it all, the state of grace Wordsworth achieved with 'Lines Written a Few Miles Above Tintern Abbey'.

This poem is actually quoted by Frankenstein himself in Mary Shelley's novel—it had by this point become part of the canon, and Wordsworth was an elder statesman. Mary was only nineteen years old when she wrote *Frankenstein*—she'd never known the world Wordsworth had been born into and was already living in a very different one. By this point, France's monarchy had been restored, and Europe had settled into a period of extreme political conservatism. The cautious reforms that many governments had been implementing in the pre-Revolutionary period were abandoned, and the general feeling was that if you give the people an inch, they'll take a mile. Frankenstein is typical of the new role of the gothic in this era. The early nineteenth-century horror story represents the threat of chaos, and perhaps even a repressed desire to see that chaos unleashed—to smash society, finish the job and see it all come down. This is why Tim Burton instinctively connected the gothic horror of *Bride of Frankenstein* with his desire to destroy his suburban surroundings. The monster himself is—like his cousin Dracula—an image of romanticism on the rampage, a terrifying, irrational force turned loose on an over-ordered world.

But Frankenstein, with its Old Testament morality, also points to another side-effect of the Revolutionary period on the romantic imagination. The failure of the eighteenth-century dream of a society based on rational principles to materialise had been bad enough; that what had emerged had been something closer to a medieval bloodbath was enough to convince the romantics that the ideal of human perfectibility was dead in the water. Indeed, the arguments for seeing humanity as basically flawed and doomed to repeat its mistakes began to look more and more convincing—especially to those who, as Leigh Hunt had said of Mary Shelley, had 'a tendency to look over-intensely at the dark side of human things'.[2]

Mystery

IN 1988 NICK Cave was flying from Australia to London. It's a long trip, and it tends to bring out the worst in people. 'The other passengers were basically gearing up to tear my girlfriend and me to bits if we continued to go the way we were going', he later confessed to Simon Reynolds.[1] On this flight, Cave almost became a born-again Christian:

> *Two days sitting on the plane and fifty bourbons later*
> *I had this young born-again advocate holding my hand*
> *and praying for me at the top of his voice.*[2]

To hear Cave tell it, the missionary was quite surprised to find that the evil-looking rock singer he'd just latched on to knew his Bible quite well—better, even, than the missionary.

> *He started quoting things from his modern*
> *translation which I find really irritating ... to find it so*
> *utterly demystified by these modern religions keen to*
> *allow people of today to understand ... it really appals*
> *me.*[3]

People have been trying to demystify the Bible since Descartes, and during the Enlightenment, it became something of a craze. In the seventeenth and eighteenth centuries, the 'mystery' Cave likes so much in his King James Bible was seen as one of those things the human race was better off without—a point of view championed by the English physicist Isaac Newton. "Tis the temper of the hot and superstitious part of mankind in matters of religion ever to be fond of mysteries, and therefore to like best what they understand least', he once wrote.[4] Mysteries, for Newton, had kept people in the dark for centuries. Therefore as a scientist and a Christian he considered it his business to rationalise his religion. This was no easy task, Christianity had over the past thousand or so years accumulated a lot of strange dogma and superstition, but Newton fearlessly set about trying to strip all of this back so as to reveal the true, rational religion underneath. Miracles, of course, would have to go, as would the doctrine of the Holy Trinity—which to Newton was a sop to the superstitious pagans. He even went so far as to deny the divinity of Christ.

The job of bringing Christianity into line with reason would continue well into the next century. This was the time during which the philosophy of Leibniz became popular. Leibniz argued that since God is all-powerful and infinitely good, he must have created our world as the best of all possible worlds. Evil, in Leibniz's system, is thus explained as a necessary part of the greater good. This was a religious philosophy which appealed to the profoundly optimistic mood of the Enlightenment. In his famous *Essay on Man*, Alexander Pope wrote:

> *All nature is but art unknown to thee;*
> *All chance, direction which thou canst not see;*
> *All discord, harmony not understood;*
> *All partial evil universal good:*
> *And spite of pride, in erring reason's spite*
> *One truth is clear, whatever is, is RIGHT.*[5]

The *Essay on Man* did much to popularise Leibniz's thought in both France and England. But though Pope's verse is impeccable, his philosophy—and Leibniz's—is full of holes. To look at the world with all its trouble and strife and say 'it's all good' seems unconscionable today—and it wasn't much better in 1732. The glibness of Pope's brand of optimism didn't escape the sharper eyed critics of the Enlightenment. The French philosopher and poet Voltaire mercilessly sent up the Leibnizians in his satire, *Candide*. Candide's tutor, Professor Pangloss, is a metaphysico-theologo-cosmolo-nigologist, who insists, in the face of a great deal of evidence to the contrary, that he is living in the best of all possible worlds. His philosophy makes him an idiot—worse, a shit of a human being, who won't lift a finger to help the victims of wars or natural disasters.

> *Candide had been wounded by splinters of flying masonry and lay helpless in the road, covered with rubble.*
>
> *'For heaven's sake,' he cried to Pangloss, 'fetch me some wine and oil! I am dying!'*
>
> *'This earthquake is nothing new,' replied Pangloss; 'the town of Lima in America experienced the same shocks last year. The same causes produce the same effects. There is certainly a vein of sulphur running under the earth from Lima to Lisbon.'*
>
> *'Nothing is more likely,' said Candide; 'but oil and wine, for pity's sake!'*[6]

Voltaire, as historian Norman Davies has said, was expert at using the techniques of the Enlightenment to expose its flaws—which, in a sense, made him the ultimate embodiment of the age.[7] The German philosopher Immanuel Kant, after all, insisted that the obstacle to enlightenment was not our lack of understanding, but our lack of courage in putting that understanding to work, and Voltaire was fearless in his unmasking of outmoded or useless ideas.[8] He saw it as his life's mission to clear away the accumulated junk of Western thought wherever he found it, and he hated dogma and superstition above all. But Voltaire would not abandon God, and he always believed Christianity was compatible with reason. Two decades after Newton's death, he laid out the principles of a rational religion in his *Philosophical Dictionary*:

> *Would it not be that which taught much morality and very little dogma? That which tended to make men just without making them absurd? That which did not order one to believe in things that are impossible …?*[9]

This reasonable Christianity, this religion for the Enlightenment, is not Nick Cave's preferred variety. Since that fateful plane trip twenty years ago, Cave has never stopped looking into his Bible. He's quoted it in his songs and caught its grave rhythms in his prose. But he never went to it looking for glorified commonsense, or with a view to hunting down inconsistencies so as to bring them in line with reason. For Cave, a religion which has been purged of its madness, sadness and bloody-minded violence is not a religion at all; and 'believing in things which are impossible'— as Voltaire put it—is both an essential part of religious experience and a key requirement of his day job as a singer of love songs.

Speaking at London's South Bank centre in 1999, Cave insisted that the words of the Old Testament Psalms and the words of a song like Kylie Minogue's 'Better the Devil You Know' are both born from the same profoundly unreasonable impulse. The love song, Cave said, 'is a howl in the void for love and comfort, and it lives on the lips of the child crying for his mother. It is the song of the lover in need of their loved one, the raving of the lunatic supplicant petitioning his god.' For Cave, both the love of God and romantic love are 'manifestations of our need to be torn away from the rational, to take leave of our senses'.[10]

To an eighteenth-century ear, this lecture would have exposed Cave as an ignorant superstitious goth. Cave, of course, has often been called a goth—even the 'king of the goths'—and just as often denied it. But if 'gothic' means—as it did in 1750—irrational, superstitious and unhealthily obsessed with hellfire and damnation, then Cave is gothic to the tips of his well-tailored black suits.

Utopia

'THE TIME WILL come,' wrote Voltaire's colleague the Marquis de Condorcet in 1793, 'when the sun will shine only on free men who know no other master than their reason.'[1] Like Voltaire, de Condorcet was a member of the society of *Philosophes* and a firm believer in human perfectibility. His *Sketch for a Historical Picture of the Progress of the Human Mind* demonstrated that science and mathematics would improve every aspect of life in post-Revolutionary France, and eventually, the whole world. Population control, sexual equality, religion, law, language and love would all benefit from the application of mathematics to their specific problems, and given time, poverty, civil strife and war would become things of the past.

As a utopian, de Condorcet firmly supported the republic, but as a liberal humanist he could not condone the execution of the king. This automatically made him a Royalist in the eyes of the Committee of Public Safety. So, even as he set down his vision of a mathematically perfectible utopia, Robespierre's police were coming for him. He spent most of

1793 in hiding, and then tried to flee France the following year. He was caught, thrown in prison, and found dead in his cell the next morning, having taken poison.

The Terror ensured that there would never be another period of sustained optimism like the Enlightenment. But the *Philosophes*' vision of a society that works remained a powerfully attractive one for many years to come. Long after the romantic movement parted company with universal reason, works such as de Condorcet's had become the basis for the nineteenth century's belief in progress, which survived virtually unchallenged in the world of industry and science right up until the mid-twentieth century. Even in artistic circles, romantic gloom would occasionally give way to bursts of utopian optimism over the next two centuries. Strong traces of Enlightenment thought can be detected in the arts and crafts movement, the Vienna Secession, at the Dessau Bauhaus, among the Russian constructivists and—curiously—in London's post-punk scene of the late '70s.

Like the Enlightenment itself, punk is often understood as a reaction to what came before—in this case, the grandiose mysticism of mid '70s prog-rock. 'We tend to keep away from the present', said Genesis's Steve Hackett in 1974, 'we're very hesitant to make any commitment to how we feel about what's happening now.'[2] Punk, on the other hand, would admit no other subject matter than 'what's happening now'. The lyrical abstractions of prog-rock, like the introverted navel gazing of the West Coast groups, seemed to create music with no social purpose beyond pure escapism—and the punks were adamant that music should be about more than that. In theory, if not always in practice, punk bands wrote songs about what it was really like to live on a council estate or what was in the papers or what their record company did last week. Heroic quests, mystical allegories and song cycles were banished, never to return.

Having cleared away the useless clutter and mystical obscurantism of prog, it was now left to the groups who emerged in the wake of punk's first wave to build a new songwriting ideal. Now, all bets were off, everything could be questioned. Gang of Four applied the *Philosophes'* favourite question: 'is it rational' to that oldest of rock institutions, the love song, and found that it was not. Guitarist Andy Gill muses on 'Love like Anthrax':

> ...*most groups make most of their songs about*
> *falling in love or how happy they are to be in*
> *love...these groups go along with the belief that love*
> *is deep in everyone's personality. I don't think we're*
> *saying there's anything wrong with love; we just*
> *don't think what goes on between two people should*
> *be shrouded in mystery.*[3]

Like Newton, Gill has no time for mystery; mysteries keep people stupid, and the mysteries of love are no exception. When Gang of Four did write about love, they stripped off the ornament and reduced love to a social agreement or a coupling of bodies; there were no hearts and flowers, no burning fire or pure desire in these songs. Love was presented as difficult but never mysterious. In the post-punk love song, as music critic Simon Reynolds writes in *Blissed Out*, 'the acknowledgement of the dark side was always grounded in progressive humanism, the belief that what was twisted could be straightened out...shadows could be banished by the spotlight of analysis.'[4] According to Reynolds, punk had established the idea that 'demystification was the road to enlightenment.'[5]

Nick Cave: Moody and miserable.

Utopiate

IF PUNK RE-ENACTED the Enlightenment, then it was left to a 'moody, miserable' kid from rural Victoria to play the part of the entire romantic movement. As early as 1977, punk's year zero, when everyone else was poring over Theodor Adorno, Herbert Marcuse and Guy Debord, Nick Cave started reading the Bible—the King James, of course.[1]

The brutal, bitter tales of the Old Testament confirmed Cave's suspicion that human beings are not infinitely perfectible, but born in sin and bound for hell. Cave knew at an early age he was either destined or damned—or maybe, like Napoleon, a little bit of both. As he grew older, he found that this basic fact of his personality remained unchanged, and nothing he saw after that could convince him that we come into the world as 'lumps of dough that are later moulded by our parents and so forth'.[2]

Cave's first band, The Boys Next Door, had a hit in 1978 with a song called 'Shivers'—a song that the producers of *Countdown* refused to allow the band to perform because the lyrics mentioned suicide.[3] 'Shivers', written by guitarist Roland S Howard, is a confessional in the early Byronic mould. The hero is detached and strangely static. He's been thinking about suicide, but he'll only do it if you're watching, and if you think it's fashionable. In the end, he remains paralysed by ennui. Howard takes up the theme with a long, plaintive guitar solo, which sounds like a lethargic replay of Pete Shelley's famous two-note refrain in the Buzzcocks' 'Boredom'.

On the day Bon Scott was buried, The Boys Next Door left Melbourne for London, changing their name on arrival to The Birthday Party. Post-punk was in full swing, and superficially, The Birthday Party fitted right in—the lopsided Magic Band guitar parts, the tribal thump of their rhythm section, their singer's anguished, alienated squawk. At a moment when Captain Beefheart's *Trout Mask Replica* represented the musical ideal, and PiL's *Metal Box* the cutting edge, The Birthday Party had every reason to think their success was assured.

But even as England learned to love The Birthday Party, The Birthday Party were learning to despise England—English bands especially. Cave quickly realised that he hated all the post-punk/new wave groups that were so heavily feted at the time. His old-fashioned sense of sin and retribution chafed badly against then-fashionable topics such as 'personal politics'. For Cave, love was not, and could never be 'a contract in our mutual interest' as one Gang of Four song put it; love was madness, sorrow, despair, violence, a deeply mysterious and irrational force.

'Zoo Music Girl', the first song on the Birthday Party's debut album is a blood-soaked ballad. 'Oh God,' cries Cave 'let me die beneath her fists!'[4] In 'Wild World' the lovers are crucified, in 'Six Inch Gold Blade' the singer sticks a knife in his girl's head. We are already a long way from the world of personal politics.

In 'Hamlet Pow! Pow! Pow!' Cave re-casts Shakespeare's tragic hero as a gun-toting gangster. 'Wherefore art thou baby face?' he sneers (having ended up, not only in the wrong century, but in the wrong play).[5] It makes perfect sense for Cave to turn Hamlet into a killer with a gun, because for the singer, the tragic Dane and the murderer are burdened with the same heavy load—passion that can find no outlet in society. They stand side by side in the Nick Cave pantheon with Saint Sebastian, Iggy Pop, Count Dracula, Beethoven, Dostoyevsky, the Hunchback of Notre Dame, Captain Ahab, Robert Mitchum (in *Night of the Hunter*) and Jesus Christ.[6] Cave will always side with geniuses, freaks, monsters and outcasts—as opposed to the society that could not accommodate them—because to him society is not only hateful, it's a bad bet; doomed to fail, no matter what the positivists, empiricists and neo-Marxists try to tell you. 'To see yourself as part of some greater humanist scheme,' he said to Reynolds in 1988, 'I can't really abide by that myself. I'm someone who has very little concern with any kind of social problems, someone who's very much concerned with their own plight.'[7]

Two years, and two extraordinary albums later, The Birthday Party self-destructed—and you can hear it happen on their swansong, 'Mutiny in Heaven'. The lyrics of 'Mutiny' run on from an earlier song called 'Dumb Europe', written with Die Haut in 1983. 'Dumb Europe' describes a night out in Berlin where 'the cafes and bars still stink'. An early draft of the song features a coda, 'Hey! Dumb Europe! Utopiate! European Utopiate!'[8]

Here, Cave stands up in his 'bleak Teutonic hole' and calls time on the *Philosophes'* dream of a heaven on earth. The perfectibility Jacques Turgot promised his eighteenth-century audience at the Sorbonne, the mathematical utopia de Condorcet was still dreaming about as Robespierre's police hunted him down, the hope of Universal Reason Wordsworth clutched at during his crisis of 1795, where are they now? Utopia, Cave puns, is a Utopi*ate*—a drug which has enslaved the European mind as surely as any of the crackpot dogmas it was supposed to destroy. And the positivist is a junky, on the nod in a corner while the Continent falls apart around his ears. In 'Mutiny in Heaven' Cave invites us to look around at dumb Europe and admit that utopia has long since turned into a slum. The place is overrun with trash and rats—and now even the rats are leaving, crawling up his arm in search of higher ground. This is never a good sign. If this is heaven, he says, 'Ah'm bailing out!'[9] But how do you get out of the modern world? Over The Birthday Party's terrifying rumble, accompanied by a guitar that sounds like the peals of a church bell, Cave talks us through it:

> Well, ah tied on…percht on mah bed ah was
> Sticken a needle in mah arm
> Ah tied off! Fucken wings burst out mah back![10]

The positivists would have you choose life. Cave—as Mark Renton puts it in Irvine Welsh's *Trainspotting*—has chosen something else.

Siouxsie Sioux: A hostile and valueless reality.

The Degraded Present

BECAUSE HE FEELS that society should be destroyed, Nick Cave is also a lover of horror—note the appearance of Count Dracula in his list of favourite things. For Cave, death and darkness—being closer to the truth of the human condition— are sublime. Luckily, his baby feels the same way:

My baby is all right
She doesn't mind a bit of dirt
She says 'horror vampire bat bite'
She says 'horror vampire
How I wish those bats would bite'[1]

'Release the Bats' was a certified Batcave floor-filler—for obvious reasons. It would also become The Birthday Party's most important contribution to the goth aesthetic. As Simon Reynolds shows in *Rip it Up and Start Again*, Goth first emerged as an alternative to two recent developments in post-punk—the rabble-rousing Oi! movement, and the anarcho-punk scene centred around Crass.[2] Goth became a home for kids who liked the energy of these bands, but were bored by the politics. Anything with a whiff of romance, darkness and mystery was bound to appeal to them—and 'Release the Bats' had plenty of all three.

When the singer in 'Mutiny in Heaven', sprouts his ungodly wings and flies out of the twentieth century, he's offering his listener something no amount of agit-prop or personal politics can provide—an escape route from the world as it is. Siouxsie and the Banshees embodied this same quality. '[*Juju*] was released at the height of the Thatcherite years,' remarked music writer Keith Cameron, talking to Siouxsie in 2008, 'yet you seemed to be inhabiting your alternative reality, a horror-show phantasmagoria: Halloween, Voodoo Dolly, Arabian Knights...'

'Right!' the singer replied. 'You're saying "Thatcherite years", and I'm going: "Really?!" I wasn't even aware! We were in our own universe.'[3]

The flight to this alternative reality is what links together the motley collection of bands who came to be embraced by the 'white faces' in the early '80s, and has been central to the appeal of goth through the decades. The Cure, for example, are not really goth. But to Geoff Rickly of Thursday, growing up in the '90s, they were of a piece with the other goth bands he liked because they seemed to offer an escape route from the present day.

'The goth and British bands I liked had the same visceral kick as regular punk but it seemed more like a place for me, a space you could inhabit. Something far away from reality.'[4]

Similarly, for Gerard Way of My Chemical Romance and Davey Havok of AFI, the appeal of goth is precisely this escape from the present day, an escape that punk with a capital 'p' can never allow. In Bauhaus, Southern Death Cult, The Damned, Alien Sex Fiend, The Virgin Prunes and The Sisters of Mercy, the Britain of 1979–84 is only suggested by its absence. All these bands made the leap out of what Alex de Jonge calls 'the degraded present' and into something out-of-time, something eternal and unchanging.[5] Siouxsie and The Banshees' 'Spellbound' invokes the world of the irrational, dreams, magic and madness. Siouxsie asks us to cast our minds back to childhood and the 'beckoning voice' that seemed to call us through the cradle bars. These deep-seated urges, she insists, cannot be ignored—they define us for all time, and all our efforts to civilise ourselves, from pre-school onwards, are reduced to nothing when we hear this siren-sound again.

You hear laughter
Cracking through the walls
it sends you spinning
you have no choice[6]

The contrast with the Leeds positivists couldn't be more complete. In 'Love like Anthrax', Andy Gill scoffs at the idea that, deep in the human soul, there are permanent emotions that everyone can relate to because they have not changed in thousands of years. If this is true, what hope do we have of perfecting society? None at all, says the goth. We can't change, because we're not lumps of dough, but unfathomable mysteries, full of primitive urges and recurring nightmares. These timeless and tragic emotions have haunted humanity for thousands of years, and will continue to haunt us for thousands of years to come.

This, for the punk activist and pop deconstructivist alike, is almost unforgivably backward. That's why, when they went looking for a name for this unwelcome eruption of romantic gloom in their new pop universe, critics of the day settled on 'gothic'. The word had almost the identical connotations it had for the reviewer of Horace Walpole's *The Castle of Otranto*—'gothic' meant superstitious, irrational and unhealthily obsessed with love, religion and death. The implication was—haven't we grown out of all that stuff?

But these criticisms ignore the fact that the goth's attachment to the timeless and the tragic is the result of the very same 'Enlightenment' that the pop optimist claims to advocate. Nick Cave, like Wordsworth, would eventually find his God, but for the majority of the romantics—including Shelley, Keats, Byron and Goethe—such simple faith was impossible. Romanticism, as Norman Davies has observed, is characterised by a profoundly religious temperament—a longing to believe.[7] But more often than not, when the romantics, having found no satisfaction in the modern world, went looking for God, they found him gone. The blame, as usual, lay with Newton and his followers, who in the rush to rid Christianity of its mystery, had rationalised God into a corner, and finally out of existence.

Blasphemous Rumours

THEY MIGHT HAVE been signed to the same label as Nick Cave, but in the musical world of the mid '80s Depeche Mode were clearly aligned with the pop positivists—those who would analyse the clichés and conventions of our behaviour with a view to creating new relations between people. And like their philosophical forebears, Depeche Mode were fearless in their quest to expose dogma and nonsense to the cold hard light of reason, even if it led them—as it had Newton—perilously close to Blasphemy. On side two of their 1984 album, *Some Great Reward*, Gahan tries to unravel the greatest mystery of all: why, if God is good, do bad things happen to good people?

> *Girl of 18*
> *Fell in love with everything*
> *Found new life in Jesus Christ*
> *Hit by a car*
> *Ended up*
> *On a life support machine.*[1]

Gahan and Gore wrote 'Blasphemous Rumours' after noticing something odd about the church services they'd attended. At the end, the priest would read out a list of those in the congregation suffering from serious illness, 'and the one at the top always died. But still everyone went right ahead thanking God for carrying out his will. It just seemed so strange.'[2] The conclusion was inescapable. In the song's insanely catchy chorus, Gahan sings:

> *I don't want to start any Blasphemous rumours*
> *But I think that God's got a sick sense of humour*
> *And when I die*
> *I expect to find him laughing.*[3]

Gahan's accusations were so bitter, and the song struck such a chord, that eventually, God's representatives on earth were moved to speak up in his defence. A priest from Depeche Mode's home town of Basildon spoke to the press, saying, 'If we can say God so loved the world that He sent His only son...if he did that, he cannot have a sick sense of humour.'[4] Which is all very well, but Depeche Mode's questions still nag. Why create us with the capacity for happiness and deny it? Why bring us into the world and then visit us with every kind of horror? Here Gahan, as Nick Cave would later put it, calls upon the author to explain.

Edward Scissorhands: 'Did I solicit thee, from darkness to promote me?'

Paradise Lost

IN *Edward Scissorhands*, Edward never gets to confront his inventor, never has the chance to accuse him of leaving him stranded in the world, half-finished, with a burning desire for love and hands that prevent him from touching anybody. But Frankenstein's monster does. What's more, his recent reading material, John Milton's *Paradise Lost*, gives him a powerful language with which to present his accusations:

> *I ought to be thy Adam, but I am rather the fallen angel, whom thou drivest from joy for no misdeed. Everywhere I see bliss, from which I alone am irrevocably excluded.*[1]

When God created Adam, the monster asserts, he provided for him, gave him guidance, direction and a companion. But

Frankenstein sees his own man of clay not as a son, but as a mistake made at work—a botched job he threw in the bin and hoped no more would be said of it. Now the botched job has learned to talk back, and is demanding justice:

> *You, my creator, detest and spurn me, thy creature, to whom thou art bound by ties only dissoluble by the annihilation of one of us. You purpose to kill me. How dare you thus sport with life?*[2]

It's all right for you, he seems to be saying to Frankenstein— you have a creator who loves and accepts you. The only thing is, we're not sure the monster is right. By comparing himself to Adam and Frankenstein to God, the monster is inviting a comparison that made Mary Shelley's readers realise how *little* difference there was between the two cases. This is the sting in Shelley's tale; Frankenstein invites us not so much to imagine Frankenstein as God, but to imagine God as Frankenstein—creating a man on a whim, and then kicking him out of doors on another, leaving him to fend for himself, like a failed experiment. The quotation from Adam in *Paradise Lost* on the title page of Frankenstein makes the point even clearer:

> *Did I request thee, Maker, from my clay*
> *To mould me man? Did I solicit thee*
> *From darkness to promote me?*[3]

Milton was a towering figure for the romantics. From 1658, the exiled poet spent seven years writing *Paradise Lost*, a Christian epic that tells the story of the creation of the world, of Lucifer's fall from heaven and of Adam and Eve's sin and expulsion from Paradise. Milton was deeply religious, yet as Karen Armstrong points out in her fascinating book *A History of God* the most likeable character in Milton's epic is not

God or Christ but Satan. 'Satan has many of the qualities of the new men of Europe,' she writes, 'he defies authority, pits himself against the unknown.'[4] In fact, it's Milton's Satan, the rebel angel, who would later become enshrined as a romantic hero—the prototype of Napoleon and Byron. When Frankenstein's monster tells his maker that he feels he has been cast out of heaven, he is, once again, being very romantic.

But if Satan is the hero of Milton's epic, where does that leave God? There is, as Armstrong points out, something truly horrible about the God of *Paradise Lost*.[5] It's not that there's anything radically out of the ordinary in Milton's portrayal of the deity. He displays the traits that have been attributed to him since the Old Testament—omniscience, omnipotence and all the rest of it. But it's precisely these traits that make him so unlovable. Milton's admirable desire to explain his religion to himself forces him to reconcile God's all-powerfulness with the suffering the human race has had to endure, and this pushes his God into some awkward postures.

God explains to his son, for instance, that he has given Adam and Eve their own free will and the power to resist the temptations of Satan. But he knows they won't, because he's God and he knows everything in advance. What's the point of allowing them free choice if he already knows they're bound to fall? God's answer to this amounts to his saying that this way, he gets to have his cake and eat it too. He can keep being all-powerful, but Adam and Eve can't blame him for the bad things that happen to them because they have free will. Thanks a lot, God.

It gets worse too. Later the archangel Michael is sent by God to reassure Adam that his descendants will find their way to redemption by discovering the true religion, Christianity. Michael treats Adam to a sneak preview of the next few thousand years of exile and suffering, culminating in God's sending his only son down to earth to redeem humankind. At this point, Armstrong writes, 'It occurs to the reader that there must have been an easier and more direct way to redeem mankind. The fact that this torturous plan with its constant failures and false starts, is decreed *in advance* can only cast grave doubts on the intelligence of its author.'[6]

This God, who appears to be either hopelessly incompetent (he can't prevent suffering) or monstrously cruel (he can, but he won't) was a particular problem of the Enlightenment. It was, Armstrong insists, the attempt to rationalise God's existence which had made him so unbearable.

The Disappearing God

BY SPREADING THEIR blasphemous rumours on *Top of the Pops* in 1984, Depeche Mode incurred the wrath of *The Sun* newspaper and Britain's self-appointed moral guardian, Mary Whitehouse. But if Martin Gore had published his verses in 1750, he would have found himself in far worse trouble— atheists were routinely locked up during the eighteenth century.

And yet many Enlightenment thinkers found that they were inexorably drawn to deny the existence of God. By looking to science for the answers religion had formerly provided, the Age of Reason had already relegated God to a less conspicuous role. Newton's scientific view of the universe held that nature and the physical world operated by a kind of clockwork. The machine was vast and complex, but essentially logical, meaning that its secrets would, given time, be discovered and understood. But the very existence of this clockwork implied for Newton that there must have been, or still be a *clockmaker*—and this is where God fits into the scheme.

Gravity may put ye planets into motion but without ye divine power it could never put them into such a circulating motion as they have about ye Sun, and therefore for this as well as other reasons, I am compelled to ascribe ye frame of this systeme to an intelligent Agent.[1]

Newton's 'Rolls Royce' universe dominated the Western imagination until long after his death, but for Scottish philosopher David Hume, writing in 1750, it wasn't nearly good enough. Hume objected to Newton's argument for God from design. If the universe is the work of a supremely intelligent overseer, he asked, then how does Newton account for the existence of evil? Does God make mistakes, or does he mean to see us suffer?[2]

Hume, as Karen Armstrong notes, chose to leave his refutations of Newton—which implied his atheism without ever stating it—unpublished, but Denis Diderot was not so cautious.[3] The French *Philosophe* was imprisoned in 1749 for publishing 'A Letter to the Blind for the Use of Those Who See'—the strongest dose of atheism yet administered to his century. The letter presents an argument between a Newtonian called Mr Holmes and Nicholas Saunderson, a blind professor. 'Diderot', writes Armstrong, 'makes Saunderson ask Holmes how the argument from design could be reconciled with such "monsters" and accidents as himself, who demonstrated anything but intelligent and benevolent planning.'[4]

They could lock Diderot up, but by this point, the horse had well and truly bolted. The rational enquiries of the Enlightenment philosophers had left humanity with a God who resembled the one in Depeche Mode's song to an extraordinary degree—a deity who was incompetent at best, malicious at worst. Diderot, for one, declared that he could do without such a being, and many more would come to the same conclusion.

The romantics inherited this unlovable and useless God, which was a shame, because with an alienating industrial future rising in front of them, and the bitter disappointments of the Revolution still lingering behind, they could really have used a 'loving father' of the kind imagined by Schiller in his 'Ode to Joy'. The great sense of crisis in romantic literature comes to a large extent from a feeling of having been shot by both sides—betrayed by the cult of reason on the one hand, and by a disappearing God on the other. Keats, in 1819, found himself in exactly this position, as his biographer Robert Gittings describes:

> *He did not believe… in the perfectibility of earthly*
> *life; indeed, perfect happiness in life, he saw, would*
> *make death intolerable… Yet the Christian idea that*
> *the common hardships of this world were only a*
> *miserable interlude before the blessed state of another*
> *struck him as 'a little circumscribed, straightened*
> *notion'.*[5]

Keats admired Voltaire. At a dinner with Wordsworth and the painter Benjamin Robert Haydon, he had raised his glass in the direction of Voltaire's likeness and drunk his good health. For Keats, Voltaire's determination to do away with the 'pious frauds of religion' made him a hero. Some time later, back at Haydon's and standing before the same painting, he placed his hand over his heart, lowered his head and said of Voltaire, 'There is the being I will bow to.'[6]

But while he admired Voltaire's intellectual bravery, the thorough-going rationalism of the *Philosophes* did not square with Keats's feeling for mystery—a quality he believed to be essential to poetry.'He could not be satisfied with a complete and negative scepticism,' writes Robert Gittings in his biography of the poet. 'Somewhere, he must find a faith.'[7]

The Age of Simple Faith

WORDSWORTH, HAVING REJECTED Revolution and Reason in quick succession, had found the faith that saved his life in nature. Likewise, after the crisis documented in 'Blasphemous Rumours', Martin Gore found himself advocating a spell in the country:

> *Come with me*
> *into the trees*
> *we'll lay on the grass*
> *and let the air pass[1]*

These lyrics from 'Stripped', a song on Depeche Mode's *Black Celebration* album, might seem like unusual sentiments coming from pioneers of industrial dance music. But the song's arrangement casts a grim cloud of irony over Gore's Rousseauish lyrics. It's an industrial symphony of steam hammers and stamping presses, and the effect is of the lovers being chased down the road by a factory even as they drive off into the country.

For the romantic, the degraded present often implies an ideal past—a Garden of Eden to which we might return. Accordingly in nineteenth-century England where the rise of industry was faster and more widespread than anywhere else, the romantic escape tended to take the form of a flight into nature. In the same way, the torturous problem of trying to accommodate God into a scientific universe led many romantics to attempt a flight back in time, to the simple faith that characterised Christianity in the Middle Ages. As the nineteenth century wore on, and the 'dark Satanic mills' continued their steady march across the landscape while God remained missing in action, later offshoots of romanticism would be motivated by an attempt to combine these two ideal

pasts—the pre-industrial society and the age of simple faith—
which were really one and the same.

Nostalgia for the Middle Ages was as Eric Hobsbawm has
noted in *The Age of Revolution*, one of the three most popular
cures for romantic displacement in the nineteenth century—
nostalgia for the French Revolution and nostalgia for the Noble
Savage being the other two.[2] Its first stirrings could be detected
by observing the crowds of tourists trekking out to see Walpole's
Strawberry Hill in the 1760s, or the even bigger crowds turning
up for the stage adaptation of *The Castle of Otranto* ten years
later. The success of Walpole's gothic novel paved the way for
later phenomena such as the historical novels of Walter Scott,
whose swashbuckling heroes were important precursors of
Byron's. Scott's stories, while not actually set in the Middle
Ages, were jam-packed with medieval paraphernalia.

Meanwhile, the gothic revival in architecture began to
gather momentum—and a new sense of purpose. By 1837 it
was virtually the national style in Britain, a moment
signalled by A W Pugin's design for the Houses of
Parliament. Some years later, critic John Ruskin went
further, advocating not just the gothic style, but the whole
medieval ethos as one worth returning to. In his essay 'The
Nature of the Gothic' Ruskin argued that industry and
progress had cut human beings off from the wellspring of
their creativity—nature. Instead of shoddy goods made by
unhappy people in ugly factories, Ruskin posited a return to
the days of the guild and the artisan; decorations, tools and
buildings made by passionate individuals with love and
creativity.[3]

Designer and social reformer William Morris began to put
Ruskin's ideas into practice when he opened the doors of his
firm, Morris, Marshall, Faulkner and Co. in 1861. Today,
Morris is best known for one of the world's most famous
wallpaper designs—but the wallpaper was in fact just a small
part of a far-reaching scheme to improve the world through

arts and crafts. For Morris, one of the most damaging effects of the industrial revolution was the standardisation and mass production of the applied arts and crafts. He hoped to reverse the alienating processes of capitalism and industrialisation by recreating, within his own firm, the world of the medieval artisan's guild. In between, he found time for pamphleteering, experiments in communal living, learning to paint, and writing fiction. His *House of the Wolfings* is both fantasy and polemic—clearly influenced on the one hand by the romances of Walter Scott, while implicitly using an imagined Middle Ages as a stick to beat the nineteenth century with on the other. Unfortunately, Morris's enthusiasm for all things medieval led him to write the entire book in some kind of archaic eighth-century dialect—which made it pretty tough going for the average reader.

> *What aileth thee, O Wood-Sun, and is this a new*
> *custom of thy kindred*
> *and the folk of God-home that their brides array*
> *themselves like thralls*
> *new-taken, and as women who have lost their kindred*
> *and are outcast? Who*
> *then hath won the Burg of the Anses, and clomb the*
> *rampart of God-home?*[4]

Morris was also closely associated with a group of painters and poets called the Pre-Raphaelite Brotherhood. The Brotherhood began in 1848, with just two brothers answering the rollcall. Painter and poet Dante Gabriel Rossetti tracked down William Holman Hunt after seeing the latter's *The Eve of St Agnes*, and the two bonded over Keats—upon whose poem the painting was based. They called themselves Pre-Raphaelites because they believed that after Raphael, European art had begun a slide into irrelevance—empty displays of technical bravado and pointless imitations of Greek or

Renaissance art—from which they hoped to rescue it. 'Study nature' was their motto, and in early successes like Holman Hunt's *Our English Coasts*, you could see that they had.[5]

But the best known of the Pre-Raphaelites, Rossetti, seemed to abandon this principle quite early on—and many younger artists followed his example. His painting is beautifully observed, but the degraded present disappears, and is replaced by an idealised fourteenth century. Rossetti's *The Annunciation* (1849–50) recreates the atmosphere of early Renaissance art, the breakthrough paintings of Fra Angelico and Gozzoli, to the letter—from the carefully planned perspective to the golden disc hovering over the Virgin's head.[6] Rossetti's paintings look back at a time when the divinely inspired artist provided people with objects and images they could believe in.

The handicrafts Morris designed and sold through his firm were undoubtedly beautiful and true in many ways to the spirit of the medieval artisan's guilds he so admired. But having insisted on the handmade over the mass produced, Morris was forced to sell his goods at many times the price of the competition—placing his wallpaper and ceramics completely out of the price range of the ordinary folk whose lives he hoped to improve. There was, it seemed, no going back. 'Dreamer of dreams', is how Morris later described himself, 'born out of my due time'.[7] This feeling of having tried to turn back the clock—and having failed—dogged both William Morris and the Pre-Raphaelites to the end of their days. To the Pre-Raphaelite painter Edward Burne-Jones, the chances that art and artists might be able to stop the industrial rot and improve the world looked increasingly slim: 'Rossetti could not set it right and Morris could not set it right—and who the devil am I? ...'[8] The age of simple faith was long gone by 1850—eroded by the achievements of the Enlightenment, and finally blown to smithereens by the shock of the Revolution—and all the golden haloes in the world could not bring it back.

Robert Smith: The pious frauds of religion.

Faith

THE COVER OF the Cure's 1981 album *Faith* looks like nothing at first—a grey, abstract blur to match the indistinct gloom of the album itself. But just as repeated listening to *Faith* will cause its clouds of sound to coalesce into songs, so too does the cover eventually resolve itself into an image. It's an out-of focus photograph of Bolton Abbey, a Gothic church in North Yorkshire. Bolton was built in 1151, and has been alternately falling apart and being restored ever since. August Pugin, the Gothic Revival architect, did some work on it during the Victorian era.[1]

Earlier in the nineteenth century, the ruined abbey had inspired a poem of Wordsworth's, 'The White Doe of Rylstone'. The story is of a woman named Emily whose brothers and parents were killed in a revolt against Queen Elizabeth. Emily finds solace from her despair—and ultimately faith—in the visits of a white doe. The doe was a childhood pet, raised by her in the days when she was still surrounded by family and the world seemed full of hope and promise. Here, as in 'The Prelude' or 'Tintern Abbey', childhood memories, nature, and the passage of time work their magic to restore faith.

Wordsworth, as Karen Armstrong has noted in her *History of God*, was a religious man, who often spoke of God when he was discussing ethics or morality.[2] But the word never appears in his verse. In 'The White Doe of Rylstone', as in many other poems, Wordsworth evokes the spirit that he felt to be moving through all things, the presence 'whose dwelling is the light of setting suns'.[3] But he never calls this 'God'. Wordsworth's Enlightenment side made him distrust organised religion, his romantic side lead him to resist categorising the ineffable. In 'Tintern Abbey,' he simply calls it a 'something'.

It's this same 'something' that Robert Smith searches for in the final moments of *Faith*. But it seems to have got away from him. The whole album feels elusive and faraway, as though it's being heard from a great distance no matter how close you put your ear to the speaker. As the singer retreats into his loneliness, the world goes out of focus. In early Buzzcocks-inspired songs like 'Jumping Someone Else's Train', Smith's lyrics described characters—now, they're just 'other voices'. It becomes hard for him to make distinctions. 'All cats are grey,' he sings.[4]

The word that emerges most distinctly from the fog of *Faith* is 'nothing'—perhaps because it's repeated so many times. The same 'nothing' Smith found when he went running into the forest on 'Seventeen Seconds' has become the whole world of *Faith*. And yet, in the album's final song—the title track—the singer dares to hope for something more. *Faith* is the epitome of The Cure's early '80s sound—guitars like distant church bells, a stripped-bare drum kit ticking away in an empty hall—a song that sounds like a memory of a song. Smith's lyrics rise fitfully out of the gloom, describing the singer's final descent into solitude. Outside, it's 1982, and New Wave pop music is taking over the world. 'The party just gets better and better!' Smith observes—he spits out that last 'better' like Johnny Rotten singing 'pretty'.[5] He's turned his back on all of it. 'I went away alone,' he says, 'with nothing left but faith.'[6] Smith, like some kind of post-punk monk (or, as he puts it, 'an unknown saint') has renounced this world of temptation and illusion—now he has only his belief to sustain him. But belief in what? At the beginning of the album, he'd rejected what Keats called the 'pious frauds' of religion, standing up in the middle of a church service, he'd screamed 'a wordless scream at ancient power'.[7] Like Wordsworth and the Romantics, he's renounced dogma and tradition in favour of a direct experience of the ineffable 'something'. This is the kind of faith people knew in the Middle Ages, the kind that drove the hands of the stonemasons who built Bolton Abbey. This is what Smith is searching for in the final seconds of 'Faith'. Even after the rest of the band have disappeared, and the drum machine has run out of batteries, Smith is still wailing in the empty church hall, 'there's nothing left but faith!'[8]

Dave Gahan: Personal Jesus.

World in My Eyes

BY THE MID-NINETEENTH century, others were more willing than the Pre-Raphaelites to look the modern world's spiritual crisis in the eye. In 'Dover Beach' Victorian poet Matthew Arnold admitted that the age of simple faith was long gone:

The sea of faith
Was once, too, at the full, and round earth's shore
Lay like the folds of a bright girdle furl'd.
But now I only hear
Its melancholy, long, withdrawing roar…[1]

Arnold, wrote William J Long in his *History of English and American Literature*, 'reflected the doubt or despair of those whose faith had been shaken by the alleged discoveries of science'.[2] In 'Dover Beach' we see clearly the despair lurking behind the uncannily still fantasies of the Pre-Raphaelites. Arnold wrote the poem on his honeymoon, while staring out at the French coast from Dover. This view gave him the poem's central metaphor—the ocean, which Arnold likens to the faith in God that once seemed so boundless. Now, he writes in 'Dover Beach', this faith has drained away from the world like water through a sieve. There is no sign, even, of the solace Wordsworth found in nature or Keats in the imagination. The world is used up, containing 'neither joy, nor love'.[3] Love, where it does exist in 'Dover Beach' is something that takes place outside of the world, in spite of it, almost. It's the love of two people who have turned their backs on the world, who find themselves unable to place their faith in anything but themselves—and each other.

> *Ah, love, let us be true*
> *To one another! for the world which seems*
> *To lie before us like a land of dreams,*
> *So various, so beautiful, so new,*
> *Hath really neither joy, nor love, nor light,*
> *Nor certitude, nor peace, nor help for pain;*
> *And we are here as on a darkling plain*
> *Swept with confused alarms of struggle and flight,*
> *Where ignorant armies clash by night.*[4]

This image of lovers united against a hostile and dangerous world would turn up more and more in Martin Gore's songs after *Some Great Reward*. In fact, the cover of that album already shows a couple who could have stepped out of Arnold's 'Dover Beach'. The scene is of a grim industrial landscape. It's night, but there are no stars—just the glare of halogen lights throwing the forbidding geometry of the factory into sharp relief. In the midst of this desolate scene, dwarfed by the inhuman scale of their surroundings, is a pair of newly-weds—just married, in fact—he in his tuxedo, she in a bridal gown. It would be wrong to describe them as happy, or even hopeful. But given that their love for each other is all they have, what else can they do but stare into each other's eyes and try to will this nightmare world out of existence?

The young couple has been left stranded in the world of blasphemous rumours—a world in which God is either cruel or incompetent, and has subsequently been relieved of his duties. This desolate landscape was the one Martin Gore began exploring on Depeche Mode's next album *Black Celebration*. In 'Nothing' Gore, like Robert Smith, waits hopefully for a word from God and hears only silence. Now his faith is long gone, and with it any meaning life might have held. He resigns himself to his fate. He will 'learn to expect—nothing'.[5] In the space of two albums, Gore has made the whole journey from the optimistic enquiries of the Enlightenment to the despair of the mid-nineteenth century. Gore has moved into the world of 'Dover Beach'—or the even bleaker one of James Thomson's *The City of Dreadful Night*, in which the poem's narrator is shown around a desolate city by a mysterious guide. The traveller is baffled by what he sees. Here, humanity seems to have reached the end of its tether: the ties that bind people together—love, family, brotherhood—have all finally snapped. Nobody here believes in anything, nothing has any meaning, no-one seems to have any reason to go on living. And yet life goes on, but why? 'When faith and hope and love are dead indeed', he asks his companion, 'can life still live? By what doth it proceed?'

...He answered coldly, Take a watch, erase
the signs and figures of the circling hours
detach the hands, remove the dial face
The works proceed until run down; although
Bereft of purpose, void of use, still go... [6]

This is Newton's universe turned ugly—a machine with no-one at the controls. Depeche Mode's Dave Gahan echoes the solitary traveller's confusion in *Black Celebration* when he wonders—a little enviously—how his friends can carry on living in the face of all this cosmic meaninglessness.

Your optimistic eyes
Seem like paradise
To someone
Like me [7]

Two albums later, Depeche Mode would do away with this simile. In the world of 1990's *Violator*, the idea of paradise in another's eyes is not just an idle thought, it's the tenet of a new religion. *Violator* was a landmark album for the band—in which Gahan and Gore seemed to have discovered an antidote, of sorts, to the despair of *Black Celebration*. The mood of *Violator* was religious—but God was nowhere to be found. His replacement was a lover. In the album's first song, the scenario of *Black Celebration* is reversed—the singer tells his beloved that there's no need to give another thought to the meaningless world outside—he's found a better one. 'Let me show you the world in my eyes,' he croons. [8] The singer has already made this leap of faith himself—he's turned his back on worldly temptation in favour of a new religion based on ... worldly temptation! In 'Blue Dress' he insists that the meaning of life is nothing more than the feeling he gets looking at a beautiful girl in a beautiful dress. Here, he seems to say, is the faith that will sustain him, and on the album's first single, Gahan takes this idea to its logical conclusion. If a woman could be God for him, then he can be God for you: 'your own personal Jesus'.[9] In the song's towering chorus, Gahan preaches his new religion to the waiting world. God has deserted you, he says, but I'm right here. 'Reach out and touch faith.'

Richard Wagner: So might we die together...

We Can Be Heroes

NATURE, MEDIEVALISM, SATANISM; of all the possible escape routes from society at the romantic's disposal, none have quite the pulling power of ideal love. Being a solitary, inspired individual acting in defiance of society's laws is heroic, but it also gets lonely—which is why the romantic goes looking for a soul mate, the perfect, untarnished love of two people united in pure feeling, who live in a zone untouched by the world of dull care. It never really works out, but this is hardly the lovers' fault. The world, with its painful compromises, social conventions and moral laws keeps coming between them. Ideal love has a hard time standing up to the onslaught of reality, and eventually becomes impossible to maintain. So love becomes a recipe for tragedy—the now-familiar stand-off between the romantic individual and society is rewritten for two. The odds, sadly, are not much better than before:

Though nothing
Will drive them away
We can be heroes
Just for one day.[1]

The lovers in David Bowie's 'Heroes'—kissing by the Berlin Wall as the bullets fly over their heads—are doomed; and they know it. The song, as Bowie admitted after it was released in 1977, is about 'facing reality and standing up to it.'[2] But the lyric is full of wrenching sadness, because the singer knows that in this contest between two people and *reality itself*, they don't stand a chance. Bowie's extraordinary vocal grows by stages from a croon to a scream as the song moves towards its end—bearing witness to his character's slow realisation that, pure though the lovers' love may be, a stone wall is a stone wall. And yet, paradoxically, even as he faces the fact that he and his beloved can't win, he insists that they can. 'We can beat them,' he sings, 'for ever and ever!'[3] The lovers are heroes—but not the kind to save somebody from a burning building or lead a nation to victory. They're martyrs to love; two people who have chosen to preserve their perfect feeling by, as Werther would say, quitting their prison. Their love is too big, and too bold for the world, they must perish.

As with 'Rock and Roll Suicide', the sentiment of Heroes—the very idea that passion cannot and should not be contained by the limits of life—would have been baffling to an eighteenth century audience. But a concert-goer of 1865, hearing 'Heroes', would understand instantly why the lovers in the song are heroic—and might not even be too bothered by the screaming guitars. Thanks to composer Richard Wagner, the nineteenth century music lover had already become quite well acquainted with romantic passion and terrifyingly loud noise.

Wagner was born in the last days of the Napoleonic wars, and grew up admiring the great culture heroes of German romanticism—Goethe, Hoffmann, and above all, Beethoven, whose Symphony No. 9 he arranged for piano at the age of seventeen. Twelve years later his opera *Rienzi* became a huge hit. More successes—artistic if not always commercial—followed, with *The Flying Dutchman* and *Tannhäuser*. Then, in 1848, Wagner embarked on the greatest project of his life—the three-part saga, *Der Ring des Nibelungen*.

In the summer of 1857 Wagner, short of funds and mentally exhausted by his monumental and as-yet incomplete trilogy, decided to try something different. This new opera would be simpler to stage, cheaper to produce, and much shorter. Compared to the mind-boggling scale of *Nibelungen*, *Tristan und Isolde* would eventually satisfy all these criteria. But if Wagner ever thought it was going to be easy to write, he was in for a shock.

Tristan was to be an adaptation of the ancient folk tale of the same name—a Celtic love story with a tragic end, kept alive as a metrical romance in medieval Europe. Versions of the Tristan story turned up in France, Italy, England and Germany. And it was a German version by Gottfried von Strassburg written in 1200 that Wagner used for his libretto. Like all medieval ballads, *Tristan* had acquired a lot of embellishments over the centuries—things that would have been entertaining to an audience of the thirteenth century, but which didn't translate so well in the nineteenth. In adapting *Tristan* for the stage, Wagner set about stripping away a lot of this incidental action, to reveal the story's core. As he did so, his *Tristan and Isolde* began to take on a life of its own. 'Child!' he wrote to the poet Mathilde Wesendonk. 'This Tristan is turning into something terrible! This final Act!!!!—I fear the opera will be banned.'[4]

The first act of *Tristan* is musically revolutionary, but dramatically nothing too out of the ordinary. The action begins on a ship. Tristan, a Cornish knight, is ferrying Isolde to Cornwall and his King Mark, whom Isolde has promised to marry. Isolde is secretly in love with Tristan. She would, she says, rather die than marry 'Cornwall's weary King'—but tragic heroines say things like that.[5] Later in the first act, Tristan snubs her, and the furious Isolde decides that he must die, and that she will die with him. They both drink what they think is poison—but is in fact a love potion. This love potion, as the British academic Michael Tanner points out in his study of Wagner, is not so important as people imagine. 'So far as its long term effects are concerned, they might as well have been drinking water—the potion enables them to release their previously hidden feelings for one another instantly, but they do that only because they believe death is imminent.'[6] The lovers embrace, and become completely absorbed in their love for one another. By this point, the ship is landing, and King Mark's royal train is in sight. But Tristan and Isolde are oblivious.

In the second act, the lovers meet in secret while King Mark is out hunting. They begin a duet with the words 'O sink hernieder, nacht der lieber' ('O sink upon us, night of love').[7] Now, the only thing real in the world of Tristan and Isolde is the dream of Tristan and Isolde—everything else, including King Mark who we know must come back from his hunt at any moment—is an illusion, albeit a persistent one. When Mark returns and confronts Tristan over his betrayal, Tristan dismisses the king and his claims as nothing more than 'Phantoms of the day! Morning dreams!' He has determined to leave this sham world, and asks Isolde to accompany him to the 'wonder-realm of night'.[8] To the king, this is all complete nonsense, but the lovers have long ago replaced sense with sensibility. Feeling, to Tristan and Isolde, is sacred—it's the only law they will accept. And since no-one else can understand their feeling, they retreat more and more from the world and go deeper into their love for one another. People say they're crazy, what do they know? Here, the loneliness that comes of solipsism is in theory redeemed by romantic love. But in a sense, Tristan and Isolde are lonelier than ever.

The climax of Tristan and Isolde's love-duet finds them singing, 'So might we die together, eternally one without end, without awakening, without fearing, nameless in love's embrace, giving ourselves wholly, to live only for love!'[9] And this is what they set out to do. Tristan fights a battle with Sir Melot, who had betrayed the lovers to King Mark. He allows himself to be beaten, is fatally wounded, and is carried off to Brittany where we find him, slowly expiring, as the curtain goes up on the third act—the one Wagner worried would be banned, or would drive people insane.

Tristan's faithful servant Kurwenal has sent for Isolde to heal his master's wound. The dying Tristan hallucinates Isolde's arrival, and this, as Tanner writes, is his happiest moment—'essentially, he has found the world he wants to be in'.[10] Tristan dies as Isolde arrives. She, devastated, expires over his body, singing her famous 'Liebestod'. The terms of the agreement they reached in the second act are fulfilled—the world could offer the lovers nothing, they will be united in death. Isolde leaves the world of day behind for ever, and joins Tristan as she sinks into 'unconscious, highest bliss!'[11]

Throughout *Tristan und Isolde*, Wagner uses the other characters in his drama to critique the lovers' behaviour. Mark and Kurwenal's dialogue gives voice to the incomprehension 'normal' people must feel in the face of Tristan and Isolde's monumental self-absorption. While Tristan lies unconscious in the third act, Kurwenal sings, 'Oh deception of love! Oh passion's force! The most beautiful of the world's illusions!'[12] Kurwenal's world, the world most of us live in, is the opposite of Tristan's—here romantic love is an illusion, a phantom which is bound to evaporate. As Tanner points out, many critics have taken Kurwenal's stance to be the true voice of *Tristan und Isolde*. They see the opera, in other words, as a critique of romanticism—as though Wagner knows better than his doomed lovers, and is subtly exposing their self-deception. In his book, *Wagner*, Tanner insists that nothing could be further from the truth. 'The trouble with accounts of Tristan which view it as in any way a critique or expose of romantic love is that that is not in the least how it feels.'[13]

The promise Bowie's King makes to his Queen is the same impossible vow Wagner's lovers make in the second act of *Tristan*. Their struggle against the world will end in their deaths, but in death their love will live 'forever and ever'. As Tanner has said of *Tristan*, it's *tempting* to interpret this as ironic, because if it's not, then the song is a sincere denial of civilisation itself. 'Heroes' indicts the whole world for letting its lovers down, and then dismisses that world as a sham, insisting that the lovers' dream world—*Tristan*'s 'wonder-realm of night'—is their true home, where they can reign as King and Queen forever. It's still possible that all this is meant to be ironic, but as Tanner says of Tristan, that's not how it feels—the quotation marks around the title appear nowhere in the song. Bowie sings it as though his heart is about to burst.

Wagnerian

OF ALL THE romantic composers, Wagner is the one most deserving of a place in the history of rock and roll. Others have had their moment in the sun—Beethoven was briefly in vogue in the late '60s thanks to Wendy Carlos's *A Clockwork Orange* soundtrack, Strauss had one of his tone poems pressed into service as Elvis's walk-on music in the '70s, and Rivers Cuomo, as we'll see later, has always had a soft spot for Puccini. But Schumann? Mahler? Berlioz? None are likely to find a place in the index of even the most exhaustive rock history, let alone have an entire genre of rock music named after them.

The phrase 'Wagnerian rock' is generally credited to songwriter Jim Steinman. Steinman adapted Wagner's *Das Rheingold* into a stage musical in 1974.[1] Three years later, he had teamed up with ex-*Rocky Horror Picture Show* star Meat Loaf to record *Bat Out Of Hell*, a hysterically over-the-top ode to American romance that turned Meat Loaf into an unlikely star, and paved the way for future Steinman mini-operas like Bonnie Tyler's 'Total Eclipse of the Heart'. But by the time *Bat Out of Hell* appeared, the term 'Wagnerian' already had some currency in the world of heavy metal. When The Stalk Forest Group changed their name to Blue Oyster Cult in 1971, rock critic Richard Meltzer suggested a way to lend their new name a bit of typographical panache. 'I said, "How about an umlaut?"' Meltzer later recalled, 'Metal had a Wagnerian aspect anyway'.[2] The heavy metal umlaut—or 'rock dots' as they came to be called—went on to have a life of their own, subsequently adopted by scores of bands from Motörhead to Mötley Crüe for their vague associations of tragedy, paganism, and above all, loudness.

By 'Wagnerian' Meltzer most likely meant 'loud and intense'—which is absolutely fair. 'I like Wagner's music better than anybody's,' says Lady Henry in Oscar Wilde's *The Picture of Dorian Gray*. 'It is so loud that one can talk the whole time without other people hearing what one says.'[3] Wagner's music was frequently dismissed as 'noise' by nineteenth-century critics. A cartoon published in 1869 showing the composer hammering a crotchet into a concertgoer's ear with a mallet sums up a fairly widespread feeling about him at the time. But Wagner intentionally strove for intensity in his music, and just like the metal bands he unknowingly inspired, if the technology of the day wasn't up to producing what he heard in his head, Wagner simply went 'one louder'. He had a specially designed Festival Theatre built in Bayreuth to accommodate his musical vision—the first stone was laid in 1872, and it would be another four years before the theatre saw its first performance.

Meanwhile, *The New York Times* reported excitedly on Bayreuth's radical new design. Wagner had the orchestra sunk below the floor so that the music would rise up before the audience as if from nowhere. The paper informed its readers that future theatregoers would watch Wagner's dramas 'through an invisible wall of sound'.[4]

Almost a century later, pop's most famous Wagnerian, Phil Spector, revived *The Times*' phrase to describe his new hit making formula, first heard on The Crystals' 'He's a Rebel' in 1962. Spector's Wall of Sound was created by a unique combination of multiple instruments, strings, kettledrums and big reverb-soaked spaces—all squeezed into a mono mix. The result was the most overwhelming noise that had ever been heard on the radio, a deep cataclysmic rumble topped with a sweet sprinkling of bells and shakers and a gut-busting vocal. Spector produced hits for The Crystals, Darlene Love and Bob B Sox, before reaching an extraordinary peak with The Ronettes' 'Be My Baby' in 1963.

Spector called these songs 'little symphonies for kids',[5] and spoke elsewhere of taking a 'Wagnerian approach' to rock and roll.[6] While the sound was radically new, Spector's fusion of teen-pop and romantic agony was by no means just a gimmick.

The eccentric producer had hit on a fundamental connection between the high school kids who bought his records and the operas of Richard Wagner. Spector had realised that in high school, every time a boy *looks* at you, let alone asks you on a date or dumps you just before the dance, it feels like *Tristan und Isolde*. So Spector decided to treat these teen tragedies with the dignity their protagonists instinctively felt they deserved. He would tell the teens of America that their emotions were every bit as important as they imagined. The Wall of Sound is not just a sound—it's a sound married to an idea.

Spector quit the business (temporarily, it later turned out) after DJs refused to play his masterpiece, 'River Deep–

Mountain High', in 1966. He would have taken his Wall of Sound with him if he could, but by the end of the '60s it was no longer exclusively his. A new generation of artists and producers who'd grown up with Spector's songs ringing in their ears was taking his sound in new directions, and using it to tell new stories. By the mid '70s the kids who'd bought 'Be My Baby' were in their twenties. Their lives had become more complicated, their responsibilities were greater, but they all still retained, somewhere in their hearts, the vision of ideal romantic love presented in that song and the sound that carried it—a vision that came to seem all the more tragic as reality closed them in its net.

Born to Run

IN 1974 'BE My Baby' still sounded like the future to Bruce Springsteen. The singer was looking for a way to refine the structure of his music while increasing its emotional impact, and Spector's 'little symphonies for kids' seemed to point the way. Not that Springsteen's new songs were 'for kids' exactly. Music writer Greil Marcus once wrote that Springsteen in the '70s took the carefree, drag-racing, soda-jerking teens of the '50s and early '60s and 'dumped fifteen years on them'.[1] Those kids who busted out of their parents' house and hit the road in search of fun and love; what did they find? And where are they now? This was the territory explored by a new song Springsteen had written early in 1974. He asked producer John Landau if he thought a Wall of Sound-style arrangement would work for 'Born to Run'.

'Born to Run' was one of the shortest songs Springsteen had written up to that point, but recording it took almost six months in the studio—twice as long as it had taken to record his last *album*.[2] The time spent paid off—'Born to Run', then as now, explodes out of the radio. As with Spector's '60s' productions, the song's deep spaces and tiny details add up to create the effect of a gigantic symphony compressed into the grooves of a rock and roll 45. But the song doesn't just sound like 'Be My Baby', it *works* like 'Be My Baby'. The music is impossibly grand, but the song is not about great men doing great deeds, it's about young Americans whose emotions will not be contained by the limits of their small-town lives. It's 'Summertime Blues' meets *Tristan und Isolde*. It's a tragic romance—and something more.

Romanticism replaced the Enlightenment's insistence on knowledge with a philosophy based on action. Goethe said, 'I am not here to know, but to do.'[3] In 'Born to Run', Springsteen's lonely rider agrees. Sensible, rational people tell him to knuckle down and get a good job—but this is second-hand philosophy, which is of no use to a young romantic:

> *... I gotta know how it feels*
> *I wanna know if your love is wild*
> *Girl I wanna know if love is real.*[4]

These lines are followed by a terrifying hallucination of America by night, lost souls drift through the mist, cars scream down the highway, the amusement park looms over the lovers like a mechanical monster. The singer and his girlfriend have to get out of this hostile world—he serenades her with the surprising lyric:

> *I wanna die with you out on the street tonight*
> *In an everlasting kiss.*[5]

This world of illusion is not for the singer and his Wendy; he proposes Isolde's 'unconscious, highest bliss' as an escape route. But he also suggests, just before the song's last chorus, that death is not the end, or that they might be headed somewhere after all:

Someday girl I don't know when
We're gonna get to the place where we really wanted to go
And we'll walk in the sun.[6]

'Born to Run' comes on as a tragedy—only to later reveal itself as something else—a religious drama based on a faith that doesn't exist yet. This, as Michael Tanner insists, is what *Tristan und Isolde* is really about. Wagner's lovers are determined to live with the consequences of their love, to see it to its conclusion. Their death is not a defeat, because they believe in something beyond the physical world. This is clearly a religious idea—but whereas Bach's *St Matthew Passion* deals with a religion everybody knows, Wagner was creating a brand-new one—a religion of romantic love.[7] 'Born to Run' and 'Heroes' both preach this religion. The singer and his soul mate place their faith in each other, knowing that this will offer them salvation in death. This is how Springsteen and Wendy can die in each others arms and 'get to the place'; Johnny and Tina can 'make it' whether they make it or not; and Bowie and his queen can be beaten and still 'beat them forever'.

This 'Passion of Passion' as Tanner calls it shares a few things in common with Christianity: the players in the Passion are forced to make enormous sacrifices and have their faith tested every step of the way. The key difference, according to Tanner, is that the Christian God makes you wait, whereas romanticism demands immediate action, with paradise as the direct result. In 'Thunder Road', the first song on the *Born To Run* album, Springsteen is standing outside his girl's house, holding out his hand and offering her a ride. She's been praying for a saviour, he tells her to get up off her knees and get in the car.

Well now I'm no hero that's understood,
All the redemption I can offer girl is beneath this dirty
hood...[8]

Springsteen is not just talking dirty when he suggests that salvation is right there under the hood of his car, and that heaven's in the back seat. He's saying: you don't have to wait, and you don't need God. He's going out tonight, he tells her, 'to case the promised land'.[9] He's more or less made up a new religion on the spot—and armed with this new faith, he assures her, the threat of death will become no threat at all. Their faith in each other, he insists, will allow them to transcend the material world.

Freddie Mercury: Compagnon de miseres.

Pressure

FOR DAVID BOWIE, 'Heroes' marked the beginning of a new, bravura-style of singing which record producer Tony Visconti dubbed 'The Bowie Histrionics'.[1] Though there wasn't much room for it on his next album, the surprisingly low-key *Lodger*, the new style did make a few appearances on 1980's *Scary Monsters*—especially on the first track, 'It's No Game'. But here, Bowie sounded more demented than heroic, as though the world he thought he could face on 'Heroes' had beaten him down again.

The Bowie Histrionics proper didn't really come out of its case again until 1981, and the occasion was not a David Bowie recording session per se, but a visit to fellow rock royalty that unexpectedly turned into a collaboration. In July of that year, the members of Queen were recording at Mountain Studios in Montreux. Bowie dropped by to say hello, and finding themselves with some time to spare, the five musicians started messing around with an idea. Before he knew it, Bowie found they were writing a song together. The music started to cook, the atmosphere in the studio grew heated, egos clashed. 'It was, er…peculiar,' said Bowie later.[2]

'Peculiar' is one way to describe the result of this unlikely collaboration. At first listen, 'Under Pressure' sounds like what it is—the sound of the two greatest hams in rock trying to out-ham each other. But it's not all empty posturing—the lyric is a little vague, but that's just because the scope of the song is so enormous that it's hard for the singers to stay focused. 'Under Pressure' is about all the trouble in the world, and what we, as mere human beings, can hope to do about it. It struck a chord—the single went to number 1 in the UK at the end of 1981. It also topped the charts in Argentina—and stayed there for the entire duration of the Falklands War. This had the leader of Argentina's military junta worried—he attacked 'Under Pressure' as a piece of British propaganda.[3]

But while it's full of rage and hope, 'Under Pressure' is not a protest song—or if it is, it's more in the vein of My Chemical Romance's 'Welcome to the Black Parade' than Bright Eyes' 'When the President Talks to God'. The singers' adversary is not a demagogue or a dictator or a corrupt bureaucracy—it's the world itself. The world, Bowie and Mercury tell us:

Breaks a building down
Splits a family in two
Puts people on streets.[4]

As the song goes on, the pressure builds and builds. The guitars brood like thunderclouds as Bowie, in his best Hammer Horror voice, sings about facing 'the terror of knowing what this world is about', as though he's finally come to understand the mysterious source of all this global chaos. Then the pressure drops, the song quietens down, and the singers ask themselves how they can live with the horror. They can't turn away and pretend it's not there, and they can't go on insisting that this is the best of all possible worlds when so many people are miserable. Then the music starts to build again, Freddie Mercury makes a vocal noise that approximates the sun breaking through clouds, and a solution comes rocketing out of the heavens—compassionate love! 'Love! Love! Love!', cries Bowie, heralding our salvation. When people understand that they need to change their way of life and start caring about one another, we will finally experience some relief from this terrible pressure. Freddie goes scatting off into the distance and the band leave the white-boy funk riff that started this whole thing lying on the floor—where Vanilla Ice would find it ten years later.

Bowie and Queen didn't stick around long enough to explain how this doctrine of compassionate love would work out in practice. But the German philosopher Arthur Schopenhauer had some ideas, which he set out in his essay, 'On the Suffering of the World', published in 1851. He was sixty-one years old, and had spent at least forty of these living with 'the terror of knowing what this world is about'. He did not believe things were about to get any better.

> If you imagine, in so far as it is approximately
> possible, the sum total of distress, pain and suffering of
> every kind which the sun shines upon in its course, you
> will have to admit it would have been much better if
> the sun had been able to call up the phenomenon of
> life as little on the earth as on the moon...[5]

Life, Schopenhauer insisted, is so bad that it can only be a mistake, and given that this is the case, and that we are all in the same unhappy boat, we owe it to one another to show a little kindness. Instead of going about calling one another 'sir' or 'monsieur' (or 'dude'), we ought to address strangers as 'fellow sufferer' or *'compagnon de miseres'*.[6]

Schopenhauer: The terror of knowing what this world is about.

Schopenhauer

SCHOPENHAUER HADN'T LIVED very long in 1805, but he'd already seen enough to convince him that Newton's clockwork universe proceeding according to some grand design was a crock. He had a clerical job in a commercial house in Hamburg, and a few weeks of this provided all the proof he needed that life was not an elegant machine, but a constant lurch between pain and boredom.

His father, whom he loved, had been found dead in a canal earlier that year, having taken his own life. His relationship with his mother was uneasy at best, bitterly competitive at worst. He'd taken a tour of the Continent, but with the Revolutionary wars still underway, had seen nothing but cruelty and unhappiness wherever he went. He hated his job, he hated his life.

Schopenhauer's Hamburg days formed his mature philosophy, a thorough-going pessimism which—as R J Hollingdale has observed in his introduction to Schopenhauer's essays—remained virtually unchanged until his death fifty-five years later.[1] He acquired more knowledge, but nothing altered his basic feeling about our existence. 'Life,' he wrote later, 'is a disagreeable thing—and I have determined to spend it in reflecting on it.'[2] This is exactly what he did. Back in 1776, the young Goethe, sitting on top of Strasbourg Cathedral, had a vision of the universe as 'convulsed with desires knotted like snakes, from which it tries to escape only to entangle itself again'. This bleak view of life is perfectly understandable as a natural outcome of Goethe's youthful angst, but, as Barker Fairley points out, it would be 'hard to sustain as a piece of philosophy'.[3] Amazingly, Schopenhauer would not only sustain it, but perfect it.

He started writing his first book in 1814. Four years later it was published—to no reviews and no sales—and this, considering the book's content, was entirely appropriate. In the two volumes of *The World as Will and Representation* Schopenhauer laid out his vision of life as a constant struggle for which there is no reward. The source of this struggle and the reason why our desires can never be satisfied is for Schopenhauer something very similar to the thing David Bowie and Freddie Mercury sang about in 1981. They call it 'pressure', but Schopenhauer called it 'Will'—the blind, striving, unstoppable force behind all perceptible phenomena. All things in our world, including ourselves, are manifestations of this Will, which means that no matter how hard we try, we can never become masters of our own destiny.

Schopenhauer replaced the *Philosophes*' infinite perfectibility with infinite struggle, the promise of utopia with an insistence that life is hell. German philosophy in the late eighteenth and early nineteenth century was, as the Australian author Robert Spillane has pointed out in his book, *An Eye for an I*, a form of revenge on the French, who had dominated philosophy as they had all other walks of cultural life in the 1700s.[4] So the Germans decided that if the French were going to be rational, they would be irrational. Immanuel Kant (who died the same year Schopenhauer went to work in his father's office) began to dismantle the apparatus of the Enlightenment by insisting, like his hero Rousseau, that the discoveries of science could have no positive effect on the lives of human beings. Johann Gottlieb Fichte, a little younger than Kant and a lot more hot-headed, proposed a philosophy of action, not knowledge, and replaced the Enlightenment's mechanical universe with a chaotic, meaningless one in which we must freely exercise our will.[5]

Schopenhauer, who admired Kant but despised Fichte, inherited the idea of a world without meaning. But where Fichte saw Will as positive—a way of imposing one's forms on reality—for Schopenhauer Will was entirely negative and destructive. The thing behind all appearances, the force that animates all of nature is, in his view, evil. That's why he was a pessimist. Optimists, like Fichte (or Nietzsche or Napoleon), believed they could impose their will on the world, that they could make a difference. But Schopenhauer looked at the actions of the optimists and concluded that their actions were usually harmful in the short term, and didn't amount to a hill of beans in the long term. For Schopenhauer, action was always subject to Will and could therefore lead to no good. So in place of action, he advocated renunciation and compassion: hence his preferred form of address.

In 1854 Schopenhauer received a letter from Richard Wagner—enclosed within was a copy of the composer's Tristan poem. Wagner never got a reply—but this, as Robert Gutman observes in his biography of the composer, is not too surprising:

> Not only must its diction have offended the great
> stylist, but, when proudly sending off this paean to
> love, Wagner was obviously unaware that his idol was
> a confirmed misogynist whose soul had found its mate
> in a white poodle.[6]

Schopenhauer was an enormous influence on Wagner at the time he was writing Tristan—and in many ways, Wagner's hero is much more Schopenhauerish than he is medieval. Tristan has seen behind the veil of illusion that disguises the true nature of the world. He knows life is a sham and cannot provide him with happiness, so he renounces the world and all its willing by allowing himself to die. His beloved soon follows suit, and they achieve redemption in death. No more willing, no more problem.

But the truth is, in welding Schopenhauer's philosophy to his tale of tragic love, Wagner took some liberties with the great pessimist's ideas. For starters, suicide for Schopenhauer 'substitutes for a true redemption from this world of misery a merely apparent one'.[7] He didn't think suicide was wrong or immoral—he just didn't think it worked. Secondly, Schopenhauer would have absolutely no time for Wagner's Passion of Passion. Tristan and Isolde reject the world's illusory values, but replace these with something Schopenhauer would see as even less helpful—a transcendent ideal based on sexual love.

The music video for Queen and David Bowie's 'Under Pressure' makes the same philosophical blunder—which is a shame, since the song itself is far more faithful to Schopenhauer's ideas than anything Wagner ever wrote. Since Bowie and Mercury barely managed to work together in the studio for the six hours it took to do the song, getting them to commit to a day of shooting together was out of the question. So the director went for the Ed Wood-style solution of assembling a clip out of stock footage, classic films and TV news images. The video shows people rushing through cities and crowding onto trains. We see riots, a burning car, a woman screaming and a building collapsing—the perceptible phenomena of the world as will. (Vampires, for some reason, also make an appearance.) But for the last section, where the singers herald compassionate love as the means to redemption, the video shows a montage of great screen kisses. As the lovers lose themselves in their ecstatic union, the world fixes itself back up again—buildings un-explode on cue. But here, compassion has been replaced with passion. And passion, as far as Schopenhauer was concerned, is the problem—not the solution.

Pinkerton

IN 1900, SEVENTEEN years after Wagner's death, *Tristan und Isolde* was scheduled to be performed for the first time at Milan's famous opera theatre, La Scala. Unfortunately, the great Wagnerian tenor, Giuseppe Borgatti fell ill, so *Tristan* was postponed, and Giacomo Puccini's *La Boheme* was substituted in its place.[1] This was fitting, since Puccini was an admirer of Wagner, and strove to match the emotional intensity of *Tristan* in his own operas. This placed him on one side of a very firm line in turn-of-the-century Italy, where many saw Wagner's influence on opera as a bad one.

La Boheme did not go well at La Scala—the cast was in a bad mood to start with, and the 'fatal silence' of the audience didn't make them feel any better.[2] *La Boheme* limped through nine more performances, after which Puccini tried to put the whole miserable experience behind him. Little did he know there was more misery in store.

Shortly before the fiasco at La Scala, Puccini had been struck with a new idea for an opera based on a play he'd seen in London called *Madame Butterfly*. The subject—an unhappy love affair between an American naval lieutenant named Pinkerton and his Japanese bride, Cio-Cio-San—was well timed to ride the wave of interest in all things Japanese that was sweeping Europe at the time. Puccini had a good feeling about *Madama Butterfly*. 'I am completely taken with it!' he wrote in March 1901.[3]

But *Madama Butterfly* was plagued with problems, and two years later Puccini was still struggling with it. Then things got worse. On 21 February 1903 the composer was on his way to dinner at a friend's house when his car drove off the road and plunged down an embankment. Puccini was trapped underneath the car with a fractured leg—a nearby doctor patched him up, but it later turned out that the leg had not been properly set and had to be re-broken. He was immobilised for almost three months, and the inertia made his bad mood worse. He despaired of *Butterfly* ever seeing the light of day, and wondered if anyone would care if he and his unfinished opera just disappeared off the face of the earth. Later that year, he wrote to his colleague Luigi Illica:

> *I am here alone and sad! If you could know my sufferings! I have much need of a friend, and I don't have any, or if there is someone who loves me, he doesn't understand me. I am of a temperament very different from most! Only I understand myself and I grieve; but my sorrow is continuous, it does not give me peace... My life is a sea of sadness and I am stuck in it!*[4]

Somehow the shattered composer managed to finish his opera, and *Madama Butterfly* premiered on the night of 17 February 1904. It was an even worse disaster than the performance of *La Boheme* four years earlier. Puccini, leaning on a cane, could hardly hear the music for the laughter, catcalls and boos. The singers could barely hear themselves. The reviews, when they appeared the next morning, were terrible. '*Butterfly*,' they wrote, 'the diabetic opera, the result of an automobile accident.' In years to come, *Madama Butterfly* would come to be seen, along with *La Boheme*, as one of Puccini's masterpieces. While the version performed at the premiere was marred by structural problems which would later be ironed out, even in this raw state *Madama Butterfly* was already full of daring formal innovations and sincere personal emotion. But in 1904 it was regarded as a bitter disappointment from the man who had been hailed, only five years earlier, as the successor to Verdi. The critics roasted him for the opera's sentimentality, the smallness of its themes, and for Puccini's failure to grow as an artist.[5]

Ninety years later, history repeated itself. Rivers Cuomo, like Puccini, was an admirer of the German romantic composers—though he preferred Mahler to Wagner. He and his band, Weezer, were hailed as the saviours of bubblegum rock in 1994. But Cuomo broke his leg at the height of their success—not in an accident like Puccini, but on purpose, to have it lengthened. He wore a painful brace for almost a year, and entered a period of deep doubt and depression. Under these circumstances, he began writing the songs that would become Weezer's second album—a rock opera called *The Black Hole*. But the opera idea was scrapped in favour of a concept album loosely based on Puccini's *Madama Butterfly*. In years to come *Pinkerton* would come to be seen as Weezer's masterpiece—full of daring formal innovations and sincere personal emotion— but in 1997 it was regarded as a bitter disappointment from the band who had been hailed, only three years earlier, as the successor to The Cars. The critics roasted Cuomo for *Pinkerton*'s sentimentality, and for his failure to grow as an artist.

Rivers Cuomo: My life is a sea of sadness.

Butterfly

IN *Madama Butterfly*, Pinkerton travels across the sea and finds himself a beautiful creature. He captures her, and immediately loses interest—he's drinking a toast to finding 'a real American wife' before he's even left Japan. He sails back to America and forgets Cio-Cio-San, and she is left staring out to sea, clinging to the promise he made that he would return 'when the robin makes his nest again'.[1] The opera ends when Cio-Cio-San, having remained faithful to Pinkerton throughout, learns that he has an American wife. Having no hope left in the world, she takes her own life.

One of the greatest challenges Puccini had faced in bringing *Madama Butterfly* to the stage was the percieved lop-sidedness of the story's plot. Puccini's collaborator Illica complained that Pinkerton virtually disappeared for most of the story, 'and his is the drama!' he wrote to Puccini, exasperated.[2] Weezer's second album would, in a curious way, make amends for this. Here, the drama is all Pinkerton—tellingly, his name has replaced hers on the marquee. There is still the unfathomable distance of the Atlantic Ocean between the young American and his Japanese love. But we never see her—while his emotional crises form the entire plot of the album. Butterfly writes adoring letters on cute stationery to her young man, he sits alone in his room and rationalises their relationship out of existence before it's begun—all the while wishing for it to come true. But it's on the album's last song, 'Butterfly', that Cuomo's feeling for Puccini's opera becomes clearest. The singer tells us he keeps going out to catch butterflies—and they keep dying on him. 'Every time I pin down what I think I want it slips away,'[3] he sings. It seems as though there's something wrong with him, as though his wants and his needs are fundamentally opposed. He wants something, he chases it and often catches it. But the object of his desire melts away as he grasps it. Understandably, he's starting to wonder if there's any point doing anything at all.

The prevailing mood of *Pinkerton* is not so much of despair as of resignation. 'Tired of Sex' is a nightmare reversal of the usual rock star brag about all the girls the singer slept with in all the different towns he played. This is not the Don Juan of the Spanish legend or the Don Giovanni of Mozart's opera, but the Don Juan of Byron, who looks back over his many conquests with an air of melancholy detachment. The joke in Byron's *Don Juan* is that the great seducer is always the seduced—he doesn't really have to try. This is the scenario of 'Tired of Sex', where the singer sounds mostly perplexed about his many one-night stands, and finally, disgusted. He feels he has been taken advantage of but, like Byron, his pose of static detachment prevents him from running away. 'Thursday night I'm naked again,' sings the tired-sounding rock star.[4] What's the point? In 'Why Bother?' the singer reveals that he's just as tired of love as he is of sex. He could ask that girl out, he could pick up the phone, he could lean in for a kiss. But he has already been disappointed so many times that he can't quite bring himself to try, he has already spent enough time chasing happiness to know that it will always elude him. So he gives up. He ignores his urges—which in any case are no match for his inertia—and resigns himself to solitude.

Schopenhauer would say that the singer is right—love is not worth the trouble. The problem with love, according to Schopenhauer, is that it's inseparable from the sexual drive, and the sexual drive is part of the great, destructive tide of birth, struggle and death that pushes life along its purposeless course. The sex drive is will manifested in the individual, and since will for Schopenhauer is always negative, allowing oneself to be driven by instinct can only lead to no good.

In the world of rock and roll, this amounts to heresy. Rock ballads—with their *we gotta* and *I wanna*—place a lot of faith in instinct. 'We gotta get out while we're young', 'we gotta hold on to what we got', 'I wanna rock and roll all night and party every day'—belief in the power of instinct is the legacy of fifty years of rock music. No wonder Cuomo sounds so confused when he sings in 'Butterfly', 'I did what my body told me to'. In chasing his Butterfly, he merely followed the advice of a thousand radio hits—do what you feel, listen to your body, go for it—and the result was tragedy. 'Tired of Sex' and 'Why Bother?' present variations on the same theme. He acted naturally, according to instinct, and all he got was... more unhappiness.

Schopenhauer would say that a moment like this is a step on the path to true wisdom. We must accept that the butterfly will always get away, that our goals will always melt into the air when we reach them—like Robert Smith's girl in 'A Forest'. In *Pinkerton* the singer has come to realise that happiness can only be found in a state of non-willing, which his new attitude of resignation and renunciation ('Why Bother?') will allow. This, as Schopenhauer himself knew, is easier said than done. The so-called 'Buddha of Frankfurt' had a surprising number of affairs and one-night stands, presumably because—like Cuomo—his inertia made him an easy target.

Wagner gave Schopenhauer a number of reasons to dismiss his *Tristan* poem. Even if Schopenhauer had managed to overlook the problems of style and the fact that Wagner wrote grand operas (which Schopenhauer mostly hated), there would still be the hurdle of the composer's insistence on love as a form of salvation from suffering. For Schopenhauer, love is the *reason* we suffer, and it ensures that we continue to suffer. In this, Schopenhauer is not, like Andy Gill from The Gang of Four, trying to say that love is a superstition which is perpetuated by love songs and grand operas, and can be unlearned. Schopenhauer accepts that our desire for love, like all our other urges and emotions, is real enough. But the fact that we are created with the desire for happiness and dumped into a world of flux and chaos in which that happiness must always remain out of reach is, for him, yet more proof that life is hell, and that it would have been better if the human race had never been born. Human life, Schopenhauer writes in his essay, 'On The Emptiness of Existence', 'is basically a mistake'—and the proof of this lies in the simple fact that no matter how hard you try, you can't get no satisfaction.[5]

Mick Jagger: Man is a compound of needs which are hard to satisfy.

Satisfaction

ON 9 MAY 1965 Keith Richards woke up in the middle of the night with a riff in his head. He grabbed his acoustic guitar, hit record on a cassette player, and got down sixty seconds of the guitar part he'd caught on the tail of his dream before going back to sleep. 'The next morning I played it back,' Richards later recalled. 'Amongst all the snoring I rediscovered and found the lick and the lyrical hook I'd come up with to accompany it.'[1] The words that had formed in his mind as he'd bashed out his dream riff in that Florida motel room were 'I can't get no satisfaction'. Sitting by the pool the next day—with a cocktail in one hand and a cocktail waitress's phone number in the other—Mick Jagger took the riff and the chorus Richards had written in his sleep, and turned it into a song which expresses better than any other the suffering of the world and the impossibility of happiness. But 'Satisfaction' was not just a song. As the Rolling Stones' former manager Andrew Loog Oldham has pointed out in his memoir, *2 Stoned*, 'Satisfaction' contains, in embryo, the entire culture of the late '60s and everything that came after—the profound refusal of the modern world that would characterise most of the important statements of rock and roll from this point on. Keith Richards, according to Oldham, 'changed life as we know it' in his sleep.[2]

In his essays, Schopenhauer accounts for the prophetic nature of dreams by explaining that the dreamer, in his unconscious state, is offered a glimpse of the world as will. The baffles and blinds that our conscious mind put around to convince us that life has some structure and meaning are removed, and the dreaming philosopher glimpses the truth of things.[3] Wagner would bestow this ability on the musician as well. He claimed, in his famous essay on Beethoven, that the dreaming artist hears sounds which provide him with staggering insights into the nature of reality. Later, in his conscious state, the composer must act as the mediator between these terrifying cosmic truths and his unsuspecting audience.[4]

This is the difficult role the Rolling Stones take on in '(I Can't Get No) Satisfaction', a song which pulls back the curtain on a world without meaning for just as long as we can stand it. The verses describe Mick Jagger trying to impose his considerable will on the world, the chorus informs us of the result: nothing. There's a lot of pushing, a lot of shoving, a lot of trouble; and no satisfaction. 'It was my view of the world,' he later explained, 'my frustration with everything.'[5] In three verses, Jagger dispenses, one by one, with humankind's traditional consolations. Knowledge, material comfort and sex—none, he decides, are worth the trouble. Even fame, which the singer had worked so hard to get up until this point, turns out to be one big hassle. Doin' this and signin' that—who needs it?

Here, 'Satisfaction' differs from earlier teenage anthems like 'Summertime Blues' in one very important respect. In the older songs the singer couldn't get what he wanted because he didn't make enough money or because his parents were a drag. But the singer in 'Satisfaction' has already broken free of all those limitations; he's a rock star with money, fame and power—and none of this has made him happy. And since being a rock star is about as good as it gets in 1965, the singer is forced to conclude that all the other goals he might move himself to pursue will turn out to be just as unsatisfying. 'Satisfaction' is not about how the singer can't get his shirts white or make out with the girl—the disgust in his voice tells us he knows, before he's even tried, that neither will make him happy for longer than thirty seconds. The sheer grinding monotony of Keith Richards' riff drives the point home—as soon as we reach our goal, a new one will appear, and the struggle will resume.

This kind of thing, according to Schopenhauer, is all the proof we need that human life is pointless. Our achievements leave us feeling unsatisfied precisely because they are, in a cosmic sense, unsatisfactory, our lives have no meaning or significance because the world is in a constant state of flux, and our efforts to impose our will on the world are doomed to fail. The world has its own way of telling us this through the feeling we call boredom.

> *That human life must be some kind of mistake is sufficiently proved by the simple observation that man is a compound of needs which are hard to satisfy; that their satisfaction achieves nothing but a painless condition in which he is given over to boredom; and that boredom is a direct proof that existence itself is valueless, for boredom is nothing more than the sensation of the emptiness of existence. For if life, in the desire for which our essence and existence consists, possessed in itself a positive value and real content, there would be no such thing as boredom: mere existence would fulfil and satisfy us. As things are, we take no pleasure in existence except when we are striving after something—in which case distance and difficulties make our goal look as if it would satisfy us (an illusion which fades when we reach it)...*[6]

Howard Devoto: Life is hell.

Boredom

IGGY POP KNEW all about boredom. On the first two Stooges albums—the self titled debut of 1969 and the towering *Fun House* released the following year—the singer sounds like a worn out Mick Jagger, whose frustrated attempts to impose his will on the world have reduced him to a near-vegetable state of inertia. Iggy can't even be bothered to advance an argument on the level of 'Satisfaction' for why life sucks. All he can do is blurt out two monosyllabic words. These two words, as it would later turn out, said more about the human condition in the late twentieth century than anyone had managed before or since: 'No fun'.

In 'No Fun' Iggy weighs up his options: 'Maybe go out, maybe stay at home, maybe call mom on the telephone'.[1] Who gives a fuck? Looking into the future, he sees no hope for improvement. In '1969' he reflects that he had no fun in 1968 and that he will most likely have no fun in 1969. He gloomily rings in the New Year; 'another year with nothin' to do'.[2] What about girls? What *about* 'em? For all his snarling and yowling, when Iggy sings about sex on The Stooges' early albums, he's mostly passive. Again, he sounds a bit like Mick Jagger, but he's nothing like the strutting Don Juan of 'Little Red Rooster' or the eager lover of 'I Wanna Be Your Man'. In 'TV Eye' the singer is a victim—it's as though he's frozen on the couch while the girl fixes her predatory stare on him.

When he does get horny, his come-on is framed as a submission. Jagger wants to be your man, Iggy wants to be your dog.

In the first phase of their existence, The Stooges were a joke in the music industry and virtually invisible to the public. After their demise, they became a legend. By the end of the '70s they were the musical and philosophical godfathers of punk, and Iggy's concerns became the concerns of the entire movement. This put boredom high on punk's agenda from day one, and punk singers came to insist on boredom as the most basic condition of life. The Slits sang about 'A Boring Life', The Clash about being 'Bored with the USA'. Punks were bored with TV, bored with sex ('Here we go,' said a thoroughly ravaged Johnny Rotten, 'another squelch session'[3]), even rock and roll itself had become boring. By 1977 boredom was already enough of a cliché for Howard Devoto to send it up in the Buzzcocks' 'Boredom'. 'Da dum-de-dum,' sang Devoto, thoroughly bored by his own boredom, and even more bored by the boredom of punk—which he ejected himself from in timely fashion only one year later.

Devoto formed a new band called Magazine, and broke two of punk's sacred commandments before they'd even played a show. He hired a keyboardist (a *jazz* keyboardist, to make matters worse), and told the band to play *slowly*. 'I don't like most of this new wave music,' Devoto told Jon Savage around the time of his great escape, 'I don't like music.'[4] But he kept making it anyway, because he had a feeling that punk had started as a way of 'diagnosing modern forms of unhappiness'—and that there was still work to be done in this area.[5] By saying that everything is boring and that there's nothing to do, punk had opened up a void which Devoto made it his business to explore. His time spent doing nothing (because there's nothing to do) eventually led him to a great insight, which he expressed in Magazine's 'Song from

Under the Floorboards' in 1980. Here, the author starts out with a brief self-portrait—'I am angry I am ill and I'm as ugly as sin'—before going on to explain why: 'I know the meaning of life it doesn't help me a bit.'[6]

In 1977 Devoto had told Savage that he was 'trying to find something to get excited about.'[7] By 1980 he had given up. In every case—love, politics, social life—Devoto tallied the reasons for doing anything at all and found them wanting. In this, the meaning of life would prove to be no use to him at all—in fact, it made things worse. Because the meaning of life, as Devoto had realised by this point, is that we are born to suffer. 'Life', he later told cultural commentator Michael Bracewell, 'is hell. I don't think I ever strayed very far from that idea since I was about twenty.'[8]

So, in 'Song from Under the Floorboards' Devoto announces that he has given up looking for satisfaction, which he knows will always elude him. He can no longer allow himself to believe in the bright dreams presented in movies, pop songs and grand operas—those chimeras of romantic love and ideal happiness that have tormented humankind through the centuries. Not for him, not anymore. 'Do you remember dreams?' Savage asked Devoto in 1977. 'I take pills to stop myself,' the singer replied.[9] 'In Song from Under the Floorboards,' he explains why. 'I used to make phantoms I could later chase,' sings Devoto. 'And then I just got tired.'[10]

The singer renounces the search for satisfaction, and downsizes his expectations to fit the small dark space under the floorboards.

Notes from Underground

IT'S 11 APRIL 2006, Morrissey is onstage at the Olympia Theatre in Paris. 'This song,' he says, 'was written before I was born.'[1] He and the band launch into a tough-sounding version of Magazine's 'Song from Under the Floorboards'. He's exaggerating a bit—the song was written a long time ago, but Morrissey is old enough to have seen Howard Devoto playing with the Buzzcocks' original line-up at Manchester's Lesser Free Trade Hall in 1976. That night changed Morrissey's life, and Devoto, with his keen intelligence, literary style and permanent air of dissatisfaction, quickly became a hero for the singer.

At the Olympia, 'Song from Under the Floorboards' grinds to a halt, and the audience cheers. 'Do any of you remember that song?' asks Morrissey, a handful of people answer in the affirmative. '*How?*' chuckles the singer, mock astonished.[2] Morrissey is making a joke about his age relative to that of his audience—which seems to get younger every year. But there's a sense in which 'Song from Under the Floorboards' really was written before he or any of his audience were born—before Devoto himself, even. Magazine's outsider anthem is a cover—not of a song, but of a book written in 1864 by Russian novelist Fyodor Dostoyevsky. The first paragraph of *Notes from Underground* reads:

> *I am a sick man…I am an angry man. I am an unattractive man. I think there is something wrong with my liver.*[3]

Dostoyevsky's book describes, in the first person, the thoughts and exploits of a mean and miserable man—an 'underground man', as he calls himself. He lives in St Petersburg though everyone tells him the climate is bad for his health. He used to have a good job in the civil service, but after he came into some money he decided, not to sell up and move to sunnier climes, but to retire into a small corner of his small house where he now sits, all alone and sick. What's wrong with his liver? He doesn't know—and even if he did, he wouldn't want to get well—the only thing he really enjoys is complaining about how sick he is.

Dostoyevsky's narrator is a liar—he makes maudlin confessions to elicit our sympathy, only to admit three paragraphs later that he was only kidding. Did he tell the truth in the first place and then try to cover it up as an afterthought? We'll never really know, so it's hard to get his story straight. But it quickly becomes clear that he was lying about his liver—his illness resides not in his guts, but in his head. He suffers from a serious case of above average intelligence. 'I swear to you that to think too much is a disease, a real, actual disease,' he says.[4]

Intelligence is a terrible affliction for the underground man because he would like nothing better than to be as stupid as an insect. He is, as you've probably guessed, a romantic—although Dostoyevsky's is a romanticism stripped of a lot of the romance. The underground man is not so sentimental as to imagine himself as a butterfly—a lowly mosquito with a simple libido would suffice. But while his prose might be less flowery, the wish behind it is the same as the one expressed elsewhere by Emerson, Keats and Conor Oberst. He accepts that he must live with desire—he'd just prefer not to have to think about it. But the simple happiness of the insect is denied him. Even the simple half-happiness of stupid men is more than he can hope for. He is overburdened with intelligence and further handicapped by a good education. Thanks to this deadly combination, there is no hope of his ever being able to 'act naturally'. In fact, most of the time he finds action of any kind virtually impossible.

For most people, action is the easiest thing in the world. If you walk up to a normal, healthy, natural man and insult him, he responds in a 'natural' way—he gives you a swift kicking, and the matter is settled. 'I am green with envy of such men,' says the underground man.[5] How do they do it? Because they're stupid, of course. Dostoyevsky explains:

I repeat, and repeat emphatically: all spontaneous people, men of action, are active because they are stupid and limited. How is this to be explained? Like this: in consequence of their limitations, they take immediate, but secondary causes for primary ones, and thus they are more quickly and easily convinced that they have found indisputable grounds for their action.[6]

Where is the underground man supposed to find the grounds for action? Let's say he did run after the man who insulted him and managed to kick him in the pants. Would it teach him a lesson? No, quite the opposite; and even if it did, so what? There's always going to be violence in the world, always someone big picking on someone small. Surely it's just foolishness to imagine that this act is of some great importance, simply because it has meaning for you, when there's so much aggression in the world that goes completely unchecked. And okay, so maybe every little bit *does* count. But in the end, what does it matter? We all die eventually, after leading long, painful lives punctuated by occasional moments of joy, and as far as we know, there's no point to any of it. And in any case, in five hundred million years time, this whole planet will crash into the sun, which means there won't even be anyone around to ask all these stupid questions—and won't that be a relief.

This is the great legacy of the Age of Reason, the underground man's birthright. He has the extraordinary ability to reason his way out of every natural impulse that comes his way. In the end, he can find no convincing argument for any kind of action at all. So he does nothing. He sits underground and stares enviously up at the men of action as they strive and achieve, turning his loathing and resentment of them over in his mind.

Morrissey: Still ill.

How Soon Is Now?

ROCK AND ROLL is full of natural men. Elvis Presley—whose genius resided not in his mind, but in his voice and his body—was the first of these. Part of the importance of Elvis as a rock myth is his almost divine naïvety, the way he seemed to act without thinking, to change the world without knowing what he was doing.

Elvis, the man of action, makes an appropriate figurehead for early rock and roll, because for the first ten years of its life, rock was all about action. The songs were invitations to dance, incitements to riot, or none-too-subtle propositions for sex. And the singer's desire was always backed up by the music—the most intensely physical music a mainstream white audience had heard up to that point. Sweat, exertion, desire and spontaneous action created the foundation on which rock and roll was built, and over this the music's architects constructed their machines for dancing and doing. By 1965 these included the Chuck Berry duckwalk, the Sun Studio slap, the Phil Spector Wall of Sound and the Bo Diddley beat.

Bo Diddley's 'shave-and-a-haircut, two-bits' rhythm is, as Toby Creswell says in his book, *1001 Songs*, 'one of the essential parts of the vocabulary of rock and roll'.[1] The famous beat first came to light on Bo's 1957 hit 'Bo Diddley'. His producers, the Chess brothers, made him change some of the song's lyrics so it would get played on the radio:

Bow-legged rooster told a cross-legged duck
Say you ain't good lookin' but you sure can...crow²

But even if he'd scrapped the lyrics entirely, no-one who heard the music would be left in any doubt as to what the song was about. The Bo Diddley beat is pure desire.

In 1964, Andrew Loog Oldham overheard Keith Richards singing snatches of Buddy Holly's 'Not Fade Away' over a Bo Diddley beat played on his acoustic guitar, and knew he was listening to the next Rolling Stones' single—it was recorded two days later.[3] 'The Bo Diddley feel is a suggestion in Buddy's version,' said Tony Calder in Andrew Loog Oldham's *2 Stoned*, 'and a call to arms in the Stones".[4] 'Not Fade Away' heralded a tough and threatening new sex drive in the Stones' music which would become a hallmark of their sound from this point on. 'I'm gonna tell you how it's gonna be,' sang Mick Jagger, not messing around any more, 'you're gonna give your love to me.'[5]

The Stooges' '1969' is also built on the Bo Diddley shuffle. But while the desire in the rhythm is still strong, the simple sense of purpose it had in the Stones' hands is gone: the song still thrusts and kicks, but in a flailing, hopeless fashion. '1969' seems to go on forever, locked in its two-chord drive to nowhere, and the wah-wah guitar solo sounds more like a tantrum than a come-on.

In 1984 the Bo Diddley beat was back—though in barely recognisable form. On The Smiths 'How Soon Is Now?', the sound that had framed a litany of desire in 1957 and a call to arms in 1964 seemed finally to have worn itself out—the song sounds like 'Not Fade Away' played on a Walkman with a dying battery. This was a dance record for those who find dancing—along with any other form of spontaneous action—impossible. The singer introduces himself in the first verse:

> I *am the son*
> *And the heir*
> *Of a shyness that is criminally vulgar*
> *I am the son and heir*
> *Of nothing in particular.*[6]

Self-loathing, self-pity, bad jokes; we're a long way from 'you're gonna give your love to me'. Where would an underground man find the grounds for a statement like that? As the song unfolds, the gloomy young man gets some unsolicited advice. Don't sit there tormenting yourself, say the men of action, go out there and have some fun. Dance! Enjoy yourself! 'You could meet somebody who really loves you.'[7] But the singer knows even before he gets in the car and drives to the club that things will end badly. In fact, he's so smart that he's seen into the future, and knows that everything, everywhere will end badly.

As with Dostoyevsky's basement-dweller and the singer's own subterranean hero Howard Devoto, Morrissey's world-weariness is a result of his intelligence—which he would *gladly* trade for the ability to act. 'I'm obsessed by the physical,' he told Simon Reynolds in *Blissed Out*, by way of explaining his ongoing fascination with criminals and toughs, 'it always works—instead of creeping around and relying on your thesaurus.'[8]

But Morrissey has not succeeded in making an insect of himself, he is decidedly not what Dostoyevsky refers to as '*l'homme de la nature*'. 'I don't feel natural even when I'm fast asleep,'[9] he sings in 'Sweet and Tender Hooligan'. Time and again, in Morrissey's songs, the hero is about to take action and finds, for one reason or another, that it's impossible. And this would be fine if he'd somehow managed to transcend his earthly desires—to make himself into the Buddha of Manchester. But as he reminds us in 'How Soon Is Now?,' he is still human, and he still needs to be loved.

Why Bother?

IN 1997, RIVERS Cuomo went into retreat. He moved into a small apartment under a Los Angeles freeway, disconnected the phone, sealed up the windows and painted the walls black. The singer's decision to isolate himself has always been seen as a reaction to the embarrassing failure of *Pinkerton*. But Cuomo's new monkish lifestyle was, in a sense, the inevitable result of that album—the philosophy of *Pinkerton* put into practice.

In 'Why Bother?' the singer thinks about finding a girlfriend, but finds insufficient grounds for action. It's like a super-pessimistic version of Wham!'s 'Last Christmas'. Before he's even picked up the phone he's reasoned his way to the following summer, when she'll no doubt dump him and break his heart. So he remains alone. The singer has proved his intelligence while ensuring that he remains miserable. This line of thinking leads to greater and greater inertia—taken to its logical conclusion, the singer must renounce the search for happiness entirely and derive whatever kicks he can from monkish self-denial.

Music journalist Chuck Klosterman described *Pinkerton* in *Spin* magazine as emo's *Sgt Pepper*. 'Philosophically, it defined what emo was supposed to feel like.'[1] Emo songs had always rated the ability to feel much higher than the ability to act, but *Pinkerton* sealed the deal, by suggesting that there was something truly noble in being broken and beaten. The intelligent but highly emotional singer has seen the horror up far too close—how can we expect him to act, let alone fight? We can't, of course, but we can applaud his inner resolve as he shuts himself away from the rest of the world while everyone else carries on with the meaningless comedy of existence.

The Get Up Kids are one of the scores of bands who followed the example of *Pinkerton*, exploring the lonely landscape Weezer had discovered long after Cuomo himself had moved on. In The Get Up Kids' 'I'm a Loner, Dottie, a Rebel', the hero tells us that last night he was in love, and that the possibility is still there. But sitting by the girl's bedside in the morning, he reasons his way out of whatever future they might have together. 'I'm afraid to try,' he admits, 'I'll keep my hands by my side.'[2] A real man, a natural man (a jock, a Limp Bizkit fan) would *do* something. But for The Get Up Kids and their fans, this kind of 'action' is deeply suspect. As Trevor Kelley and Leslie Simon have observed in their book *Everybody Hurts: An essential guide to emo culture*, non-athleticism is one of the sacred commandments of emo.[3] It's reflected, on a very simple level, by the fans' fashion accessories. Emo replaces nu-metal's trainers and baseball caps with black-rimmed glasses and Penguin classics. And it means that the heroes of the scene tend to be of the static, intellectual type—Rivers Cuomo, not Zack de la Rocha; Morrissey, not Metallica.

In *Nothing Feels Good*, Greenwald argues that emo's roots can be traced back to an unholy coupling of Washington DC hardcore with The Smiths that took place in the late '80s.[4] This partnership is not as odd as it might first seem. Hardcore, essentially, is about resistance. But as Greenwald points out, there are different types of resistance. Hardcore in its pure strain made a spectacle of political protest. But The Smiths' music, in its fey, unassuming way, mounts a much more challenging refusal. Morrissey might not be a 'natural man', but his stance is, in its way, as tough and intractable as any of the thugs and gangsters he admires so much; and more than a match, as Greenwald insists, for the hardcore bands he found himself sharing shelf-space with toward the end of the decade.[5]

Morrissey, in his songs, demands the right to be miserable and alone. This doesn't sound like too much to ask—but the world keeps telling him he has to cheer up and get over it ('There's a club, if you'd like to go').[6] And since he steadfastly refuses to do this, his position has, over the years, become more and more entrenched. What started out as a polite request has turned into a war of attrition, with Morrissey as the unlikely heroic general, who refuses to give up one inch of his territory no matter what the enemy throws at him. You might say he's taking it too personally, but what other way is there to take it? The world has refused to accept his personality. No wonder he's determined not to give up the fight. In this war, what's at stake is nothing less than the human soul.

Dostoyevsky: Smashing things can sometimes be very pleasant.

The Crystal Palace

THERE'S A GREAT deal of masochism in the underground man's miserable stance—he enjoys his suffering, and enjoys complaining about it even more. And since his pain is now his only real source of pleasure, he refuses to get over it. Reasonable people could reasonably accuse the underground man of being horribly self-indulgent. But this accusation raises a question—why are reasonable people so offended by an individual who demands nothing more than the right to be broken, bitter and dissatisfied? Whether he set out to do this or not, the man under the floorboards has exposed a terrible flaw in modern society.

By the time Dostoyevsky sat down to write *Notes from Underground* in 1864, reason, empiricism and mathematical perfectibility should all have been well and truly trashed by almost a century of romantic philosophy—from the counter-Enlightenment of Rousseau and Kant to the view of life as chaos and flux expounded by Schopenhauer (who had, by this time, become one of Europe's best known and most quoted thinkers). But while romanticism did much to form popular taste and opinion in the nineteenth century, for all the difference it had made in the world of industry and commerce, it might just as well have never happened. While the romantic individualist was developing his philosophy of feelings, dreams and the irrational; the businessman—who could have no use for this sort of stuff—simply continued the project of the Enlightenment, but to quite different ends.

This time the goal was not the perfectibility of human life, but the perfectibility of human life in the pursuit of profit. Business, with its eternal worship of the bottom line, will always look to rationalise and systematise human behaviour. And since the fate of nations was increasingly tied up in the fortunes of business, the shopkeeper mentality gradually spread to influence every aspect of modern society during Dostoyevsky's lifetime. Goethe had remarked, a few years before his death, that 'wealth and speed are what the world admires and strives for'.[1] By 1864 belief in technical progress had become a sort of secular religion in Western Europe, the idea being that the perfection of industry would lead to greater profit, and greater profit would increase the amount of human happiness in the world accordingly.

The triumphant symbol of this ideal—the St Paul's cathedral of progress—was the Crystal Palace, a shimmering glass and steel building created to house London's Great Exhibition of 1851. This, according to the marketing puff, would 'unite the whole world in the quest to apply the latest advances in science and industrial production for the benefit of all'.[2] But who was really benefiting? William Morris walked out of the place disgusted, seeing nothing but mass-produced junk, entirely lacking in that particular, personal sense of beauty that had guided the hand of the medieval craftsman in days gone by. The individual's feeling for expressive form had, it seemed, been ruthlessly snipped out of the manufacturing process for the sake of a better looking profit margin—a more efficient machine. For Dostoyevsky, the Crystal Palace was equally hateful, but for slightly different reasons.

In 1864, Dostoyevsky had had forty years to think about man's ability to reason and where it had got the human race so far. For him, the Crystal Palace was a monument not to progress, but to stupidity, the extraordinary stupidity of a culture that had convinced itself that the application of reason and commonsense would improve the lives of human beings.

> What does reason know? Reason only knows what it has succeeded in finding out…but man's nature acts as one whole, with everything that is in it, conscious or unconscious, and although it is nonsensical, yet it lives.[3]

The application of reason could guarantee that a railway will run on time or that a factory will produce more ceramic plates per year. But human happiness, he insisted, cannot be calculated mathematically. Our desires are, and always will be, irrational; and a society that tries to systematise every aspect of life will not be able to accommodate them. In *Notes from Underground*, the underground man—in one of his many imaginary confrontations with the surface dwellers—

puts forward the case against the positivists and their cathedral of commonsense:

> *You believe in an eternal and indestructible crystal building, in which you won't be able to stick out your tongue in secret, or even make a rude sign in your pocket. But perhaps I fear that building precisely because it's indestructible and made of crystal, and you won't be able to stick your tongue out, even in secret.[4]*

Dostoyevsky saw that the attempt to rationalise all of human life 'for the greater good' would eventually lead to a situation in which bad behaviour is no longer tolerated. Spite, malice, shoplifting and the irrational desire to smash things are all bad for business and bad for the state. But all of these things make us happy—as the underground man, who loves nothing better than to complain, knows all too well.

> *And why are you so firmly and triumphantly certain that only what is normal and positive—in short, only well-being—is good for man? Is reason mistaken about what is good? After all, perhaps prosperity isn't the only thing that pleases mankind, perhaps he is just as attracted to suffering...whether it's a good thing or a bad thing, smashing things is also sometimes very pleasant. I am not here standing up for suffering, or for well-being either. I am standing out for my own caprices and for having them guaranteed when necessary.[5]*

How much of our happiness are we prepared to give up for the greater good? And what is the greater good if not the sum total of human happiness? We'll never know, because you can't calculate happiness. Scientific analysis might prove that a henhouse is enough to keep a man dry when it rains. But that won't stop him from wanting a mansion.[6] You can only stop human beings from wanting what they want, says the underground man, by altering their nature. This, Dostoyevsky believed, was impossible. We are not perfectible, we are ridiculous, and a society that pretends this is not the case— that tries to tell a man that he is better off with a henhouse when he wants a palace or that he should be cheerful when nothing makes him happier than being miserable—does so at its great peril. Eventually, he warns, desire will escape whatever restraints the positivists place on it.

> *I am certain that underground people like me must be kept in check. Though we may be capable of sitting underground for forty years without saying a word, if we do come out into the world and burst out, we will talk and talk and talk…*[7]

Morrissey has always suspected as much. The Smiths' 1987 single, 'Shoplifters of the World Unite', is a paean to human happiness in one of its most irrational manifestations, and a call to arms for the malcontents of modern society. The shoplifter just has this thing he likes doing—it hurts no-one, but because he stands in the way of money being made, the government says he must be stopped. This is the same government, he notes, that is busy figuring out how to put more missiles in space so as to be able to kill a few more million people in some future war. And they call *him* a criminal! His self-righteous proclamations are interrupted, he feels a 'heartless hand' on his shoulder, his happy dream shatters at the same moment as the alabaster vase he was busy lifting. The state tries to rehabilitate him, to teach him to accept a reasonable amount of happiness. 'I was bored before I even began,' sighs the singer.[8] He's not satisfied with what he's been offered—and he knows he's not the only one.

The Broken, the Beaten and the Damned

THE SMITHS' ALBUMS were to the solitary young romantics of the 1980s what *The Sorrows of Young Werther* was to those of the 1780s—a friend to the friendless. In America they sustained many a lonely soul through the materialist wasteland of the late '80s. And long after the band had broken up, The Smiths continued to speak for those who weren't being spoken for elsewhere. By the '90s, 'alternative' music was everywhere, and misery, alienation and disaffected rage flooded the radio and the mall in ways that would have seemed unthinkable five years earlier. Paradoxically the orgy of self-congratulation that surrounded Lollapalooza and the mainstream success of Nirvana alienated the very people alternative music was supposed to represent.

The lonely and disaffected fled the suddenly exposed world of alterna-rock like vampires caught in a searchlight. They sought out the more rarefied pleasures of *Pinkerton* or *Diary*, hit 'play' on their copy of *Siamese Dream* for the hundredth time or turned—as Gerard Way did—to The Smiths. For a kid who wears black and feels different to everyone else, a song like The Smiths' 'Unloveable' is a way of explaining yourself to yourself and maybe, one day, to the world that doesn't understand you. 'I wear black on the outside because black is how I feel on the inside,' sings Morrissey, 'and if I seem a little strange—well, that's because I am.'[1] For Way, Morrissey was more than just a human voice in an inhuman world, he was an inspiration—one of a few guiding lights he would later follow when he started a band of his own.

I've always seen My Chemical Romance as the band that would have represented who me and my friends

were in high school, and the band that we didn't have
to represent us—the kids that wore black—back then.[2]

My Chemical Romance would take up Morrissey's plea for acceptance and turn it into a battle cry. In 'Welcome to the Black Parade', the singer sees that, like himself, the kids who wear black are threatened on all sides by behaviourists and rationalists who are determined to rid them of their irrational desires for the sake of the greater good. The singer, still haunted by his father's words—'will you be the saviour of the broken, the beaten and the damned'—and determined to make good on his promise, leaps into the fray. 'Let's paint it black and take it back!' he shouts.

Gerard Way's heroes—Morrissey, Robert Smith and Billy Corgan—all expressed dissatisfaction with modern life. But their protests mostly took on the form of a hunger strike—the singer would suffer publicly until the world recognised his needs. Unfortunately, outside the proscribed limits of indie rock, the world takes no notice of this kind of thing. So the singer in 'Welcome to the Black Parade' has decided to try something new. He has decided to do the one thing the world will not expect from a gloomy young man with a sensitive temperament—to form an army and start marching. This, he has realised, is the only language the world understands. Pretty soon, he has a ragtag mob of fellow revolutionaries, an army of loners which he leads, Napoleon-like, to the gates of civilisation.

The word 'cult' was often used by music journalists to describe the bands Gerard loved in high school. Singers that speak for those who don't have a voice tend to attract committed followers, and sometimes slavish imitators. By standing up and saying 'I don't feel like everyone else', Morrissey and Robert Smith became role models for anybody who ever felt like they weren't like everybody else. And since this was the task Gerard Way set himself—to speak for those who are not like others—it was inevitable that My Chemical Romance would attract its own legion of devotees.

But Gerard was never comfortable with the word cult— not because of its religious or pagan overtones, but because it seemed offensively small-minded. Cults meet in secret, communicate in code and die tragically in mass suicides. Gerard Way had a world to change, and he refused to see his fans' energy and ambition curtailed by a word. 'You should all know,' he told his audience from the stage in 2006, 'if you support us … you are not a cult; you are a fuckin' ARMY!'[3]

Alex: A sprig in a barrel-organ.

Teenagers

'WELCOME TO THE Black Parade' is something new in the world of rock and roll. There have been songs that angrily demand that the kids be granted the right to party, and there have been songs where the singer says he won't go to the party with all the other kids because he's too full of despair. But there's never been a song that angrily demands that the kids be granted the right to be full of despair. This is what the army of the black parade wants as it rattles the gates of the crystal palace. Here is the underground uprising Dostoyevsky imagined, thousands of human individuals who insist on being useless—broken, beaten and damned—in a utilitarian world. Their slogans are carefully calculated to annoy positivists and empiricists: 'We're all gonna die', 'I think I'm gonna burn in hell', 'What's in is despair'.

But the right to be sad is one that the modern world can't allow, and as the black parade began its march around the world in 2007, the media began a severe crackdown on sadness. The word 'cult' began to be thrown around. Old folk devils were revived: *The Black Parade* contained suicidal messages; the singer was using his shows and web forums to encourage his impressionable young fans to dive, lemming-like, into oblivion with him; links were implied between emo (the band members gritted their teeth) and recent high school shootings. The quiet, lonely kid with the overactive imagination, the notebook full of visions of impending doom, the black clothes and the long fringe. 'If you think your child might be at risk, go to our website…'

Way, understandably, was spooked by this media panic, which had in fact been building since the release of My Chemical Romance's second album. The huge spike in the band's sales and concert attendances after *Three Cheers for Sweet Revenge* was largely due to an influx of very young fans, and Gerard felt an enormous sense of responsibility to them. But the singer could see through the fear-mongering of the news networks and the tabloids to a much more serious malaise lying beneath. On tour, he poured his frustration into a song— a Bon Jovi-ish anthem recorded for *The Black Parade*, in which middle-America, picking up the tune laid down for them by Fox News, bawls out the refrain, 'Teenagers scare the livin' shit outta me!' This song, 'Teenagers', warns us of the lengths the state may go to in order to pursue its war on sadness.

> *They're gonna clean up your looks*
> *with all the lies in the books,*
> *to make a citizen out of you*[1]

'They've got methods of keeping you clean,' sings Gerard Way, hinting at more sinister procedures to come—drugs, surveillance and mind control. Why would they go to all this trouble? Because they're *scared* of you! If those underground types keep talking, word will get around that the limits imposed on human desire by the state are arbitrary and false, and people will start demanding all kinds of things that modern society is in no position to offer them. Dostoyevsky's underground man warned that happiness is not synonymous with wellbeing. A complete list of the ridiculous activities that make human beings feel good would have to include sulking, stealing and 'smashing things' which, the underground man insists, can sometimes be 'very pleasant'.

Alex, the protagonist of Anthony Burgess's *A Clockwork Orange*, would agree with this. Burgess's 1962 novel accelerates teenage delinquency into a nightmare future, where Alex and his gang of beautiful young men in eye make-up and bowler hats terrorise the city's streets with 'ultraviolence'. Alex is not interested in the greater good—but he knows what he likes: rape, ultraviolence and Beethoven's Ninth Symphony. These things make him happy—isn't that what life is all about? Of course, that's not how the state sees it. After a night of ultraviolence gone horribly wrong, Alex is thrown in prison, and soon becomes a candidate for a very promising new rehabilitation technique. When the underground man argued in 1864 that the state could only stop him from wanting the things he wants by altering his nature, he didn't believe for a second that this might be a possibility. But perhaps he should have—de Condorcet, in his sketch for a mathematically perfectible utopia, had already suggested that careful breeding might, given time, eventually iron out some of the kinks in the human organism.[2] Now, in Alex's time, science has progressed to the point where unreasonable individuals can be 'perfected' more or less on the spot.

But making a citizen out of Alex comes at a terrible cost. Dr Ludovico's brutal aversion therapy and high-powered drug injections rip up Alex's head and rob him of his free will. He can't be 'bad' anymore, and while the government might herald this as a great leap forward, the true meaning is not lost on Alex. He finally realises that, in his society's crystal palace, flipping the bird is not allowed. 'They of the government and the judges cannot allow the bad, because they cannot allow the self,' Alex muses. 'And is not our modern history, my brothers, the story of brave malenky selves fighting these big machines?'[3]

Alex is a nasty piece of work, but he's no dummy—and he knows his history. The big machines have been a problem for romantic individuals since William Blake wrote his preface to *Milton: A Poem* in 1804. Blake gave the nineteenth century one of its most indelible images when he described 'dark Satanic mills' rising over 'England's green and pleasant land'.[4] In 1811 one of these bleak-looking intrusions on the landscape erupted in violence: textile workers in Nottingham, angry about the introduction of a new stocking weaving frame that would, it was said, speed up production and reduce the number of workers needed in the factories, took up arms against the new frames. Many of them found themselves sentenced to death (or worse, sent to *Australia*) as a result.

But the frame-breakers—or Luddites as they became known—found themselves with an unexpected champion in Lord Byron, who argued passionately in the House of Lords against the introduction of the new laws, and later took the case to the streets with an article in *The Morning Chronicle*. This, at first, seems a little out of character for the poet, who had little love for the common man. But a letter to his mother, written around the time of the dispute, reveals the source of his sympathy for the Luddites:

> *If I could by my own efforts inculcate the truth, that a man is not intended for a despot or a machine, but as an individual of a community…I might attempt to found a new Utopia.*[5]

Here Byron is making a case for the dignity of the solitary citizen over the interests of states or systems. People want more and cheaper stockings, so it makes good rational sense to install machines that will make more stockings more quickly—more people will get what they want. But here we have already lost sight of the individual human being, and individuality is everything to Byron. This helps unravel the paradox behind Byron's support of the Luddites—how he could despise the mob, and yet stick his neck out to help a mob. The former is an individualised mass, the latter is a mass of individuals.

England embraced industry more quickly and effectively than any other nation in the nineteenth century, which is why the image of nature opposed to the rise of the machine, and the individual man opposed to totalitarian systems, became such a hallmark of romantic poetry in that country. It's a vein of imagery that can be traced all the way from Blake to Morris and the Pre-Raphaelites to Tolkien—whom they inspired—through to the strain of medievalism that runs through the hippy movement and right up to Pink Floyd.

Animals, Pink Floyd's eleventh studio album, released in 1977, painted a bleak portrait of English life after two centuries of progress and industry—from the dark Satanic mills on the album's cover, to the dog-eat-dog world described within. The album begins by wondering what would happen 'if you didn't care what happened to me and I didn't care for you', and quickly gets worse.[6] Later that year, while touring the album, songwriter Roger Waters discovered that he was far from immune to the social collapse he'd just described when he spat on a fan at a show in Montreal.[7] Much soul-searching followed, which eventually lead to the band's next project, 1979's *The Wall*. Waters' epic study in alienation traces the roots of his character's soul sickness back to the public school system. In the classroom children are treated as though they are empty vessels, ready to be filled up with correct ideas which will equip them for the workforce. Of course, human children, Waters insists, are not empty vessels. They're unique individuals with strange dreams and irrational urges. But since the behaviourist state cannot admit this even for a moment, they have to beat those dreams out of you. Producer Bob Ezrin, fresh from recording the kids choir on Alice Cooper's 'School's Out', assembled a gang of English school children in the studio to sing Waters' immortal lines: 'Hey! Teacher! Leave them kids alone!'[8]

Though Waters, like Byron, is hardly a man of the people, he is a staunch individualist—so he will never accept the idea that human beings are merely part of a system. But this is exactly what modern government wants: another brick in the wall, a human being reduced to what Dostoyevsky calls a 'sprig in a barrel-organ'—or, as Gerard Way puts it in 'Teenagers', 'another cog in the murder machine'.[9]

With this line, Gerard exposes the real irony in America's War on Sadness. Society considers it dangerous for a band like My Chemical Romance to promote despair, because despair is a drag on productivity—it sends a bad message to the kids who are the workforce of the future. You can't go around telling people life is pointless. It happens to be true, but how will we get anything done if people find that out? The valuelessness at the heart of modern society will be revealed for all to see, the jig will be up, the machine will be prevented from working.

But Gerard suspects, as Dostoyevsky did in his day, that the machine itself might be the real reason the kids are unhappy in the first place. By enshrining progress over real values, to the point where nobody knows what values are anymore, science and industry have created horrors that Rousseau, Wordsworth, Morris and Dostoyevsky could barely have imagined. How can we expect the workforce of the future to put on a happy face while contributing to a society that has produced the atomic bomb, missiles in space, the greenhouse effect and the War on Terror? The world produced by reason and commonsense is a nightmare. So, because utilitarianism has proved incompatible with real human happiness, the romantic artist, as Bertrand Russell has observed in his *History of Western Philosophy*, tends to replace utilitarian standards with aesthetic ones.

The earth-worm is useful, but not beautiful; the tiger is beautiful, but not useful. Darwin (who was not a Romantic) praised the earth-worm; Blake praised the tiger. The morals of the Romantics have primarily aesthetic motives.[10]

Byron will support the Luddites over the government; Morris the solitary artist over the big factory; Tolkein the hobbits over Saruman's industry; Nick Cave the murderer over the state that wants to reform him; Morrissey the shoplifter over the cops; Jon Bon Jovi the outlaw over the sheriff; Tim Burton the monster over the suburban world that won't accept him. The factory and the police force are useful, but not beautiful. The monster and the sulky teenager are beautiful, but not useful. In any contest between the big machine and Alex's 'brave malenky selves', the romantic has to side with the 'brave malenky selves'.

Gerard Way: Making a difference.

I've Gotta Get Out of the Basement!

IN AN INTERVIEW conducted shortly after the release of *Three Cheers for Sweet Revenge* the members of My Chemical Romance were asked about their goals as a band and whether they felt they had met them. Frank Iero had a detailed answer ready to go.

> When we started this band we set mini goals and then we had our ultimate goal... We met all our smaller goals...we've been able to reach an exorbitant amount of kids that we never thought we would reach. Our major goal was to make a difference, and I think we are on our way to that goal.[1]

In the mythical universe of *The Black Parade*, this goal was entrusted to My Chemical Romance on that fateful day when the singer's father took him to see the marching band. In the real world, the story gets a little more complicated. Gerard Way spent his formative years locked away in his bedroom, living in a make-believe world of comic book superheroes and Dungeons & Dragons (D&D). Later, he discovered music— his first concert was Springsteen in New Jersey, followed by those other local heroes, Bon Jovi. As high school wore on, he moved on to darker, heavier stuff: The Smiths, The Cure, and other bands who spoke for the loners and losers. Way remembers making the hour-long round trip from his parents' house in Belleville, New Jersey, to the nearest mall to buy The Smashing Pumpkins' *Siamese Dream* on the day it came out.[2]

All of these—the comics, the Springsteen and Bon Jovi concerts, the cult bands, the punk 7-inch singles he was starting to collect—would provide important cues for Way when he started making his own music in his late twenties. By that time, Way was living in his parents' basement, trying to make it as a commercial artist. He interned at DC Comics and pitched an idea to the Cartoon Network, which they very nearly picked up, about a flying monkey who talked like Björk and could make breakfast foods appear out of nowhere. But he was unhappy. He drank too much, he popped too many pills, and occasionally thought about suicide.

Then, driving in to Manhattan on 11 September 2001, Gerard had an epiphany. 'I've gotta get out of the basement,' he said to himself, 'I've gotta make a difference!'[3]

At this point, Gerard Way's story really does begin to resemble the superhero comics he devoured so eagerly as a young man. Way's response to global catastrophe and personal meltdown was ... to form his own superteam. He, his brother Mikey and neighbourhood friend Frank Iero banded together as My Chemical Romance. Their mission? 'To deal with the post-traumatic stress disorder of 9/11.'[4] In the beginning, the band's role was therapeutic. Gerard thrashed and howled and let off steam, and felt much better for it. But he also realised that he had created art. Art had healed his bruised psyche and given him a reason to live. Might it not be able to accomplish the same task on a larger scale? The world was in crisis, society was falling apart (again), everybody he met seemed so loaded up with stress that they might explode at any moment. Could art *make a difference*?

The answer was almost irrelevant, since Gerard and the band felt as though they had no choice but to do what they were doing anyway. But after the adrenaline rush of those early gigs had worn out, Gerard began to think more carefully about *how* to do it. The clues turned out to be in his own childhood and adolescence—in the music, comics and movies that had shaped his imagination. The gothic gloom of The Cure, the horror business of the Misfits, the Old Testament morality of Nick Cave and the Bad Seeds, the high romance of Queen, Bowie and Springsteen, the cosmic allegories of power and responsibility in the superhero comics, and the medieval escapism of D&D. These were the myths that had sustained him, that had given his life meaning and purpose in his darkest moments—and these became the raw materials for the great multimedia art project that would be My Chemical Romance.

Role-playing games and comics have never really been cool, exactly. But they got a boost in the early '90s from the patronage of Rivers Cuomo. Weezer's song 'In the Garage' describes the place the singer goes when normal life drives him round the twist. Here no-one can tell him what to do—he's got his Kiss posters, his X-Men comics, and his twelve-sided die. But we wouldn't know that he's into any of that stuff, the singer tells us, because we're not allowed in here. 'In the garage where I feel safe,' he croons, 'no-one knows about my ways.'[5]

With 'In the Garage', Cuomo made himself a martyr to geekiness. Thanks to the Weezer singer's groundwork in establishing such nerdy pursuits as part of the aesthetic of twenty-first-century pop-punk-whatever, the modern rock star no longer has to hide his Dungeon Master's guide in the garage. The members of My Chemical Romance are not so shy about their obsessions. While all the other musicians on the 2006 Warped tour were getting loaded and chatting up groupies, *Rolling Stone*'s contributing editor Jenny Eliscu followed the members of My Chemical Romance around the local Wal-Mart as they looked for Spiderman pyjama bottoms and plastic racks to organise their D&D books. 'They prefer to think of themselves as superheroes rather than rock stars,' Eliscu noted, as the band climbed beneath their Teen Titans bedspreads and bid each other goodnight.

> *And, like any respectable superheroes, the members of My Chemical Romance get their own action figures later this year. 'I don't think that having a My Chemical Romance action figure will make a kid start his own band,' Gerard says. 'I like to think it will make him save children from a burning building.'*[6]

This is about much more than merchandising for Gerard Way—more than music, even. It's about finding a way out of the shallow materialism of his age. It's about giving fans something to believe in.

Myths of the Near Future

THE PROBLEM WITH reason—as Rousseau realised—is that it's essentially amoral. Logic, science and mathematics can help us figure out how to do things better, but they can never tell us whether the thing was a good idea in the first place. So a society that enshrines science and reason above all else is, in the end, guided only by the spirit of competition—the race to see who can build a more efficient mill, a faster steam engine. Progress can never tell us how to live or why we should carry on doing so. For that, Dostoyevsky believed, you need religion. But the new ideology of commonsense had rationalised religious faith out of existence. Here again Dostoyevsky saw the dubious legacy of the Enlightenment at work. A society based on rational principles can have no use for things that don't make sense—and Christianity, like all major religions, is full of nonsense. A virgin birth? A man who dies and comes back to life? Three persons who are the same person? Enlightenment philosophers jumped through hoops to reconcile all this mumbo jumbo with reason—and what they couldn't explain, they did away with.[1]

This, for Dostoyevsky, was the greatest mistake of the age. The empiricists and positivists had created a world in which behaviour was only tolerated if it was rational and useful. This left no room for tradition or faith, which are irrational and therefore useless. But again, Dostoyevsky asks, how did reason become the measure of all things? Myths, as Isiah Berlin points out in *Against the Current*, are not 'false statements about reality corrected by later rational criticism'.[2] What's important about mythology will never show up on the rationalists' radar—so of course they'll assume that it's useless. But what if there was something wrong with the system? What if the most important element in our lives, the one thing that can give meaning to what otherwise seems like a brute struggle for existence, cannot be weighed on a scale or calculated by an adding machine? Dostoyevsky believed that the erosion of faith by science had created a world without meaning in which the spirit of competition and one-upmanship was the only rule. Now society, which had once been bound together by real values, was falling apart at the seams.

Against his degraded present, Dostoyevsky opposed the image of a specifically Russian Christian tradition, rooted in the soil of the nation and flowing through the veins of its people. This, as Alex de Jonge points out in his book *Dostyevsky and the Age of Intensity* is closely bound up with his idea of the 'living life'—a Rousseau-ish vision of human beings connected to their natural impulses.[3] The underground man is envious of the natural men and the men of action precisely because they seem to be in touch with this 'living life'. He, on the other hand, is unnatural—a test-tube man— the inevitable result of the fragmented and meaningless world created by reason and enlightenment.

Dostoyevsky was not alone in voicing his discontent with modern society—nor was he the only one to posit national folk traditions as the remedy for its ills. Richard Wagner, like William Morris, advocated a return to the artisan's communities of the Middle Ages, and found the materials for his dramas in medieval folklore. He believed these indigenous traditions could provide German people with the kind of spiritual satisfaction that the modern world, with its flimsy material consolations, could not. And Wagnerians—following the composer's lead—loved Wagner's music in a completely different way to that in which, say, the French concert-goer of the eighteenth century would have enjoyed Mozart. Wagner was not entertainment, his operas were, as Eric Hobsbawm puts it in *The Age of Empire*, 'all-purpose providers of spiritual content'.[4] And Wagner was not just a composer, he was—as he was the first to insist—a maker of myths.

This new role for the artist came to seem more and more important as the world created by money and business proved to be not only immoral, but far less stable than the positivists would have you believe. The Great Depression of the late 1800s, as Hobsbawm points out, seems like a barely perceptible blip compared to the financial crises of the twentieth century.[5] But it was enough to shake people's faith in economic progress, and it certainly lead to a great deal of 'I-told-you-so'-ing from the nineteenth-century's discontents. In his study of turn-of-the-century culture in Vienna, Carl Schorske explains how this new instability gave extra momentum to the Wagnerians' cause. 'The crash of 1873', he writes in *Fin-Du-Siecle Vienna*, 'made particularly attractive [Wagner's] glorification of the Medieval Artisan community against modern capitalist society.'[6] Addressing a meeting of Vienna's Wagner society in 1875, August Sitte told his audience that '[t]he essence of the modern condition being the fragmentation of life, we stand in need of an integrating myth'.[7]

Showing how these unifying myths could be created by artists was, Sitte argued, Wagner's great achievement. Just as Wagner's Siegfried forges a new weapon from the fragments of his father's sword:

> *So too must the modern artist generate, by the example of his art, the strength to overcome fragmentation and provide a 'community life-outlook' for people as a whole.*[8]

In a meaningless and chaotic world, a world in which social relations have broken down and the old faiths have disappeared through neglect, it was the artists' job, the Wagnerians believed, to heal society's wounds.

Gustav Klimt

TOWARD THE END of 1895 the Austrian painter Gustav Klimt was commissioned to paint three pictures for the great hall of a Viennese university—one for each of the university's three main faculties: medicine, philosophy and law (jurisprudence). The board of trustees wanted something inspirational, something that communicated in every possible way that the combined forces of knowledge, reason, and intellect would, in the fullness of time, lead humankind out of the wilderness and into the light. Something modern as well—that went without saying—but not *too* modern. What they got was a shock—to say the least.

Klimt's first effort, 'Philosophy', was an overwhelming avalanche of human joy and tragedy—birth, death, agony and ecstasy cascaded past the viewer, springing from nowhere and, it seemed, going straight back there. As Schorske says, 'The ideal of mastery of nature through scientific work was simply violated by Klimt's image of a problematic, mysterious struggle in nature.'[1] The university politely asked for its money back.

A painting that represented the thing-in-itself as imagined by an Enlightenment philosopher would be harmonious and elegant. But Klimt had decided to give them Schopenhauer—so it's little wonder the thing turned out looking nasty. For Schopenhauer, the thing-in-itself, the world as will, is senseless, destructive and evil. The university's trustees worried that, faced with such a heavy dose of romantic despair in the great hall, students would simply throw their books in the air, turn around and go back home—there to spend the rest of their days in contemplation of the suffering of the world. This is actually not too far from Klimt's intention, and very close to Schopenhauer's idea of redemption—the one piece of good news in his otherwise gloomy philosophy.

Schopenhauer insists that as long as we're pursuing our interests—food, shelter, sex, material possessions or power over others—we're being driven by will, which can never be satisfied. For this reason, he dismisses the Rousseauian idea of a 'natural' state to which modern people can aspire. For Schopenhauer, our natural state is the problem—we've complicated matters by becoming as self-aware as we have, but the source of our unhappiness is the sheer pointlessness of life itself. We must pursue our interests, knowing that they must leave us unsatisfied.

But if we can somehow become *dis*interested, we are no longer willing—and the result is a feeling of bliss. This, Schopenhauer believed, is what art does for us.

> *When an aesthetic perception occurs the will*
> *completely vanishes from consciousness...this is the*
> *origin of the feeling of pleasure which accompanies the*
> *perception of the beautiful...*[2]

As we contemplate art, we are able to see life—with all its striving and willing—in a detached, aesthetic way. We are freed, briefly, from the desiring that takes up so much of our time, and leaves us so unsatisfied, as we look at life from the artist's point of view. In this way, the suffering of the world becomes bearable, and art, according to Schopenhauer, becomes our most important consolation for the pain of life. It's little wonder that, of all philosophers, he's the artist's favourite.

Schopenhauer's formula for redemption through aesthetics explains, among other things, how it is that a song about how life sucks can make us feel good. 'How Soon is Now?', 'Blasphemous Rumours', 'Butterfly', '(I Can't Get No) Satisfaction'—these songs are full of bad news about the human condition, and all have the power to make us feel fantastic. Even as we recognise the sincerity of the artist's view of life, and the honesty with which he's portrayed it, the feeling we get as we listen to his song about how life is hell is not the same as the feeling of living in hell—quite the opposite.

It's as though the singer, by giving us such an unflinching portrayal of the world as will, has shifted our position in relation to it. If life could be compared to a giant traffic jam, the song has the effect of lifting us high above the traffic in a helicopter. We can still see the chaos on the roads, but we're no longer directly involved in the struggle—where previously we were interested (because we have to get to work on time), now we are disinterested—and from this new aesthetically detached point of view, the traffic jam becomes beautiful, a glittering mosaic winding its way around the city. We no longer experience the pain of the world as sufferers but as spectators.

The university trustees needn't have been so worried about Klimt's *Philosophy* mural after all. Far from spreading despair, a painting like that—in which the suffering of the world is presented as an aesthetic spectacle—would, if Schopenhauer was correct, become a means of redemption. This idea proved to be enormously popular and durable in the late nineteenth century. It formed the backbone of Wagner's conception of music and opera as a substitute for religion in a fragmented modern world. And it gave a young philologist from the University of Basel—a man much admired by Klimt—the necessary foundation on which to build a career that would take romantic philosophy in undreamt-of new directions.

Nietzsche: 'I discovered all these abysses in myself ...'

Nietzsche

IN 1865 TWENTY-ONE-YEAR-OLD Friedrich Nietzsche walked into a second-hand book shop in Leipzig and purchased a copy of Schopenhauer's *The World as Will and Representation*. This was good news for Schopenhauer (who unfortunately was dead by this point) because it's safe to say that even if only two people had ever read his books, as long as those two people were Richard Wagner and Friedrich Nietzsche, his place in history would be assured.

Schopenhauer's philosophy of disgust spoke to Nietzsche with a voice he was ready to hear, a voice that seemed to confirm what he already suspected—that the optimism of his age was a thin veneer over a meaningless abyss. He stayed up all night sitting on the family sofa, reading *The World as Will and Representation* over and over again. 'Here where every line cried renunciation, denial, resignation,' he later wrote, 'here I saw a mirror in which I observed the world, life and my own soul in frightful grandeur.'[1] Nietzsche was, by this point, extraordinarily well acquainted with his own soul, having written the autobiography of his emotional life at least six times (he would make it nine by the time he was twenty-three).[2] He had already seen enough to convince him that the world was not an elegant system into which the individual could be inserted like a sprig in a barrel organ, but a dark, mysterious, violent struggle in which he must either fight or perish. Now, in the book he held in his hands, he had finally found a writer who was willing to admit this, and who seemed to offer a solution.

Nietzsche came to realise through Schopenhauer that he had sound reasons for being dissatisfied with life—only a stupid man could find life satisfying, and Nietzsche knew he was not stupid. But, Schopenhauer insisted, the man of intelligence could redeem himself through music, philosophy and renunciation. Here was a man who could explain to the young Nietzsche why music had such a tremendous effect on him. Life is unbearable but music, incredibly, allows us to see it as beautiful. Thus, music becomes a consolation for suffering. The man of intelligence must take an aesthetic attitude to life. Finally, Nietzsche thought to himself, someone who understands me! For a period of two weeks, Nietzsche took this business of renunciation more seriously than Schopenhauer himself ever had. He horrified his mother by adopting a monkish lifestyle—keeping a very strict diet and depriving himself of sleep, human company and material comfort. He became obsessed with a certain atmosphere he'd detected in Schopenhauer, 'the ethical air', as he described it, 'cross, death and grave'.[3]

Nietzsche loved Schopenhauer for the same reason that he loved Wagner—as a teenager, he'd spent hours at the family piano pounding out the chords of *Tristan und Isolde*.[4] Both confirmed his instinctive belief that the optimism of the nineteenth century was a sham, and that tragedy and violent struggle constituted the true essence of life. And since Wagner himself was so heavily influenced by Schopenhauer it seemed only natural to Nietzsche to develop a system of aesthetics that incorporated the two. In any case, as Colin Wilson points out in his classic study of the artistic personality, *The Outsider*, Nietzsche had by this point consigned every other major intellectual figure of his century to the scrap heap—there was no-one else left. 'Nietzsche stood alone,' writes Wilson, 'except for the two men for whom he still felt respect: Schopenhauer and Wagner. Three men against the world ... but what men!'[5]

In 1868 Nietzsche, now a professor at Basel University, began writing what would become his first book, *The Birth of Tragedy*—a meditation on the origins of Greek tragedy out of what Nietzsche called 'The Spirit of Music'. Nietzsche had by this point become quite a close personal friend of Wagner, and a firm believer in the composer's propaganda. Wagner, in turn, was enormously impressed by the young professor. After reading the manuscript of *The Birth of Tragedy*, Wagner declared it to be the finest thing he'd ever read. But then, he would say that—Nietzsche had devoted the last quarter of his treatise on Greek drama and music to building a case for Wagnerian opera as the true revival of tragedy in the modern world and the future of music for Germany. This cost him his career—and in the long run, his sanity. After *The Birth of Tragedy* was published in 1872, Nietzsche was more or less laughed out of the academic world for good. Despite (or perhaps because of) his enormous popularity, Wagner was not considered cool in the Philology Department of the University of Basel, and Nietzsche misjudged the mood of his colleagues entirely by spending the last four chapters of his book mounting a vigorous argument in favour of a composer who catered to the tastes of emotional young girls and girlish, emotional young men.[6]

Nietzsche himself later disowned *The Birth of Tragedy* completely. He came to regard it as a ridiculous book, in which he'd tried to do something impossible—to reconcile the three things he happened to be into at the time—Schopenhauer, Wagner and Greek Tragedy—into a single system. The young professor jumps through hoops to make Schopenhauer more Greek and the Greeks more Wagnerian, and ends up falling on his face.[7] But while *The Birth of Tragedy* is a deeply strange book, it's crucial to understanding Nietzsche's mature philosophy, (in which, as Colin Wilson has noted, he eventually came back around to the position he'd staked out in *The Birth of Tragedy*),[8] and contains many striking insights in its own right, particularly as regards its central subject—tragedy. How are we redeemed by tragedy? asks Nietzsche, and what is the role of the tragic hero in relation to music? His answers have as much to teach us about Wagnerian rock as they do about Wagner himself.

Freddie Mercury: Not to be born, not to be, to be nothing.

A Night at the Opera

'COME ONE, COME all to this tragic affair.'[1] Gerard Way's opening words on *The Black Parade* let us know what we're in for immediately. A man will be wheeled out on stage, and we will be told the story of his life. He'll grow up, fall in love, fall out of love, face terrible obstacles and painful decisions. He'll come to understand, at the end of the show, the meaning of life—which is that life is a joke with a terrible punch line. And this knowledge won't help him a bit, because this is a tragedy, and the rules of tragedy say the hero must die. How can we stand it?

The hero's theme song, 'Welcome to the Black Parade', is a multipart epic, which draws on a number of different musical styles. The first part is a stately ballad in the vein of 'My Way', the second act sounds a bit like Green Day, and the final section is pure Wall of Sound—the noise of teen angst inflated to epic proportions. But the single biggest influence on the song—and the album as a whole—is, as many fans and critics have noted, the operatic bombast of mid '70s Queen. In fact, the whole pocket epic form of 'Welcome to the Black Parade' is virtually unthinkable without the precedent of Queen's own rock opera classic 'Bohemian Rhapsody'. In 1977 Queen found themselves recording in the same studio as the Sex Pistols, and Sid Vicious decided to drop in and meet the neighbours. 'Hullo Fred,' said Sid Vicious. 'So you've really brought ballet to the masses then?' 'Ah, Mr Ferocious!' replied the flamboyant frontman. 'Well, we're trying our best, dear!'[2] Welcome to the Black Parade's Queen-meets-punk arrangement imagines a parallel universe where Mercury had invited Mr Ferocious in for a cup of tea, and the two bands had ended up writing a song together.

Two years earlier, in 1975, Queen's producer Roy Thomas Baker had dropped by Freddie Mercury's apartment in Kensington. The singer sat down at his piano and told Baker that he'd like to play him something new he'd been working on: 'So he played the first part and said "this is the chord sequence"…He played a bit further through the song and then stopped suddenly, saying, "This is where the opera section comes in". We both just burst out laughing.'[3]

It took weeks of painstaking work in the studio for Baker and the members of Queen to get Mercury's ambitious new song into shape. In the process, the 'opera section' grew and grew—'just one more Galileo!' Mercury would insist, while Baker watched the master tape wear away to nothing.[4] When it was finished, the band liked it so much they decided it would be their next single, an idea which was met with hoots of derision from their record company. A six-minute single with an opera in the middle of it? Are you mad? In the end, however, EMI's hand was forced by Capitol Radio presenter Kenny Everett, who broke the song on his show. 'Bohemian Rhapsody' was rushed into stores, and spent eight weeks at the top of the British charts.[5]

'Bohemian Rhapsody' begins with the singer pondering the eternal romantic dilemma. His life is awful, but his dreams are beautiful—is it possible he has been deceived? Are his dreams real, and 'reality' simply a sham? 'Do I wake or sleep?' He tries, like Tristan, to wave these *morgentraume* away only to find that he cannot quit his prison so easily. The only escape route lies in death. Our hero is not quite ready to commit suicide, but now that the world has been exposed as a cruel deception, he can't really be bothered doing anything with his life either. What's the point? 'Anyway the wind blows', he sings, 'doesn't really matter'.[6] The tragic hero has been afforded a glimpse behind the screen of bourgeois life and has seen the eternal chaos and flux of Schopenhauer's world as will—how can he be expected to show up to his classes or clean his room now?

Here, the opera section kicks in, and 'Bohemian Rhapsody' turns from a lyrical poem into a mythic drama, in which Beelzebub and a chorus of angels battle it out for the hero's soul. This metaphysical argy-bargy recalls many similar scenes in Goethe's *Faust*. Faust, like the hero of Queen's epic, believes that life can show him nothing, and thus becomes the subject of a wager between God and Mephisto. God believes Faust's disillusionment with earthly pursuits will eventually lead him to religion. The Devil is certain he can get Faust interested in *something*. It was these alarmingly casual chats between God and Mephisto that led early British critics to condemn Goethe's drama for its 'blasphemous levity'.[7] The light-hearted tone of *Faust* suggests that human life might be no more than a joke—and 'Bohemian Rhapsody' (which was funny long before it appeared in *Wayne's World*) leaves us with much the same feeling.

In any case, the hero eventually storms out of his own scene of heavenly judgement, insisting that he can beat anything the Devil throws his way. He's gone from being a hopelessly static whinger, like the Byron of *Childe Harold*, to a proper romantic hero, the later Byron so admired by Goethe for his determination to push against all natural laws. 'So you think you can stop me and spit in my eye!,' he snarls.[8] But he quickly runs out of steam. Reality, it seems, is a stone wall. Our hero falls back, exhausted, and makes ready to die—his tragedy has run its course.

In *The Birth of Tragedy* Nietzsche repeats Schopenhauer's assertion that life can only be made bearable by philosophy and art. Nietzsche insists that this is what art is for; to create a space from which we can begin to see suffering on an enormous scale as an aesthetic phenomenon. He then goes on to fuse Schopenhauer's idea of redemption through non-willing with his understanding of Tragedy, formed during those marathon sessions at his parents' piano, and further honed by his long walks and talks with Wagner at Tribschen. For Nietzsche, the role of the tragic hero is to confront the world as will head on. He sees behind the veil of illusion, stares into the horror and is crushed by it. By doing this, he effectively takes the whole weight of existence on his back, and relieves us of its burden momentarily.[9]

By contemplating the nature of this burden, Nietzsche finds the link between Schopenhauer and the world of the Greeks that forms the foundation of his thoroughly mad, but strangely convincing book. Schopenhauer, bored out of his skull by his dumb clerical job in Frankfurt, had looked around him and realised that the meaning of life was precisely nothing. And given that life is painful, boring *and* pointless, he concluded that it would be far better in the grand scheme of things if the human race had never existed. The Greeks, Nietzsche insists, were well acquainted with this truth. Not the Greeks as the eighteenth-century classicists liked to imagine them, the white-marble world of clarity and Apolline perfection so admired by the likes of Joshua Reynolds and Gottfried Lessing; but the real Greeks, who knew Apollo as just one of many deities, and not the wisest among them. In *The Birth of Tragedy*, Nietzsche writes,

> *According to the old story, King Midas had long hunted wise Silenus, Dionysus' companion, without catching him. When Silenus had finally fallen into his clutches, the king asked him what was the best and most desirable thing of all for mankind. The daemon stood silent, stiff and motionless, until at last, forced by the king, he gave a shrill laugh and spoke these words: 'Miserable, ephemeral race, children of hazard and hardship, why do you force me to say what it would be much more fruitful for you never to hear? The best of all things is something entirely outside your grasp: not to be born, not to be, to be nothing. But the second-best thing for you—is to die soon'.*[10]

This, for Nietzsche, is the burden the tragic hero takes up on our behalf. And this is why he must die—because no-one can go on living knowing what he knows. The wisdom of Silenus condemns the hero to death, because understanding—as Nietzsche says of Hamlet—kills action. That's why we know, sometime between the moment when the young Bohemian realises that nothing really matters and the bit where he wishes he'd never been born at all, that he will not survive this drama. And if Gerard Way's spruiking his rock opera as a 'tragic affair' wasn't enough of a giveaway, we should know by the last line of the first verse where things are headed. As the song's acoustic strum gives way to an avalanche of orchestral noise and Brian May-style multitracked guitars, Gerard screams: 'When I grow up I want to be NOTHING AT ALL!'.[11]

This is the wisdom of the woods—or, if you like, the wisdom of the Frankfurt clerical office—which no-one can survive. The tragic hero knows it so that you don't have to.

The Wisdom of the Woods

IN SEEKING THE roots of tragedy in Greek art and music, Nietzsche discovered that the Greeks knew 'two worlds of art, utterly different'. On the one hand is the Apolline world of the representational arts, of painting and prose; on the other is the wild abandonment of the Dionysiac, which produces music. Nietzsche, as Colin Wilson points out in *The Outsider*, understood the Dionysiac instinctively. Listening to Wagner, he felt the pull of the dance, of the passions, of the half-crazy impulses that lurk beneath our civilised exterior.[1]

It was the spirit of Dionysus, Nietzsche believed, that had inspired the folk dances that swept through Germany in medieval times. Nietzsche writes admiringly of the way the dancers allowed themselves to be pulled along by instinct, leaping, singing, shouting at the top of their lungs; they indulged their senses and lost their minds. It was this spirit, too, that Schiller caught in his 'Ode To Joy'—which is why the young German philosophers of the early nineteenth century liked to recite it while getting drunk and dancing around in the fields. But Nietzsche also observed that the spirit of Dionysus is not for everyone:

> *Some people turn away with pity or contempt from phenomena such as these 'folk diseases', bolstered by a sense of their own sanity. These poor creatures have no idea how blighted and ghostly this 'sanity' of theirs sounds when the glowing life of the dionysiac revellers thunders past them.*[2]

This is still a problem in nightclubs today, as The Chemical Brothers' 'The Salmon Dance' shows. Typically when poets address small animals in verse no-one really expects the animal to answer back. All this changes in 'The Salmon Dance' where the poet, MC Fatlip, actually invites the fish into the studio to trade a few lines. Unfortunately, the fish has not a scrap of romantic sensibility, he talks like a nature documentary produced for school children in the '70s. 'My peeps spend part of their lives in fresh water, and part of their lives in salt water,' he drones. 'Wow, very interesting,' says Fatlip unconvincingly.[3]

Fatlip never promised us poetry; he told us we were going to learn fun facts about salmon, and a brand new dance. But the facts about salmon are less fun than we had been led to expect, and the brand new dance is, at first, a disaster. Fatlip finds that he is the only one in the club doing the salmon, hands pressed to his sides, swaying like a fish swimming upstream. Everyone else just stands there looking at him (bolstered by a sense of their own sanity). 'What the fuck is that?' they say to each other.[4]

But by the end of the song, everyone is dancing like a salmon. What changed? Simple, Nietzsche would say. The people in the club simply surrendered to the Dionysiac urge. They gave up the struggle to maintain a rational attitude to an irrational world, and immersed themselves in the ceaseless flow of life, the same flow that sends a salmon swimming upstream, the very *will* that pushes the world and everything in it along its purposeless course.

> *Singing and dancing, man expresses himself as a member of a higher community: he has forgotten how to walk and talk, and is about to fly dancing into the heavens ... he gives voice to supernatural sounds: he feels like a god.*[5]

The romantics tended to see all art as an attempt to say things that could not be said any other way. Paintings, poems and symphonies will all, in the end, resist our attempts to analyse and explain them—as though turning art back into ordinary language were like translating a newspaper article from French into English. And of all the arts, music is the hardest to explain because music, unlike painting for example, doesn't represent the world. Music does not present facts—it *is* a fact. (Musicians still use this romantic article of faith as a way of not answering interview questions when they say 'the song speaks for itself' or 'it's all *there* man ...')

This lead Schopenhauer to the curious (but poetic) idea that music must be made of the same stuff that life is made from. It is, in other words, a pure expression of will. This explains music's effect on us: in surrendering to the power of music, we feel ourselves transported back to a primitive state, outside custom and convention, pulled along by the same forces that cause the grass to grow and the fish to swim upstream. Nietzsche, in *The Birth of Tragedy*, agrees with this theory, and uses it to explain how it is that the lyric poet comes into contact with the world as will, in order to bring back the terrible insights that he later shares with us.

Nietzsche observes that Schiller, when asked how he composed his poems, replied that he never started with a preconceived idea, but rather with a certain 'musical mood' that came over him.[6] This, Nietzsche notes, squares with the origins of lyric poetry itself, which the Greeks always recited to the accompaniment of music. The conclusion he draws is that the poet, when this musical mood comes over him, is absorbed in the spirit of music—which is a manifestation of will. Thus he confronts the great metaphysical truths hidden from the rest of us, and somehow lives to tell the tale. This all sounds a bit far-fetched, to be sure—but it would explain how it was that Keith Richards accessed the wisdom of the woods in a hotel room in Florida, and how the lyrics that came to him from that musical mood could subsequently go on to change the world.

In *The Birth of Tragedy* Nietzsche quotes Wagner as saying: 'Civilisation is annulled by music as lamplight is annulled by the light of day.'[7] Lamplight is a symbol of our mastery of nature; scientific man on the move, shining a light into the dark spaces of the world. Music is nature's revenge. It sneaks up on us, attacking via—what Nietzsche called 'the organ of fear'—the ear. Music cracks our civilised veneer, one blast, and we turn back into cave people, standing dumbstruck before a thunderstorm.

Nietzsche's view of the world as will is, as you've no doubt noticed, slightly different from that of Schopenhauer. Right from the beginning, his descriptions of the flux and chaos of life are shot through with a feeling of excitement that would be entirely abhorrent to the older philosopher. Nietzsche still sees will as irrational—and in some ways he still sees it as evil. But when he contemplates this evil, he finds that it makes him feel *good*.

In 1865, the same year he discovered Schopenhauer, Nietzsche wrote to his friend von Gersdorff:

> *Yesterday an oppressive storm hung over the sky, and I hurried to a neighbouring hill called Leutch … At the top I found a hut, where a man was killing two kids while his son watched him. The storm broke with a tremendous crash, discharging thunder and hail, and I had an indescribable feeling of well-being and zest … Lightning and tempest are different worlds, free powers, without morality. Pure Will, without the confusions of intellect—how happy, how free.*[8]

Even as he was being seduced by Schopenhauer's view of reality, Nietzsche was turning it on its head by treating it as positive, rather than negative. Instead of renouncing life, he would embrace it—*all* of it. That's why Nietzsche approves of music and dancing, but also of electricity and bloody violence—all represent will, and will for Nietzsche is sublime.

Dave Gahan: a new sense of power.

Personal Jesus

FOR TEN YEARS after the fiasco of *The Birth of Tragedy*, Nietzsche embraced philosophy—truth became his goal, and thought was exalted above emotion. But he found he couldn't keep this up for long. In 1882's *The Gay Science* he declared himself disgusted with the 'will-to-truth' of the philosophers. From this moment on, he said, he would embrace life, not thought. 'I wish to be at all times hereafter only a yea-sayer,' he wrote.[1]

By being determined to say 'yes' to life, Nietzsche became the natural enemy of Christianity with its seven deadly sins and its thou-shalt-nots. For him, what Christians call 'good' behaviour is perverse. In 1883's *Also Sprach Zarathustra*, Nietzsche's wild-eyed prophet drops this reversal of morals on the unsuspecting townspeople. 'It is not your sin, but your moderation that cries to heaven,' Zarathustra tells his baffled audience.[2] This news has turned their world upside down, but it's all in a day's work for the prophet. It's a sin! the people say. So what? says Zarathustra. Sin more! 'Your very meanness in sinning cries to heaven!'[3] Zarathustra sets himself as a Christ-in-reverse: 'It may have been good for that preacher of the petty people to bear and suffer the sin of man. I, however, rejoice in sin as my great consolation.'[4]

Zarathustra's reversal of morals is almost incomprehensible to his audience—but quite familiar to us after fifty years of rock and roll. The rock star knows instinctively that one must say 'yes' to life, and his career serves to demonstrate Nietzsche's philosophy in practice. In 1989 Depeche Mode singer Dave Gahan—the lapsed church-goer whose faith had been shattered five years earlier by the experiences described in *Blasphemous Rumours*—decided that Christian morality was something he could do without. He decided, as he put it, 'to become a monster...I wanted to live that very selfish life without being judged'.[5]

Depeche Mode's 1990 album, *Violator*, had cemented his anti-religious stance with searing indictments of the confessional ('Policy of Truth') and of Catholic guilt ('Halo'). And on the previous year's 'Strangelove', Gahan had hinted that he might try being a sinner—if only to stave off the boredom of a meaningless existence:

I give in to sin
Because you have to make this life liveable.[6]

After the extraordinary success of *Violator* and the *Music for the Masses* tour, Gahan suddenly found himself with the means to find out just how much sinning he could do. Accordingly, on the band's next tour, Gahan drank, snorted and shagged his way around the world, alienated everyone who ever cared for him, became addicted to heroin, destroyed hotel rooms, broke up his marriage and nearly got kicked out of his own band. And it all felt...fantastic. 'I'd be lying if I said it didn't make me feel...like I'd never felt before. Like I belonged. To what, I've no idea.'[7]

Thanks to Nietzsche, we are in a position to fill in the blanks in Gahan's account. The singer felt like he belonged because he was living authentically, according to his desires. He had said yes to life, and this, as Nietzsche discovered on that day when he watched the storm break, feels incredible. This is romantic optimism in a nutshell. In his *History of Western Philosophy*, Bertrand Russell says that the individual who throws off social bonds and indulges his instincts gets 'a new sense of power from the resolution of inner conflict'.[8] He already sees himself as actively inspired, rather than passively 'getting along'. Now he wonders if he hasn't become some new kind of human being—outside convention, social bonds and even morality. Nietzsche would say that he has; he called these exceptional individuals 'artist-tyrants', and insisted that we could not expect them to operate according to society's laws. 'Morality,' Nietzsche declared, 'is the herd instinct in the individual.'[9]

To live in society while demanding the right to ignore its rules makes no sense—and the romantic individualist knows it. That's why he tends to justify his irrational philosophy by claiming the authority of a mystic, or a prophet. The 'fire inside' from which romantic poets and philosophers draw their inspiration is not unlike the voice that speaks to the prophet or the saint, which is why romantics—from Goethe to Nietzsche, Springsteen to Gerard Way—slip so easily into those roles. To do what they do, these individuals believe they must obey the true voice of feeling in their hearts, which inevitably means they must, to a large extent, renounce the practical, material world. When the strain of keeping this up becomes too much, they quickly make the transition from saint to martyr—which is why Bowie describes Ziggy as a 'leper messiah', and Billy Corgan imagines 'secret destroyers' roasting him over flames in 'Bullet with Butterfly Wings'. Gahan, who ascended to megastardom on the back of a spooky glam-rock stomp called 'Personal Jesus' saw his way clearly marked out for him. In 'Personal Jesus' he'd proposed himself as a secular messiah: first in the intimate context of the song, as one to another; and then, inevitably, in the stadium, where he'd invited his fans to reach out and touch faith. Now, Gahan began to grow his hair long and to cultivate a beard. He took to appearing onstage shirtless, with his arms spread in a crucifixion pose. The follow-up to *Violator* was full of gospel choirs and lyrics about repentance and salvation, and the band named it *Songs of Faith and Devotion*. In 'Walking in My Shoes' the singer's stance is Byronic—he's done bad, bad things, he tells us. But don't think for a second that he was just having a good time. He also suffered terribly for his reversal of traditional values, and his belief that moral laws should be destroyed:

> *I'm not looking for a clearer conscience*
> *Forgiveness for the things I do*
> *but before you come to any conclusions*
> *try walking in my shoes.*[10]

Gahan's story—like all rock and roll tragedies, had a spiritual rather than a moral purpose. The singer was not a moral example; he was a martyr to a new, anti-Christian faith. And like the Nazarene preacher he not-so-subtly evoked on stage, he inspired followers. Both Marilyn Manson and Nine Inch Nails' Trent Reznor were as much inspired by Gahan's gloomy nihilism and Dionysiac excess as they were by his band's industrial-strength synth-pop. Both deliberately set out to explore the limits of morality by identifying with anti-social monsters like Charles Manson and flirting with images of evil—Nazism and Satanism. Marilyn Manson's reversal of good and evil inevitably lead him to Nietzsche, whose aphorisms he paraphrased in interviews, and who could have written the lyrics to 'Beautiful People' himself:

> *It's not your fault you're always wrong*
> *The weak ones are there to justify the strong.*[11]

Like Gahan, Manson practised what he preached, embracing hedonism with a vengeance, and going so far as to style himself as 'The God of Fuck'. But by 2004 he was feeling like a martyr to his own revolt. In an interview for *Kerrang!* entitled 'Twilight of the Gods' (a reference to Wagner's opera of the same name), he claimed that his new greatest hits collection represented 'ten years of fighting to get where I am', and that he'd decided to cover 'Personal Jesus' because, '"Personal Jesus" says more than anything I could say myself right now'.[12]

Nietzsche—who spent many years in exile, driven by neglect into a state of acute paranoia, reached the end of his life in a similar state. In 1889, just before he went completely insane, he began signing his letters 'The Crucified One'. It was no great leap for Nietzsche to imagine himself as a martyr, because he had always seen himself more as a prophet than a philosopher. Philosophers sit down with the works of other great philosophers and subject their methods to empirical tests to see if they hold true—if they don't, they reason their way to new truths. For Nietzsche, such people were 'blockheads'. His insights came from his direct experience of the world, visions that descended upon him as he contemplated nature and his own soul. 'I have seen thoughts rising on my horizon the like of which I have never seen before,' he wrote in a letter, around the time he was working on *The Gay Science*. He went on:

> *The intensity of my emotion makes me tremble and burst out laughing. Several times I have been unable to leave my room for the ridiculous reason that my eyes were swollen—and why? Each time I have wept too much on my walks of the day before—not sentimental tears, but actual tears of joy. I sang and cried out foolish things. I was full of a new vision in which I forestalled all other men.*[13]

Nietzsche's temperament was religious, but it was also artistic. His insights came from intuition rather than intellect, and this put him much closer to the poets, painters and composers than to most philosophers. Because of this, he understood instinctively that the artist is always amoral. This, as you can imagine, was a quality he admired a great deal. In *The Gay Science* he asks: 'Do you suppose that Tristan and Isolde are preaching against adultery when they both perish by it?'[14] Nietzsche saw that for the great artist, the pursuit of beauty outweighed all other considerations, including moral ones. Furthermore, he knew that this approach was fundamentally right—that is, that it was desirable to take an aesthetic attitude to life. That's why, to him, the artist was a 'higher man'. Artists have no use for morality, because their only allegiance is to beauty. And since beauty redeems us from suffering, no-one could say that their attitude is wrong.

The only problem for the 'higher man' is that of the masses—the little party of regular folk from Don Giovanni who seek to impose their standards of normalcy on the fearless artist-hero. This is what finally defeated Nietzsche—his books were full of earth-shattering revelations, but the critics and academics saw only the ravings of a lunatic. This, too, was the snag Dave Gahan ran into as he tried to live his life artistically.

In 'Condemnation', the artist–martyr shakes his fist at the heavens and demands to know why he is made to suffer. Of course, he already knows the answer: 'My duty was always to beauty,' he confesses. 'That was my crime.'[15]

Kanye West: Power increases, resistance is overcome.

Stronger

WHILE HE ADMIRED Napoleon a great deal, Nietzsche had nothing but contempt for the French Revolution, with its Liberty, Equality and Fraternity. Democracy to Nietzsche is a travesty. In a democracy, or any other variation of 'rule by the people', the vision of a great artist-tyrant can be compromised and undone by the petty wants of the bungled and the botched—the masses. Nietzsche says the suffering of one great man is more important than the suffering of millions of ordinary people. 'What do the rest matter?' he asks. 'The rest are merely mankind—one must be superior to mankind.'[1] Nietzsche always sides with the individual genius against the world that doesn't understand his vision.

This is exactly the point of view expressed by Kanye West in his 2007 hit, 'Stronger'. 'There's a thousand yous there's only one of me,' raps the artist-tyrant.[2] Accordingly, when it came time to give his song a chorus, Kanye fused the musical mood of Daft Punk's 'Harder, Better, Faster, Stronger' with one of Nietzsche's best-known aphorisms: 'What does not kill me makes me stronger.'[3]

The song's action takes place at a nightclub. We fade in on Kanye West tuning the 'black Kate Moss'. Like all romantics, Kanye takes a dim view of convention and the artificial refinements of modern life—looking around, all he sees is fake shit. 'Does anybody make real shit anymore?' he asks, rhetorically.[4] For Kanye—as for Nietzsche and Dostoyevsky—authenticity is a big deal. But while he knows he's more authentic than everybody else, he's also become lonely as a result. He believes he can still be redeemed by love, and yet it seems that the perfect union of souls he imagines is constantly under threat from the world, with all its worn-out morality. Before he and the black Kate Moss have even swapped digits, he's already lost in narcissistic fantasies in which he and his soul mate fly away to another world:

> *Let's get lost tonight*
> *You can be my black Kate Moss tonight...*
> *Y'all don't give a fuck what they all say, right?*
> *Awesome, the Christian and Christian Dior.*[5]

Kanye, as is fairly well known, is a Christian. But at this same party, barely thirty seconds into the same song, we find him standing on a table with a few Cristals under his belt, espousing some very un-Christian sentiments:

> *Bow in the presence of greatness,*
> *'Cause right now thou hast forsaken us*
> *You should be honoured by my lateness*[6]

Kanye's philosophy as presented in 'Stronger' is clearly much closer to Nietzsche's than to any flavour of Christianity. As a student of philology, Nietzsche was always fascinated by the Titans—the monstrous race of super-beings who spawned the Greek deities. He was, as Rüdiger Safranski observes in *Nietzsche: A Philosophical Biography*, far more impressed by those who *make* gods than by the gods themselves. In *The Birth of Tragedy* he relates how the Titans became the first tragic heroes of the Greek stage. Oedipus and Prometheus pushed against all natural laws, and when they died, they died heroically, for the sake of their ambition. Nietzsche warns his readers at the start of the book that if they approach the world of the Greeks looking for the type of morality found in the New Testament—or in the sickly productions of the nineteenth-century stage—they will be sorely disappointed. In stark opposition to the myths of Christianity—in which humankind is always punished for its sins—Nietzsche places the myth of Prometheus, who is heroic in his determination to push against the limitations placed on him by Zeus, who sees him as a threat. Hence Nietzsche's admiration for strength, and the importance he places on the testing of will: 'What does not kill me, makes me stronger.'

In this, the tragedy of Kanye West is exactly the type Nietzsche would admire. In 'Stronger', Kanye's will is constantly being tested by haters. But the rapper insists that he will prevail: he will continue, in the face of ridicule and indifference, to preach 'the new gospel', and he will impose his forms on the world.[7] This applies to his public life as much as his art. At 2007's Video Music Awards, Kanye—having learned that he'd lost the best video award to Justice vs Simian's 'We Are Your Friends'—crashed the stage. 'Oh, hell no!' he exclaimed, interrupting Justice's acceptance speech and angrily protesting that his video for 'Touch the Sky' should have got the gong. He started out listing its merits, 'This video cost a million dollars! I got Pam Anderson! I got 'em jumpin' across canyons and shit!'[8]

But this was not really the point. Kanye knew his video should have won because he knew it was the best video. Even as he was apologising to the bemused members of Justice whose acceptance speech he'd hijacked, he was insisting that his video was better than theirs, even though he'd never seen it. 'It's nothin' against you man, I've never seen your video.'

Kanye then went on to suggest that the show's judges were effectively sabotaging the credibility of their own show by not giving him the award, after which he suggested that the whole show might as well go fuck itself. Couldn't he be more polite and gracious? Wouldn't that be good? What do you think Nietzsche would say to that?

> What is good? All that heightens the feeling of power,
>   the will to power, power itself in man
> What is bad? All that proceeds from weakness
> What is happiness? The feeling that power increases—
>   that resistance is overcome.[10]

By his determination to impose his forms on the world, regardless of the petty complaints of the bungled and the botched, Kanye has become one of Nietzsche's 'Higher Men'. Nietzsche first encountered the higher man in the person of Lord Byron. In his youth Nietzsche had an intense admiration (as all gloomy young men of the nineteenth century tended to do) for the author of *Childe Harold* and *Manfred*. Nietzsche admired Byron's energy and drive, and the way he seemed to live the exploits described in his poetry and to embody the characters he described—as though his life and his art were one.[11] It could be argued that Byron was playing a role. But it was a role he could only play because he knew it. 'One cannot guess at these things.' Nietzsche wrote, 'One simply is it or is not.'[12] To Nietzsche, Byron seemed superior to other men because he was active, immoral and free from restraint.

Later in life, after shifting from his initial ultimate yes, to a brief dalliance with ultimate no, and then back to yes again, Nietzsche started to dream into existence his ultimate yea-sayer—a man who could say yes to all of life, for whom there were no limitations, no restraints. Would such a man, he wondered, be something a little more than human? In coming up with a name for this new creature, Nietzsche revived a word he'd first used to describe Byron in his student days—*Ubermensch*—Superman.[13]

Richard Strauss: The dance that everybody forgot.

Also Sprach Zarathustra

IN THE SUMMER of 1972 Elvis Presley played a record-breaking run of dates at the Sahara Tahoe hotel in Nevada. Elvis was in high spirits, the band was on fire, and the set-list—including 'You've Lost that Loving Feeling' and 'The Impossible Dream'—was generally regarded as topnotch.[1] But what really set the tone for the show was a number Elvis didn't sing on at all. It was his walk-on music, a majestic theme beginning with a simple but tremendously powerful sequence of three notes—C, G, C. This little fanfare was written not by bandleader Joe Guercio or any one of the dozens of songsmiths-for-hire in Freddy Bienstock's little black book but by a Munich-born romantic composer named Richard Strauss.

Like every other German-speaking composer of the late nineteenth century, Strauss grew up in the enormous shadow of Richard Wagner, and his operas and symphonies sometimes sound like they're trying to out-Wagner Wagner for sheer emotional drama and intensity of sound. Sometimes, he comes close—as in the piece Elvis included in his show at the Sahara Tahoe. The King's walk-on music began life as the opening theme for a symphonic tone poem Strauss wrote in 1896 called *Also Sprach Zarathustra*—inspired by Nietzsche's book of the same name. Strauss had first read Nietzsche four years earlier while on a holiday in Greece, and it had transformed him—and his music—immediately. After reading Nietzsche's denunciations of Christianity, Strauss tore up the last act of his (very Wagnerian) opera, *Guntram*, and re-wrote it so that it ended with the hero turning his back on society and organised religion and going it alone. Friends were horrified, and advised him to go back to his Bible—but Strauss, ever the romantic individualist and now a confirmed Nietzschean, refused to budge.[2] Three years later he started work on his homage to *Also Sprach Zarathustra*. Strauss later explained his aims in composing the piece:

> *I did not intend to write philosophical music, or to portray in music Nietzsche's great work. I meant to convey by means of music an idea of the development of the human race from its origin, through the various stages of its development, religious and scientific, up to Nietzsche's idea of the superman.*[3]

The human race, Nietzsche explained in *Also Sprach Zarathustra*, is in a transitional phase. Or rather, the human race *is* a transitional phase. We are, as Nietzsche puts it, standing on a makeshift rope over a great abyss. As we sway uncertainly over the deep, we look behind us and see our past—the ape—and when we do this we feel pretty proud of ourselves. Zarathustra points us toward the other end of the rope, ahead of us in the distance. That, he says, is where your destiny lies; the new form humanity must take; the means by which man will be superseded—just as man superseded the ape. 'Behold,' says Zarathustra. 'I teach you ... the superman!'[4] Humankind, in Zarathustra's opinion, has wasted a lot of time and effort trying to safeguard the future of humankind. What we should really be asking ourselves is: 'how shall humankind be overcome?'[5] The superman is this next stage in human evolution. And it's this great event that Strauss's magnificent fanfare is meant to announce.

Joe Guercio, who would arrange Strauss's piece for Elvis's band and lead them through it hundreds of times in the '70s, first heard *Also Sprach Zarathustra* the same way most of us did—watching Stanley Kubrick's *2001: A Space Odyssey*.[6] The film begins on prehistoric earth, at the moment when man first learns to impose his will on the world (by picking up a bone and using it to smash things), and eventually progresses to impose his will on others (by smashing them in the head with the very same bone). Kubrick marks this as the moment when man takes the first step toward his destiny by scoring the scene with Strauss's *Zarathustra*—and then cheekily suggests that we haven't got much further in the last few hundred thousand years by cutting from a shot of the bone flying through the air to a bone-shaped spaceship tumbling through the void. Kubrick's vision of humanity in the twenty-first century is a little like Nietzsche's estimation of the nineteenth. 'Even now,' he wrote, 'man is more of an ape than any ape.'[7]

Sitting in the movie theatre watching *2001*, Joe Guercio heard Strauss's massive chords heralding the arrival of humanity's successor and thought of Elvis. Elvis, watching the film a few days later, thought of himself.[8] This is not too surprising. The idea that Elvis might in fact be some completely new kind of human being—or not a human being at all—had been implicit from the moment he first appeared on TV in 1956. (Charles Laughton once introduced him to the audience as 'that man, Elvis Presley' as though he didn't know what he was.)[9] Ten seconds later, he'd awakened teenage America's suppressed longing for Dionysiac revelry, lifted the Judeo-Christian God's veto on the passions, and signalled a complete reversal of morals that would last, happily, until the present day. 'Yeah, that was the dance that everybody forgot,' said country singer Butch Hancock—echoing Wagner. 'It was the dance so strong it took an entire civilisation to forget it, and ten seconds to remember.'[10] An American evangelist famously grumbled that Elvis was 'morally insane'.[11] Zarathustra had warned in 1882 that the superman would be 'a destroyer of morality', and that his arrival would be heralded by madness and lightning.

Ziggy Stardust: Free power, without morality.

Homo Superior

IN 1969 RCA records released a single called 'Space Oddity' that was perfectly timed to cash in on the popularity of Kubrick's film. The song was a strange, psychedelic folk number—a meditation on cosmic alienation, sung by a man who lives outside everything in a tin can in space. 'Space Oddity' was a hit and David Bowie, who'd been mounting a series of increasingly desperate-looking attempts on the charts since the mid '60s, finally breathed a sigh of relief. But Bowie was not quite home and dry. Two years later, 'Space Oddity' was starting to feel more like a millstone around his neck than a foot in the door to superstardom.[1] He was in danger of disappearing into the 'where-are-they-now?' file: David Bowie? Oh yeah, the guy with the stylophone! What happened to him?

In 1971 Bowie released *The Man Who Sold the World*, and its cover appeared to be yet another attention-grabbing Bowie stunt—the singer wearing a flowing blue dress and reclining on a divan, playing with his hair. The photo was based on a painting by onetime Pre-Raphaelite Dante Gabriel Rossetti, and the mood of medievalism persisted on listening to the album. But this was no exercise in Tolkienesque whimsy—Bowie's new songs had taken on an apocalyptic tone—he sang about madness, death, and in the last song, a race of long-dead supermen.

The following year, Bowie finally caught a break: a song he'd written and sold to ex Herman's Hermits singer Peter Noone became an unlikely hit. 'Oh You Pretty Things' is one of Bowie's catchiest songs, but it's also one of his most frightening. What starts out as a normal day, getting dressed, making breakfast, takes an extraordinary turn in the very first verse. The singer, stirring his coffee, looks out the window and sees a great hand coming out of a crack in the sky, reaching toward him. The singer has been chosen as a prophet, his task is to announce the end of the human race as we know it. 'Homo sapiens', says the singer, 'have outgrown their use. You'd better make way for the homo superior'.[2]

The singer's prophecy soon came true, as the *ubermensch* arrived on earth only six months later. He did not appear, as Nietzsche might have imagined, on a dramatic mountain peak silhouetted by a flash of lightning—but in the slightly less impressive surrounds of the Toby Jug pub in Tolworth. The lightning was provided by a hand-painted banner hung from the back of the stage—a red flash zigzagging across a white disc. In front of this stood a rock and roll band with 'The Spiders from Mars' painted on their drum kit. And towering over all (thanks to a pair of shiny stack-heeled boots) was the homo superior: David Bowie, now reborn as the alien rock singer Ziggy Stardust. Bowie as he later admitted, 'always had a repulsive need to be something more than human'.[3]

Bowie had read his Nietzsche, along with his Brecht and Burroughs. He'd also spent a lot of time watching Stanley Kubrick films like *2001* and *A Clockwork Orange*, from which he'd picked up the idea, as he later put it, that 'nothing was true'.[4] Over the next two years, the singer would set out to prove it.

What really pushed Bowie over the top was a 1972 interview in *Melody Maker* wherein the singer declared: 'I'm gay', and a nation choked on its tea.[5] This was the first open admission of homosexuality by a British pop star. It was also, it later transpired, a flat-out lie—but Bowie had a point to make, and the fuss his confession caused served his purpose well. His new plastic pop star had to be seen to be a destroyer of morality because morality, as Nietzsche said, is the herd instinct in the individual, and Bowie was never going to be one of a herd. The *Melody Maker* writer picked up on this immediately. Noting that Bowie, while claiming to be gay, refused to identify with or make himself available to the cause of gay lib in Britain, Michael Watts concluded that the only cause David Bowie was really interested in was David Bowie. 'It's individuality he's really trying to preserve.'[6]

'Starman', the first single from 1973's *The Rise and Fall*..., was the sound of Ziggy beaming in a message through the static and the space junk. The kids huddled around their radio in the middle of the night can just make out Ziggy's hazy cosmic jive. 'Let the children lose it...fzzzzzt...let all the children boogie...' It's been suggested that Ziggy's message, and his mission on earth, was supposed to bring peace and love to humanity, but this is not at all what he meant to do. Ziggy's arrival (heralded by a new star in the sky), his martyrdom and his resurrection undoubtedly make him a Christ-like figure, but his message is not one of tolerance, forgiveness and brotherly love. He wants us to realise our potential ('use it'), discard our moral standards ('lose it') and—in a final directive which combines the previous two in their highest form of expression— dance ('boogie'). But he is not a man of the people—he is aloof, superior and aristocratic.[7]

British critic Herbert Read has suggested that Christ's sermon on the mount—'love thy neighbour'—contains the essence of the democratic ideal.[8] Ziggy, like Nietzsche, wants nothing to do with this ideal. He is the 'special man'—the strong individual who acts in defiance of his community, the one who realises his visions at the expense of others. Ziggy is able to do this partly because he's an alien—but mostly because he's an artist. In 'Star', Ziggy contemplates the suffering of the world, and realises that it can only be redeemed by art. 'I could make it all worthwhile as a rock and roll star,' he muses.[9] His ability to view suffering as an aesthetic phenomenon means he is unlikely to be troubled by morality.

Bowie chose the lightning bolt as Ziggy's insignia because lightning is the perfect symbol for such an individual. Lightning, for Nietzsche, represented 'free power, without morality'.[10] His superman was a result of his attempt to imagine a man who could accept, and conduct such vast energies. Nietzsche is not asking us to imagine some God-like being—a blonde giant with lightning coursing through his veins. The Superman, for Nietzsche, is nothing more than a man who can accept everything—beauty, sadness, joy, madness, the awful, destructive force of nature itself, and still say 'yes' to life. That's why Zarathustra asks the people:

> *Where is the madness that will cleanse you?*
> *Where is the lightning to lick you with its tongue?*
> *behold: I teach you The Superman*
> *he is this madness, he is this lightning!*[11]

For his follow up to Ziggy Stardust, Bowie fused these two supremely anti-social motifs—madness and lightning—into one image. The cover of *Aladdin Sane* shows Ziggy with a lightning-flash painted across his face and a mercury tear pooling on his snow-white collarbone.

Bowie's magpie eye had first spied this lightning logo on the equipment cases used to carry the band's gear to his shows— 'Danger: High Voltage'.[12] Contemplating the vast energies that surge through the mains power supply and into the Spiders' amplifiers, Bowie had an epiphany—a modern-day variation on Nietzsche's lightning-storm. Bowie's rock star ideal would be a man who could accept these vast energies and dispense them freely, joyfully, immorally. It worked—as *Mojo*'s Ben Fisher must have realised when, in 1997, he described Bowie's guitarist Mick Ronson as 'a Nietzschean ubermensch, hatched straight from Bowie's consciousness'.[13] And it may have worked too well—within a couple of months the lighting flash seemed to have been appropriated by a group of rival super-beings. 'I was not a little peeved when Kiss purloined it,' Bowie later recalled. 'Purloining, after all, was my job.'[14]

Destroyer

LIKE WAGNER, PAUL Stanley understood the need for new myths in the wasteland of modern life. His first band, Wicked Lester, was going nowhere precisely because it had failed to grasp this principle. One night in 1972, Stanley's bandmate Ace Frehely symbolically killed Wicked Lester when he wrote the band's new name—which Stanley had just recently come up with—over the old one on a poster outside a club. Frehely took out a texta and wrote the word 'KISS', stylising the two 's's to make them look like twin lightning-bolts.[1]

In re-inventing themselves as a readymade rock and roll myth, the members of Kiss combined two ideas—both of which are Nietzschean. One is the lightning motif, the other is the Superhero. Inspired by the Marvel and DC comics they loved, the members of Kiss transformed themselves from a mere rock band into a league of supermen—the demon, the cat-man, the space-man, the star-child. Kiss was the first band to spell out the connection between power-chords and super-powers, first on their album covers and in their live shows; and later when they became stars of their own Marvel Comics series in 1977. The rock and roll superman now shared shelf-space in the newsagents with the *real* Superman.

In *Men of Tomorrow*, Gerard Jones traces the development of Jerry Siegel and Joe Schuster's original man of steel, Superman, to Nietzsche's ideas, which by the 1930s were popular not just in Germany—where he had been ignored for so long—but in the United States as well.[2] In Siegel's 1932 short story, *The Reign of the Superman*, the teenage author re-imagined Nietzsche's ubermensch for the readers of his self-published magazine, appropriately titled, *Science Fiction—The Advance Guard of Future Civilization*. Like many Nietzscheans of the early twentieth century, Siegel misunderstood the ubermensch—in *The Reign of The Superman*, he becomes a fantasy of personal power instead of a religious idea of transcendence. But Nietzsche might still have enjoyed Siegel's story, in which the protagonist is not the upholder of 'truth, justice, and the American way' he would later become, but a moral monster, who uses his super-powers to trample and destroy.

Superman, in his final form, would vow to constrain his elemental power in the interests of good-old-fashioned morality. But the danger implied by such power would be constantly invoked over the next seventy years of his life—not just in the Superman comics, but throughout the Superhero universe. This barely concealed threat is what draws the rock singer to the super-being. In the storylines of Superhero comics, the questions of power and responsibility that nag at the thoughtful young rock star are played out on a cosmic scale. The rock singer, as a romantic outsider, senses the tremendous power that awaits the individual who throws off social bonds forever and enjoys free energy without morality. But the singer is also burdened with a feeling of social responsibility—a burden which becomes heavier as the band's audiences start to fill stadiums. In the comic books, these two conflicting ideas are usually split between the Supervillain and the Superhero—

the first is a threat because he is powerful and selfish; the second is still powerful but feels he must help others. Glam rock stars like Bowie or Kiss tend to be more like Supervillains than superheroes—they're a-moral destroyers and corruptors, whose existence poses a threat to the status quo. But in the mythical universe of My Chemical Romance, it's not so simple. By embracing symbols of death and evil, and by portraying himself as a Byronic super-sinner, Gerard Way at first seems to be of the same type as Ziggy—who he admires intensely. But Gerard is too moral (and, as we'll see later, too democratic) to embrace this idea completely. He knows that a Kiss comic book will very likely inspire its young reader to want to play guitar, score with groupies and flirt with Satanism. But he hopes that the kids who buy My Chemical Romance action figures will grow up to be super-heroes, not a super-villains.[3] They might accidentally destroy civilisation with the awesome power of their shredding; but they'll use that same power to rescue babies from the rubble after they've done it.

Rilke: Love your loneliness.

Such a Special Guy

IN 1992, RIVERS Cuomo was still hiding in the garage with his X-Men comics and Kiss posters. Back then, he was worried we might call him a nerd or a dork. Now, he couldn't care less what we think of him. He has become the thing he used to dream about—an axe-guitar-wielding superman, a not-so-teen Titan. He can do what he likes—in or out of the garage. In 'Pork and Beans' he sings:

I'm-a do the things that I wanna do
I ain't got a thing to prove to you[1]

With 2008's *The Red Album*, Rivers Cuomo seemed finally to have busted out of the underground. The self-loathing and self-denial of the late '90s was long gone. Part of Cuomo's disgust with the cult of *Pinkerton* stemmed from his belief that emo's insistence on misery and the inability to act was profoundly unhealthy. Andy Greenwald has observed that post-*Pinkerton* emo—the period that produced lyrics like 'I'm afraid to try, I'll keep my hands by my side'—was defined by 'an arrogance derived from superior humility'.[2] Greenwald's description of emo ethics here echoes Nietzsche's thoughts on Christianity in his *On the Genealogy of Morals*. In Nietzsche's view, Judeo-Christian morality is a fairy story invented by the weak to justify their weakness. 'They are stronger,' say the oppressed, 'but we are more virtuous.' For Nietzsche, nothing could be further from the truth:

All truly noble morality grows out of triumphant self-affirmation. Slave ethics, on the other hand, begins by saying "no" to an 'outside' an 'other' and that "no" is its creative act.[3]

A rock-and-roll superman could have no use for such perverse ethics. With *The Red Album*, Cuomo traded slave morality for triumphant self-affirmation—emo self-denial for the Nietzschean philosophy of Queen's 'We Are the Champions'. The new Cuomo had no time for losers. 'One look in the mirror and I'm tickled pink,' he sang in 'Pork and Beans'. His mood was proud and defiant. No wonder he never fit in—he's not one of a herd, but a lone, inspired individual. In 'Troublemaker', Cuomo boils the romantic philosophy down to one sentence: 'There isn't anybody else exactly quite like me.'[4]

While the self-asserting superman of *The Red Album* might seem worlds away from the human wreckage at the centre of *Pinkerton*, one very important trait connects the old Rivers to the new Rivers. In 'Troublemaker' he reminds us he's a big star, and that everyone wants a piece of him. But the grabbing hands will never touch him. You won't see Rivers out having fun like everybody else—and even if you do, you might as well not be there. Here's why:

> When it's party time
> Like 1999
> I'll party by myself because I'm such a special guy[5]

In this one important respect, the new Rivers is not that different to the old Rivers. Because whether he's living in a black box, hiding in the garage, meditating, or just partying by himself, Cuomo needs solitude. But it's not just because he enjoys it, and it's not even because he needs the angst. The success of *The Red Album* shows that meditation wasn't so bad for his art after all. Turns out it wasn't the angst he needed so much as the isolation that produced it. It took him fifteen years to figure this out—Cuomo might have saved himself some trouble by reading Rainer Maria Rilke's *Letters to a Young Poet*.

Rilke was a Czech-born poet whose first mature work was produced at a time when Nietzsche's influence was virtually inescapable. Rilke's poetry is steeped in Nietzsche's proto-existentialism—his insistence on life over thought, his search for redemption in this world rather than the next. Rilke also inherited Nietzsche's supreme subjectivity—his belief that the artist creates truth rather than merely recording or revealing it.

In 1903 Rilke received an unsolicited book of poems from a young soldier named Franz Kappus, with a note asking whether the poet would mind reading them and sharing his thoughts with the author in the form of a critique. Rilke politely refused, but he and Kappus struck up a correspondence in which Rilke, while never dealing specifically with Kappus's poems, offered the young man a lifetime's worth of advice on the subject of being a poet. First of all, Rilke advised, you should stop asking for advice.

> *You are looking outside, and that is what you should*
> *most avoid right now. No one can advise or help*
> *you—no one. There is only one thing you should do.*
> *Go into yourself.*[6]

Rilke returns to the theme in his sixth letter, sent shortly before Christmas. Knowing that Kappus would be alone for the holiday season, Rilke urged him not to be frightened of loneliness, but to embrace it.

> *What is necessary, after all, is only this: solitude, vast*
> *inner solitude. To walk inside yourself and meet no*
> *one for hours—that is what you must be able to*
> *attain.*[7]

Over and over in the course of the ten letters, Rilke returns to this theme. 'Love your loneliness,' he says. This is not an easy thing to do. But Rilke suggests to his protégé that if he's really a poet, he'll find that solitude suits him, that he'd rather be there than anywhere else.

We already have an idea why. Being weird and lonely at school was a blessing in disguise for Rivers Cuomo (as it was for Billy Corgan and Gerard Way) because it gave him the experience and the insight to write his earliest songs. He made use of his melancholy by writing profoundly affecting music about his condition. But just when it seemed like he'd broken through his loneliness and connected to the world, he went out of his way to make sure that he stayed lonely—moved out of the big world, and back into the garage. Now he's triumphantly solitary—indeed, he insists on aloneness as a condition of his existence. That's because Cuomo feels that being lonely is an important part of his job, and Rilke would agree.

Rilke insists that for a good poet there is no poor subject matter since all his experience is filtered through the unique prism of his own sensibility. That's why he advises the young man to look inside himself to find out whether or not he is a poet. Cuomo insists in 'Troublemaker' that he doesn't need books because he learns by studying the lessons of his dreams, and Rilke confirms this. The outside world is overrated, he says: learn to do without it.

> ...even if you found yourself in some prison, whose walls let in none of the world's sounds—wouldn't you still have your childhood, that jewel beyond all price, that treasure house of memories? Turn your attentions to it. Try to raise up the sunken feelings of this enormous past; your personality will grow stronger, your solitude will expand and become a place where you can live in the twilight, where the noise of other people passes by, far in the distance. And if out of this turning-within, out of this immersion in your own world, poems come, then you will not think of asking anyone whether they are good or not.[8]

It's exactly this self-reliance that Cuomo developed during his long and painful apprenticeship in the garage. In 'Troublemaker' he realises it was this, and not any of the dumb stuff they tried to teach him at school, that made him an artist. At school, they'd tried to teach him arts and crafts; in his garage, he taught himself to shred on his axe guitar while gazing up at his posters of Kiss and reflecting on his emotions. Who looks stupid now? 'You wanted arts and crafts?' sings Cuomo. 'How's this for arts and crafts!' He unleashes a face-melting guitar break, and the world is put in its place.[9] This, he explains in 'The Greatest Man...' is how it's going to be from now on.

> If you don't like it—you can shove it,
> But you don't like it—you love it[10]

Cuomo knows he is a great artist because...he knows he is a great artist. Society's pronouncements on his worth have proven to be consistently unreliable—why should he care what we have to say about him or what he does? He is expressing himself authentically. What could be more important than that?

Conrad Veidt: The notions of sick brains.

Expressionism

THE AUSTRIAN PAINTER Oskar Kokoschka had an intense admiration for children's art. When children draw people, they don't worry overly much about details—unless the details are emotionally important to them. An aunt's curly hair will be obsessively laboured over if that's what the artist loves about the aunt—who cares how many fingers she's got or whether or not she has a nose? Kokoschka would maintain this attitude to portraiture all his life. 'When I paint a portrait,' he declared in his autobiography, 'I am not conerned with the externals of a person.'[1] For Kokoschka, such things were the business of the photographer, or the lawyer drawing up a will.

In his autobiography, he admits he may have given one of his portrait subjects only four fingers on one hand: 'Did I forget to paint the fifth? In any case, I don't miss it. To me it was more important to cast light on my sitter's psyche than to enumerate details like five fingers, two ears, one nose.'[2]

Kokoschka was a truth-teller—as Viennese painters were expected to be. But his truth was internal, not external, and was celebrated as such. 'I am proud of a Kokoschka's testimony,' wrote the poet Karl Kraus, 'because the truth of a genius that distorts is higher than the truth of anatomy, and because in the presence of art reality is only an optical illusion.'[3]

Kokoschka first made a name for himself as an artist in 1907 with a book of poems and woodcuts called *The Dreaming Boys*. This highly symbolic little book, which the artist dedicated to his mentor Gustav Klimt, was inspired by Kokoschka's life as a teenage monster. To his horror, at the age of thirteen, the artist had grown freakishly tall, sprouted hair in obscene places, given voice to guttural growls and bat-like squeaks, and felt overcome by unspeakable longings. In his verses Kokoschka described:

A hesitant
desire / the unfounded
feeling of shame before
what is growing / and the
stripling state / the over-
flowing and solitude[4]

Just as he dispensed with traditional rhyme schemes in his poems, in the wood-cut illustrations that accompanied *The Dreaming Boys* Kokoschka took gross liberties with the proportions of the human body to give his readers a sense of how isolated he felt, and how freakish and unwieldy his new body seemed to him. Inspired by Van Gogh's portraits, and by his own training as a children's art teacher, he simplified his drawing into brutal, expressive shapes and thick black lines.

In 'The dreaming boys', Kokoschka warned polite Viennese society that a monster had grown up in its midst, and was even now staring hungrily at those well-fed children through the gap in the hedge:

> *When the evening bell dies away*
> *I steal into your garden into your pastures*
> *I break into your peaceful corral*[5]

The teenage Tim Burton also expressed his alienation from society by imagining himself as a monster—first in his sketch for the character who would become Edward Scissorhands, and later in the character of Vincent. Vincent, as Burton's poem reminds us, only looks like a normal seven-year old boy— inside, he's a diabolical fiend, obsessed with visions of madness, death and despair. Actually, Vincent doesn't really look that normal either, with his sharp, angular cheekbones, deathly pallor and sunken eyes. But it's hard to tell, because there is no objective reality in *Vincent*—everything—including our image of Vincent himself, is distorted through the prism of Vincent's sensibility. And whatever there was of external 'reality' at the start has disintegrated by the end, as Vincent's torments overtake him. In the 'nightmare' sequence in his Tower of Doom, Vincent's psychic stress expands out from his head to warp the architecture of his little room. As he struggles to get to the door, the walls and ceiling become horribly distended, and the door itself looms up like a crooked tombstone.[6] Here, as always, Burton insists on showing us how things feel rather than how they look. In *Edward Scissorhands*, the castle's lurching architecture is impractical—if not impossible. In his previous film, *Batman*, the city belches steam and the buildings loom threateningly over the populace. Elsewhere, trees curl up their branches like Art-Nouveau latticework, and hallways disappear into infinity—in Tim Burton's world, reality does not conform to the evidence of photographic records. But this approach is not without precendence.

Burton rejected the idea that art could be taught or learned. But he learned that he didn't need to be taught—that he should trust the peculiar visions in his own mind—by watching old horror movies. In the classic horror films of the 1920s and 30s, extreme emotions—fear, paranoia, madness—tend to be expressed in 'stressed out' visual forms. In *Bride of Frankenstein*, Dr Praetorius's laboratory is architecturally insane, but perfectly expressive of the mood in which he works. And as his efforts to create a mate for the monster reach fever pitch, the walls themselves seem to pull back in horror at his perversion of nature.

The roots of this approach can be traced back to one of the very first horror films, Robert Wiene's *The Cabinet of Dr Caligari*. Almost sixty years separate Wiene's silent classic and Burton's first films—but the family resemblance is so strong that, looking at stills from Caligari, with its lurching cityscapes and gothic curlicues, we half expect to see Winona Ryder peering out of the shot. Conrad Veidt as Cesare, dressed from head to foot in black, his face a white mask slashed with black marks, looks uncannily like Johnny Depp in *Edward Scissorhands*, and the pasty, shabby-looking Dr Caligari seems to be the not-too distant ancestor of Danny DeVito's Penguin in *Batman Returns*. Burton, with his intensely subjective approach to movie making and his artist's flair for visual interest, was always going to be susceptible to the idea contained within *Caligari*, that form can—and should—be altered by feeling. Of course, they never showed old German silent films at the drive-in in Burbank where Burton grew up. But they did show Tod Browning's *Dracula* and James Whale's *Frankenstein*—both of which owe a considerable debt to *Caligari*. And considering that these two films are the foundation upon which the whole monster / horror film genre is based, it's no wonder Burton should end up showing the influence of Caligari in his films—even if he didn't actually see it until much later.

The story of Caligari is presented to us in the film by the mentally deranged Francis—and Francis's world, acccordingly, looks completely deranged on the screen. When the mysterious Caligari makes his way through the city, the city itself seems to close in on him—the houses and shopfronts behave more like trees in fairy-tale forest than buildings. In the background, staircases disappear at impossible angles, and windows curl upwards into crooked smiles. Later, we catch Caligari's sleep-walking servant Cesare in the act of committing a horrible crime. He steals into a woman's bedroom and stabs her with a knife. But even before he does, it looks as though the whole room is conspiring to murder the hapless victim, shadows point threateningly to the corner of the room where she sleeps, even the crazy angle at which the window frame bisects the glass suggests violence.[7]

In *Caligari*, as in Kokoschka's portraits, 'correct' appearances are pushed out of shape by intense feelings. This is no coincidence—the artists who created *Caligari*'s striking backdrops moved in the same circles as Kokoschka. Weine commissioned designs from three artists: Hermann Warm, Walter Rohrig and Walter Reimann, all of whom were associated with a Berlin art magazine called *Der Sturm*. *Der Sturm* was the brainchild of Herwath Walden, a tireless promoter of modern art in Germany, whose Cologne Sonderbund exhibition of 1912 had introduced many German painters for the first time to the works of Gaugin and Van Gogh. He also organised and promoted Oskar Kokoschka's first exhibition in Germany.[8]

The artists associated with *Der Sturm* could be said to have one important idea in common—all were trying to find a way of expressing intense psychic or emotional states using paint on canvas. And by 1911, people had started calling this kind of art Expressionism. It was never a movement as such, but the term now serves to cover a number of 'mini-movements' active in Germany before, during and after the First World War. These included the group centred around Walden's gallery and publishing house—including Kokoschka, Wassily Kandinsky, Franz Marc and Arnold Schoenberg, as well as another group from Dresden known as *Die Brücke* ('The Bridge').

For the founding members of *Die Brücke*, extreme emotion was the only place left to go in art. Objective reality, which had already been undermined by the Impressionists, had been completely discredited by Munch and Van Gogh. Now, the artist must turn inward in search of truth. Art teachers could teach them nothing—as Fritz Schumacher, who instructed many of the early Die Brücke artists in drawing, would discover. Schumacher recalls a particularly heated exchange with a young Erich Heckel:

> *When I criticized the drawing for its carelessness he invoked his right to stylise. I put it that a person must be able to draw correctly before going on to stylisation … but I did not convince him. He said that the only important thing so far as he was concerned was the seizure of a total expression.*[9]

Heckel's colleague, Emil Nolde agreed. 'The art of an artist,' wrote Nolde, who joined *Die Brücke* in 1906, 'must be his own art.'[10] In their paintings, Kirchner and Nolde took the lessons they'd learned from Klimt, Munch, Gaugin, African and Islander art and Gothic prints, and synthesised them into terrifying visions of the human soul under stress. Early Expressionist painting takes a crucial extra step away from so-called 'objective' reality. Where in Van Gogh and Munch reality is strained, but remains recognisable, in Kirchner and Nolde the world of appearances seems fatally cracked. Perspective collapses, shadows abruptly reverse direction, human faces are sawn off into primitive masks or stripped of their flesh to reveal grinning skulls.

This decisive move from outer appearance to inner truth opened up exciting new vistas for artists, but it lead to enormous problems when it came time for these painters to meet their public. Expressionism precipitated what the art historians like to call 'a crisis of subjectivity'—which in layman's terms means that viewers, by and large, thought Expressionist art looked horrible, and that the artists who made it were incompetent—if not actually insane. Who looks at a beautiful woman's face and sees a flat mask with a stripe for a nose? What kind of degenerate is this painter if he can't even put a wall at a right angle to the floor?

That Expressionist art was generally thought to represent the visions of madmen made it the perfect visual language for *Caligari*, which, after all, is a story told to us by a madman. This made its radical designs acceptable to the public, in the same way that atonal noise, while deemed inappropriate for the dinner table or the nightclub, is regularly used to indicate warped mental states in thrillers and horror movies to this day, where it goes by virtually unnoticed—at least on a conscious level. One reviewer of Caligari noted that:

> *The idea of rendering the notions of sick brains…*
> *through expressionist pictures is not only well*
> *conceived but also well realised. Here this style has a*
> *right to exist…*[11]

But Wiene let his expressionist scene painters have the last laugh. As Siegfried Kracauer points out, the final episode of *Caligari* is *not* told from Francis's point of view. So, since we're no longer seeing the world through the eyes of a mental patient, the wonky chimneys of *Caligari*, should—in theory—straighten themselves out in accordance with the laws of 'correct' visual perception.[12] But this is not what happens. Expressionism, Weine seems to be saying, has a right to exist in any case, because this is what life in the early twentieth century feels like—and if it looks horrible or insane, that's because modern life is horrible and insane.

The Pain Threshold

It is hard to live in the age of psychoanalysis and feel oneself detached from the dominant public savagery. In this way, at least, the makers of horror films are more in tune with contemporary anxiety than most poets.[1]

A ALVAREZ WROTE those words in 1962, the same year *A Clockwork Orange* was published. In Burgess's novel, when Alex likes something a lot, he says it's 'real horrorshow', and Alvarez, too, had the feeling that horror might be closer to modern truth—and therefore beauty—than what we usually think of as beautiful.

This is an idea that was unthinkable in 1750, already in sight by 1850 and artist's gospel by 1900. When Gustav Klimt was accused of flinging filth in the faces of Vienna's youth with his philosophy mural, his defenders argued that the vision of horror in Klimt's painting was simply the truth, and that a society can only ignore the strong and bitter realities presented by artists at its own risk.[2] This kind of argument was guaranteed to hit the late nineteenth century bourgeois where it hurt. Thanks to Wagner, the Viennese middle classes had come to accept as gospel the idea that art is a form of spiritual instruction, and the artist a kind of prophet, whose dire warnings the populace ignore at their peril.

The artist's stance as misunderstood prophet only grew more entrenched as the twentieth century got under way. 'Our age seeks much,' wrote composer Arnold Schoenberg in 1910. 'What it has found above all is: comfort. That permeates full-scale into the realm of ideas and makes it too comfortable for our own good.'³ When Schoenberg talked about lighting a fire under the Viennese bourgeois's comfortable behind, he wasn't just striking a pose. Schoenberg was many things—a rebel, an outsider, a pretty good expressionist painter, a great musical mind and a hugely influential writer and teacher, but no-one could make a case that either he or his music were in any way pleasant. Nor was he popular; in fact, he often seemed to go out of his way not to be. Aside from some early efforts in commercial dance music, Schoenberg was swayed very little by the currents of popular taste, critical opinion or his own economic situation. He was influenced, as far as possible, by only one thing: himself. He set out his case for self-expression at all costs in a letter to the painter Wassily Kandinsky in 1911:

> ...art belongs to the subconscious! One must express oneself! Express oneself directly! Not one's taste, or one's upbringing, or one's intelligence, knowledge or skill...⁴

In this, Schoenberg was very much a product of the Viennese milieu that produced Kokoschka and Gustav Klimt. Like them, he believed that the purpose of art was to 'show modern man his true face', and that the artist had no hope of doing this if he was not, first and foremost, honest with himself. He felt he could no more ignore the dictates of his heart and his emotions than a biblical prophet could ignore the voice of God.

In his music, Schoenberg faithfully and unflinchingly presented his appalling truths—the things he saw in the darkest recesses of his heart. But he found that, by and large, the people who heard them turned away—closed the door on his truth and settled back into their easychairs. Now he knew he was right! Of course his art was terrifying to them—*life* is terrifying. The more uncompromising and truthful Schoenberg was in his art, the greater his isolation from society became. But he kept going, because he believed in only one kind of truth—subjective truth. And even as his own psyche began to fall apart under the strain, he found himself more and more determined to confront the fact of his own crack-up in his art, because here, he felt was the greatest thing he had to offer the world.

In 1912, Schoenberg found the perfect vehicle to express these anxieties. He was commissioned by a Viennese actress named Albertine Zehme to compose some piano music for a recitation she was planning. Her songs were to be adaptations of a series of poems by the Belgian Albert Giraud. In Schoenberg's hands, *Pierrot Lunaire* became, as the expressionist painter Paul Klee put it, 'a mad melodrama'.[5] Pierrot, being a clown, is in the entertainment business. But he chafes against this—he stops doing comedy and starts expressing his emotions because he feels he has important truths to share with humanity. The audience, predictably, hates this. 'Do something funny!' they demand. Funny? Pierrot climbs up on an altar and rips open his clown-suit:

The hand, consecrated to God,
tears the priest's habit
to celebrate the gruesome eucharist
by the dazzling glare of gold.

With a gesture of benediction
he shows to the fearful souls
the dripping red Host
with bloody fingers: his heart—,
to celebrate the gruesome eucharist.[6]

The spectators would much prefer that the sad clown put his horrible guts away and got on with the business of making them laugh. But Pierrot will not be deterred. Of course they would rather be pleased than appalled, of course they hate him for showing them what they would prefer to see hidden. But he has a heart that is bigger and braver than anything they can throw at him. 'Look,' he seems to be saying, holding this still-beating heart out to the people. '*This* is what I am prepared to do for you.'

Gerard Way strikes a similar pose in 'Welcome to the Black Parade'. The singer looks around at the chaos of the world, and tries to make sense of what seems like madness. He sees 'the rise and fall, the bodies in the streets', and a great tide of misery and hate. But these horrors only make him more determined than ever to carry on showing the world its true face. This, after all, is his job. Gerard—who once confessed he was 'addicted to truth and honesty'—fulfils the role society has demanded of artists since the late nineteenth century—to be the bearer of bad news. In a conversation with Liza Minnelli in *Interview* magazine in 2007, Gerard made his position clear:

> *I think we just went into it with the attitude that we're going to be different to everybody else because we're simply going to be ourselves. We're going to sing about things that other people wouldn't sing about…that is to say, we're going to sometimes put extremely difficult subjects in pop music…*[7]

Gerard means to make us uncomfortable. He knows we'd *like* it if he just sang about 'driving a truck, smoking weed and objectifying women'—as he put it on another occasion.[8] But he knows that what we *need* is the truth, and that this truth is, by nature, unpleasant.

Sprechstimme

IN *PIERROT LUNAIRE*, Schoenberg portrayed a performer who was out of phase with his audience's expectations by giving his singer music that was out of tune. This was no accident—Schoenberg knew what he was doing, and had already been doing it for a couple of years. Back in 1864, Wagner's *Tristan* had suggested, with its famous opening chord, that the rules of music could be broken if they could no longer contain the force of the composer's emotion. Strauss, inspired by Wagner's example, would bend musical relationships further out of shape in *Salome*. But it was left to Schoenberg to break the chords that bind forever with his first atonal works in 1908.

These pioneering works of Schoenberg's were sometimes referred to as 'expressionist'; and like the painters with whom he associated, Schoenberg found that by allowing his emotions to dictate the form of his music in defiance of all rules, he had completely alienated himself from his public. But as with Wiene's canny use of Expressionist décor in Caligari, Schoenberg discovered he could get away with his mad music within the context of *Pierrot*, since he was using it to express madness. Here, this style had a right to exist, and *Pierrot* was—unusually for Schoenberg—a hit.

But atonality wasn't the only trick Schoenberg had up his sleeve in bringing the eerie emotional world of *Pierrot* to life. Instead of arranging Giraud's poems as songs, Schoenberg gave his vocalist what he called 'Sprechstimme'. Here, the singer talks in rhythm over the music, suggesting—rather than singing—the pitches, and only occasionally holding sustained notes. Again, within the context of *Pierrot*, this unusual technique worked a treat. As Allen Shawn puts it in Arnold Schoenberg's Journey:

What pushes [Pierrot Lunaire] over the edge into the world of the sublimely bizarre is how the music combines with the singer who isn't quite singing. Here, a kind of universal madness has been fixed on paper with clarity and art.[1]

Appropriately for a meditation on the divide between art and entertainment, Sprechstimme was a technique Schoenberg had become familiar with when he was employed in show business. Between 1901 and 1902, the young composer had worked for a cabaret company—Baron von Wolzogen's *Überbrettl*—writing popular songs for drinking and dancing. Later, after he'd made the most gut-wrenchingly confessional music of his early career, and then forced himself to confront the fact that people just wanted him to be an entertainer, he would refer to his cabaret music again, pressing it into service to describe his painful alienation from his audience. The Sprechstimme technique he'd learned writing for the cabaret was used to suggest a singer who was somehow dangerously detached from his material, and by extension, his life. Schoenberg's music for *Pierrot Lunaire* is cabaret gone horribly wrong—the singer was supposed to pull out his hits—but what's this? He's pulled out his heart!

Today, musicians routinely espouse Schoenbergian philosophy. Billy Corgan echoes his insistence that 'one must express oneself' ('I do feel a responsibility to articulate what I feel') and draws the same conclusions from this as Schoenberg—that is, that if the artist's emotions lead him into territory that is alienating or confusing to the listener, then the listener had better suck it up. Corgan insisted that the future of rock and roll lay in music 'so emotionally explosive it's hard to listen to'.[2]

But, as we've seen, not one of the thousands of kids in Zero shirts at Lollapalooza had any trouble listening to Corgan's emotionally explosive music. In fact, they wanted him to keep exploding. The situation of *Pierrot Lunaire* was reversed; here, the audience *insisted* that the singer rip out his heart. This demand for emotional intensity nearly killed Robert Smith in the early '80s, and it scared Rivers Cuomo away from emotional music for almost a decade. In the meantime, the modern misery industry grew to spectacular proportions. In Saves The Day's 'Jukebox Breakdown', Chris Conley—who was starting to feel like some kind of automated human unhappiness dispenser—accused his audience of conspiring to kill him.

> All you want from me
> Is a broken heart
> and a mouthful of blood.[3]

Yes, we do! said the kids in the crowd. Schoenberg didn't know how easy he had it. He railed against his audience for wanting the happy clown when he was dying inside. He had to rip out his heart to show them just how bad he was feeling. But in the twenty-first century this situation is reversed. The modern emo audience demands nothing less than the artist's still-beating heart, served up fresh, every night of the week for the length of a twelve-month tour.

Needless to say, ripping out your heart on a nightly basis is hard to sustain. By the end of My Chemical Romance's *The Black Parade*, Gerard Way is starting to feel the long-term effects of all this soul-baring and blood-letting. On the album's final number, he sings:

> Give them blood, blood,
> gallons of the stuff
> give them all that they can drink and it will never be
>   enough.[4]

The situation is terrifying, but Gerard sings this in a light, jaunty ironic way—you can almost see him tipping his hat and twirling his cane. The arrangement has just a touch of dissonance to indicate the artist's impending crack-up, and Gerard deploys a little Sprechstimme to give the song that weightless 'I've lost too much blood and I'm getting dizzy' feel. The music is pure cabaret—a small group wheezing out a steady oom-pah. Gerard's voice is even put through an effect that makes it sound like he's singing through a megaphone—a popular means of getting the audience's attention in the pre-amplification days of the literary cabarets. But the effect the band are aiming for is not so much the Überbrettl of 1901 as the Troika circa 1930.

Siouxsie Sioux: Brand new people...

Everything Collapses

MY CHEMICAL ROMANCE weren't the only post-emo outfit to revive the spirit of the literary cabarets in the early twenty-first century. *The Black Parade* appeared hot on the heels of Panic at the Disco's debut album, *A Fever You Can't Sweat Out*—a record shot through with hot jazz rhythms and dressed to the nines in high literary style. Songwriter Ryan Ross poured ironies on his agonies and crammed so many sub-clauses into his parentheses that singer Brendan Urie just barely managed to fit the words between the beats. And yet the band always kept their cool—Ross's tales of bad sex, cheap laughs and existential boredom were presented with a lip-sticked pout and a mascara-ed wink. Emo kids the world over fell head-over-heels in love.

Caberet, as music writer Norman Lebrecht has observed, thrives in societies in decline. This might seem odd at first. Civilisation is falling down around your ears—is this really the best time to be drinking absinthe until two in the morning and experimenting with make-up? But for the cabaret singer, there is no better response to social collapse. Panic at the Disco know this instinctively. 'Looks like the end of history', sings Urie on Panic's 2008 single, 'Nine in the Afternoon'. 'Oh, no—it's just the end of the world.' Urie delivers these lines like he's seen it all before, and will see it again. In a sense, he has, and he will.

In Berlin, following the end of the First World War, the world was also about to end. Faced with a pile of war debts—debts which the shattered nation was in no position to repay—the German chancellory came up with the novel solution of simply printing more money. The value of the Deutschmark plummeted, and the moral standards of the capital fell quickly in its wake. Dostoyevsky, it seemed, had been right. The modern world's shopkeeper philosophy had effectively replaced real values with monetary ones. Now that money was worth nothing, life had become meaningless. 'Standards and values disappeared,' writes musicologist Douglas Jarman. 'Berlin was transformed into the Babylon of the world.'

But the collapse of morals turned out to be good news for the owners of nightclubs, where—as Jarman observes—business continued as usual. In the Berlin cabarets of the early 1920s, jaunty, jazz-inflected pop tunes told tales of political subversion and sexual perversion. Even after the mark stabilised in 1923, and Germany regained some sense of order, the cabarets continued to flourish as hotbeds of satire and sleaze. But after the Wall Street crash of 1929, Germany's economy spiralled out of control again. Predictably, in the cabarets, business boomed. Once again, all bets were off, and everything was permitted, with the sole exception of bourgeois conformity—the cabaret's arch-enemy.

In 1931—with unemployment creeping toward the six million mark and the capital edging toward civil war—an English expat named Christopher Isherwood described a typical night on the town, in his novel, *Goodbye to Berlin*.

> *The couples were dancing with hands on each other's hips, yelling into each other's faces, streaming with sweat. An orchestra in Bavarian costume whooped and drank and perspired beer. The place stank like a zoo.*[1]

Christopher's closest friend in *Goodbye to Berlin* is a nightclub singer called Sally Bowles. Sally seems to survive on a diet of Prairie Oysters and cigarettes. She refuses Christopher's offers of more substantial fare by saying:

> *I just don't want to eat anything at all. I feel all marvellous and ethereal, as if I was a medieval saint or something. You've no idea how glorious it feels…Have a chocolate, darling?*[2]

Like many of Christopher's friends in *Goodbye to Berlin*, Sally has lost the trick of acting naturally, if she ever had it. But to compensate, she has become very good at acting—and not just on the stage. Sally is unconvinced by life—reality seems unreal to her. Nazi Putsch or Communist Revolution? Eat and live or starve and die? Have another chocolate, darling? But despite Sally's inability to take it seriously, reality won't go away either. So Sally—being a consummate professional—has resolved to put in a convincing performance.

Isherwood had no way of knowing it, but his snapshot of Berlin on the brink would go on to become one of the founding texts of glam rock. Isherwood's portrait of a decadent society in decline in *Goodbye To Berlin*, his characters' ironic, detached attitude to life—even the book's title—would provide David Bowie with the atmosphere of his sequel to

Ziggy Stardust, Aladdin Sane. In *Goodbye to Berlin*, the news is all bad; one newspaper headline reads
EVERYTHING COLLAPSES.[3]

And this is precisely the reason why no-one seems to care very much about anything besides having a good time. In the face of the apocalypse, what else can you do? Bowie's *Ziggy Stardust* had begun with the news that the world would end in five years. Now, in *Aladdin Sane*, Bowie announced that there was no reason why you shouldn't do whatever you liked. Life was simply a tragedy, which would soon be over. Might as well have some fun. 'Panic in Detroit' describes a society in its death throes—the kids turn up at school and find that their teachers have simply stopped work. Sure, children are the future—but what if there's no future? The kids scream, run out into the street and start smashing things. Bowie reports on this with his usual combination of alien detachment and high melodrama.

On the album's best song, 'Time', Ziggy puts the fate of humanity into perspective. It's a cabaret number—the singer sits on a bar stool smoking a cigarette while pianist Mike Garson throws Schoenbergian shapes over his keyboard, complicating 'Time''s Weimar-jazz arrangement with expressionist dissonances. 'Time!' sings Ziggy,

> *He speaks of senseless things*
> *His script is you and me*[4]

'Time', like many of Bowie's songs, betrays the influence of composer Kurt Weill—a songwriter who virtually epitomised the cultural world of the Weimar Republic. In his memoir, *A Little Yes and a Big No*, the painter George Grosz recalled that 'you could hear [Weill's] songs everywhere you went in those days'.[5] Weill inherited the Wagnerian ideal of music-theatre as a means to repair a fragmented society. But he had no time for Wagner's emotional excesses. Weill replaced the

Ring of the Niebelungen with the *Threepenny Opera*, the most famous of his collaborations with Bertolt Brecht. The opera's best-known song, 'The Ballad of Mack the Knife', is typical Brecht–Weill. It observes the worst aspects of human behaviour in a society on the brink, but does so over a tune that once heard, never leaves your head. Later in the 70s, Bowie would record Weill's 'Alabama Song', perform many of his songs live, and come very close to starring in a film adaptation of *The Threepenny Opera*.

Bowie's interest in Weill's music was part of a larger fascination with Weimar culture. He was (and still is) a keen admirer of expressionist painting and film—the set designs for his *Diamond Dogs* tour were strongly influenced by *The Cabinet of Dr Caligari* and *Metropolis*. Later, when glam rock went mainstream, he said he felt very upset that 'people who'd obviously never seen *Metropolis* and had never heard of Christopher Isherwood were becoming Glam Rockers'.[6] In the summer of 1976 he and Iggy Pop moved into an apartment in Isherwood's old neighbourhood, the Schoneburg district of Berlin. On the cover of *Heroes*, he made an explicit homage to the expressionists, posing in imitation of an Erich Heckel painting he'd seen at Die Brücke museum. In the photo, Bowie's hands are raised at an awkward, theatrical angle, bent out of shape by the stress of modern life. His face has been reduced to a black and white mask, his cheeks are hollow, his eyes have a haunted look.

This portrait of Bowie is also a very close cousin to the one of Iggy Pop on the cover of *The Idiot*—an album Bowie produced and played on while the two were living in Berlin. On 'Nightclubbing', the pair takes us with them on one of their nocturnal escapades through the divided city:

> *We're seeing people*
> *Brand new people*
> *They're something to see.*[7]

The brand-new people do brand-new dances, he tells us, 'like the nuclear bomb'. This, as you've probably guessed is the dance of the damned. Why not twist your body out of shape and wreck yourself with pills and liquor? With everything collapsing, anything goes.

Bowie's timing was, as usual, impeccable. The same year, the Sex Pistols declared that, in the face of the apocalypse, morality was bunk. 'When there's no future, how can there be sin?' asked Johnny Rotten. 'We're the future,' he insisted, pointing to the nocturnal freaks crawling out of the city's garbage, 'your future!'[8] Sure enough, Iggy's new people had appeared, growing out of the city the way Cesare seemed to grow out of the expressionist décor in *Caligari*. Drawn by the aura of sin and subversion around the Sex Pistols and their manager, Malcolm McLaren, a strange crowd of teenagers from the London suburb of Bromley joined the group's entourage early in 1976. Siouxsie Sioux was eighteen at the time, and was determined to propel herself as far as possible from the stifling conformity of Bromley. She'd already tried to find work as a model, but the agencies had rejected her because she was too skinny and wore too much make-up. Anyone else might have been disheartened by this, but Siouxsie was already cultivating a personal style that had nothing whatever to do with the blonde, healthy, suntanned look the agencies were after. She'd first seen the light three years earlier while lying in a hospital bed, recovering from a serious illness. Switching on *Top of the Pops*, she saw David Bowie singing 'Starman'. It was, as Siouxsie's future collaborator Robert Smith once told Richard Kingsmill, the sort of thing that changes lives.[9] Bowie looked deathly pale, painfully thin, generally unwell…and fabulous! Siouxsie cheered up instantly. 'I'd lost so much weight and got so skinny that Bowie actually made me look cool.'[10]

By the time she'd fallen in with the Sex Pistols, Siouxsie had turned ill-health into a fashion statement—and something more, an existential protest against bourgeoise comfort. Pale skin and dark eyes said to the world: 'I am a creature of the night—I stay up too late and punish my body in unthinkable ways. But I do it because I will never settle for the half-life of the suburbs, the stifling comfort of work, dinner, TV, sleep, work ...' Siouxsie and her friends—John, Blanche, Tracey and Berlin—knew they were better than this, and set out to prove it in every way. 'The only thing that was looked down upon,' she told Jon Savage, 'was suburbia. I hated Bromley: I thought it was small and narrow-minded. There was this trendy wine bar called Pips, and I got Berlin to wear this dog-collar, and I walked in with Berlin following me, and people's jaws just hit the tables ... People were scared!'[11]

Berlin was only fifteen years old, but had already reinvented herself as a Weimar-era nightclub singer in bowler hat and fishnets. Cabaret, as Norman Lebrecht has observed, thrives in societies in decline[12]—which is why Bowie used it as one of the harbingers of the apocalypse on *Aladdin Sane*. Berlin from Bromley sensed this connection between England circa 1976 and Germany 1929 intuitively. 'I can't tell you the parallels between those days and *Goodbye to Berlin*,' she told Jon Savage. 'We were living it out, the whole bit.'[13]

Berlin knew what a society in decline felt like from Isherwood's novel. But she knew what it *looked* like because she'd seen the movie. *Goodbye to Berlin* had first been adapted as a popular play called *I Am a Camera*, then a musical with songs by Fred Ebb and John Kander in 1966 (which Bowie saw as a teenager and loved), and finally, as a film directed by Bob Fosse and released in 1972 as *Cabaret*.[14] Joel Grey, who plays the MC at the Kit Kat Klub, was one of the few actors to be retained for the movie from the stage version. In the film, Grey wears a thick mask of black and white make-up that pushes his face into an exaggerated smirk, like an expressionist painting come to life. 'Wilkommen, Bienvenue, Welcome!' he sings, by way of greeting the assortment of local scene-makers and gawking tourists who've come to see the show. He hams, winks and mugs his way through his duties, a model of ironic detachment and nocturnal sleaze. For the Bromley contingent, Grey's show stealing performance embodied a whole philosophy of life.

Liza Minnelli: Where are your troubles now?

Life Is a Cabaret

IN *Cabaret*, THE world is about to end. But in the Kit Kat Klub, it might as well not exist. 'Where are your troubles now?' Grey asks the audience after another bawdy, gut-busting tune: Forgotten! In here, life is beautiful...[1]

The song the audience have just heard is 'Life is a Cabaret', the singer is Sally Bowles—played in the film by Liza Minnelli. In the song, Sally tells a story about a friend she knew in Chelsea who did whatever she liked and never thought about tomorrow. Elsie lived in a tiny rented room and died alone. At her funeral all the decent respectable folk from the neighborhood snickered self-righteously; 'Well, that's what comes of too much pills and liquor'.[2] But this is not the moral of the story. The moral of the story is: Elsie from Chelsea is a hero. Why? Because life is pointless, work is futile, love is fleeting, and the world is steadily marching toward the brink of war. Again.

So why not kill yourself with booze and pills? Why not sin, and sin proudly? At least you'll enjoy yourself while you're here. All you respectable folk can do what you like, says the singer, her voice starting to tremble, her eyes starting to pop.

> *As for me*
> *I made my mind up*
> *Back in Chelsea*
> *When I go*
> *I'm goin' like Elsie!*[3]

At this point, Liza Minnelli's performance takes on an almost religious intensity, as she sings us through Sally's epiphany, the means by which she has learned to transcend her meaningless life and the world's meaningless collapse.

> *Life is a cabaret old chum*
> *It's only a cabaret old chum*
> *And I love a cabaret!*[4]

Now, as the MC says, life is beautiful. *Cabaret* is not just about distracting yourself from the threat of social collapse with a bit of harmless fun. It's about learning to see life aesthetically. It's about seeing the suffering of the world turned into a song, and then beginning to understand that the song is not only a consolation for suffering—it *justifies* the suffering.

If this sounds a little Nietzschean, it ought to. Cabaret—the style, and by extension, the movie—owes a great deal of its character to Nietzsche. German cabaret began with Baron von Wolzogen's *Überbrettl* in 1900. *Brettl* is the German word for the 'little boards' upon which the cabaret performers plied their trade—Wolzogen attached the Nietzschean prefix, *über*, to his company name, to show that, while the boards might be little, the ambitions of his new cabaret were anything but. The

Nietzschean overtones, as Peter Conrad explains in *Modern Times Modern Places*, were absolutely intentional. 'The Berlin cabarets, explicitly invoking Nietzsche as their founder, encouraged the uprising of rude, savage nature against anaemic society.'[5] The German cabaret was intended as a place where one could sin boldly, and reflect on suffering with the mocking laughter of the 'higher man'. The high romantic irony of Bowie's 'Time', Kander and Ebb's 'Life Is a Cabaret' and Lou Reed's 'Satellite of Love' (which Bowie produced), all retain this Olympian perspective—a residue of the cabaret's original manifesto—which is crucial to their appeal.

In the brief period of optimism preceding the crash of 1929, Brecht and Weill re-imagined the cabaret as having a constructive social function. Cabaret during this time took on a strong left-wing flavour. But the presence of Nietzsche in the cabaret's history explains why the genre tends to appeal to those with an aristocratic, rather than a democratic attitude to life and art. In *Stardust*, Tony Zanetta remarks on Bowie's superior attitude to his audience at his first Ziggy shows—so different from the 'I'm just a regular guy like you' image cultivated by the Californian bands of the day. Bowie, says Zanetta, 'projects an upper-middle class patrician quality, and seems impressively elegant.'[6] This aristocratic quality in Bowie made it very easy for him to slip into the role required of him in a song like 'Time', that of the aloof observer to whom suffering is merely a form of play. It also made him an important reference point for those who were caught up in the energy of punk, but unable to relate to its democratic ideals. The Clash used to invite their fans, en masse, to sleep on the floor of their hotel rooms after shows. Siouxsie and her Banshees were having none of it. 'I mean, no!' laughed a horrified Steve Severin in Simon Reynolds' 'Rip it Up'..., 'we'd let them stay out in the rain!'[7] When Siouxsie says that the only thing she and he friends looked down upon was suburbia, she echoes Nietzsche's horror at 'the mob hotchpotch'. 'Oh disgust! Disgust! Disgust!' wrote the most un-democratic philosopher in 1884.

In 1972 Bowie's *Ziggy Stardust* and Bob Fosse's *Cabaret* were ideal companions. Both offered a view of a society on the brink of collapse, and both suggested an aesthetic view of suffering as the solution. Both end heroically—the world is shown to be cruel, dangerous and corrupt, but the hero takes the stage for one more song with a great 'nevertheless'. Liza Minnelli's 'Life is a Cabaret' and Bowie's 'Rock and Roll Suicide' both insist that tragedy will redeem us and justify our suffering. But where *Ziggy Stardust* ends with a grand flourish of strings and a decisive 'home' chord, *Cabaret* strikes a more ambiguous note.

'Where are your troubles now?' asks the MC. 'Forgotten!' We have to admit he's right. The singer has stood up on stage and said 'yes' to life—to all of life. In doing so, she has become that thing that Nietzsche could never have imagined (because he was scared of women)—a superwoman. Here is a woman, we think, who cannot only cope with madness, death and societal collapse, but actually enjoy it—even laugh at it. We imagine, as we watch her, that we might be that brave and that bold. And here, in the cabaret, where everything is permitted, it seems possible. To be always a yea-sayer, to take the worst that life can throw at us and laugh at it.

But as Nietzsche knew, being a yea-sayer is not the same as saying 'all is for the best in the best of all possible worlds' or 'it's all good'. To know whether you have what it takes to be a superman or superwoman, you have to be able to grasp suffering on an endless loop, you have to be able to swallow the notion that the war you have just lived through will be followed by another, and another and another. Now, as the MC goes backstage to wipe off his make-up, Fosse's camera pans around the bar, and our new aesthetic attitude to life is put to its most gruesome test. Refracted through the prism of a whisky glass, we can see a group of men in brown shirts with red armbands sitting in the corner of the bar. Life, Fosse seems to be saying, will not be beautiful much longer. Can you say yes to World War Two?

Mother War

GERARD WAY FIRST saw *Cabaret* when he was just 'a little kid'.[1] It didn't just happen to be on TV one night, it was shown to him—as part of a broader education in art, theatre and music—by his grandmother, Elena Lee Rush. The film had a tremendous impact on him—the sound and style of Kander and Ebb's songs, the atmosphere of the Kit Kat Klub, and the strange combination of power and fragility in its leading lady. All of these things would stay with him forever, and would go on to shape his own music in important ways. Right from their humble beginnings, My Chemical Romance stood out from its punk and hardcore peers because of Gerard's exaggerated sense of melodrama, and his understanding of the importance of wardrobe and make-up. In fact, Gerard was still avidly studying *Cabaret* as My Chemical Romance wrote and recorded *The Black Parade*—and it shows.

There are plenty of stylistic references—the hot jazz rhythm and Sprechstimme of 'Dead' and 'House of Wolves', the demented Bavarian oom-pah of 'Mama' and 'Blood', the jaunty phrasing of 'Teenagers'. But the influence goes deeper— beyond the surface of the music and into the realm of ideas. *The Black Parade* is full of suffering, but in almost every case Gerard presents his pain as a show. He invites his audience to watch the spectacle of his demise with the knowing wink and insinuating leer of Joel Grey's MC. He knows they'll get their money's worth. 'Gather 'round piggies and kiss this goodbye,' he sings in 'The End', 'I'd encourage your smiles I'd expect you won't cry!'[2] His tone is mocking, superior and ironic...most of the time.

Gerard didn't learn all of this by sitting on the couch watching *Cabaret* on video—a lot of it he learned the hard way, by treading the *brettl*. Here, again, he had his grandmother to thank. Elena didn't just introduce him to musicals—she gave him the confidence to star in them. Elena encouraged Gerard to try out for the leading role in his school's production of *Peter Pan*—she made him a costume and everything. This was another milestone in Gerard's life. 'I discovered I could sing,' he later recalled, 'which was pretty interesting.'[3]

What's even more interesting is that Gerard should find himself, in 2007, telling this story to Liza Minnelli, the star of *Cabaret*. Liza with a Z has a few Peter Pan anecdotes of her own. 'When I see you,' she says to Gerard, 'remind me to tell you about the dress rehearsal for *Peter Pan* with Sandy Duncan.' Liza and Gerard are pals now ('you are my new baby, who I adore' she gushes) since the legendary actress made a guest appearance on *The Black Parade*.[4]

Minnelli's cameo appears in 'Mama'—one of the strangest, fiercest and most emotionally raw songs on the album. 'Mama' begins with the sound of a city under siege, the muffled crack of distant explosions. The band picks up the rhythm implied by the steady fall of the bombs, and pretty soon they're playing a song. Gerard steps into the spotlight and—in the time-honored tradition of the avant-garde artist—tells it like it is. 'Mama,' he sings, 'we're all gonna die.'[5]

It's not just a figure of speech. The song is addressed to Mother War, a Shiva-like goddess of destruction who forms part of the pantheon of The Black Parade. On the album's inner sleeve photo, she stands alongside the band and the other characters from the album wearing a Victorian gown and a gas mask. Like the Belle Dame of Keats's poem, or the embodiment of hopelessness in AFI's *Love Like Winter* video, Mother War is a variation on that great romantic obsession, the femme fatale—the eternal fusion of love and death.

In 'Mama', Mother War is played by Liza Minnelli. She

tells the singer, her voice muffled through the gas mask, that she wishes he would call her his 'sweetheart'. But the singer resists, because he's seen through Mother War and the things she promises. She's the personification of the will to war in both society and the individual, the collective insanity that drives people to commit murder in the name of their country or their religion. The singer has had enough of it. He's seen the truth—that there's no glory in war, no victory, no eternal reward for the soldiers or anyone else, just a pile of corpses as far as the eye can see. 'Mama', he sings, pouring on the scorn, 'we're all full of lies, Mama we're meant for the flies.'[6]

Here, something goes badly wrong with Gerard Way's ironic detachment. He wishes he could be Ziggy, observing human suffering with his Martian cool, or Nietzsche, admiring the strength and power of the 'will to war' in a troop of soldiers marching off to battle. But he can't stand it. His disgust cracks the form of the song—Sprechstimme goes out the window, he starts howling like a dog or a baby, 'Ma-Maaa!, Ma-Maaaa!' The world is going to hell, and everyone just keeps drinking and dancing. Why won't anyone listen to him? More importantly, why won't they *do* something? This is not the aloof stance of the artist tyrant, but the rage and disgust of a man who, having set out to change the world, finds himself trapped in the music hall.

This is where we leave Gerard as *The Black Parade* draws to a close—stuck in the endless limbo of entertainment. He ripped out his heart to show the audience the truth of modern life, and they just sat there and clapped, and yelled for an encore. He sounds crushed, because he's realised—as Nietzsche always knew—that tragedy doesn't improve the world. The audience in the club or the opera theatre are redeemed, but outside the world will continue to suffer. It *has* to, so that the artist's tragic attitude to life can be maintained.

Gerard Way will not accept this. He loves art, but he's too democratically minded to be able to stomach the idea that it justifies the suffering of the world. The engine that drives My Chemical Romance is powered by the perpetual push-and-pull of Gerard's contradictory impulses—his desire to create tragic spectacles on the one hand, and his need to help the world on the other, his love of the emotional and the irrational versus his determination to make a difference in the real world. *The Black Parade* is, in a sense, an album length rewrite of 'Life is a Cabaret', a record in which the hero takes everything the world can throw at him, and does his best to celebrate suffering, to always be a yea-sayer. But in 'Mama', looking around the bar and listening to the bombs fall outside, he realises he can't say yes to a third World War. Is there some way, he wonders, of making art *and* making a difference? This after all, is why Gerard started the band in the first place. On the morning of 11 September, 2001, Way had officially renounced art for art's sake, and resolved to help the world.

> *Something just clicked in my head that morning … I literally said to myself, 'Fuck art. I've gotta get out of the basement. I've gotta see the world. I've gotta make a difference!'*[7]

George Grosz: Fuck art!

Artists are Cleaners

THE GERMAN PAINTER George Grosz decided, at the end of the First World War, that he could not simply stand around sketching the collapse of his society. It gradually became clear to Grosz—as it did to many Euopeans during the '20s—that the unfinished business of the First World War was about to result in a second. Surely, he thought, as an artist, there was something he could do to prevent this catastrophe. His pre-war art training had not prepared him for this at all. He'd learned how to describe, how to decorate and—thanks to Van Gogh and Gaugin—how to express himself. But what the world now needed was art to inflame, art to shock, art that would slap the people on the street in the face, make them realise the danger lurking on the horizon and show them how to do something about it. Grosz's work took on a cold-blooded objectivity. 'I considered myself a natural scientist,' he explained. 'I spared no one.'[1] Grosz's new art wasn't pretty—but what good was pretty art? What good was art at all, unless it helped the world? 'I considered all art senseless,' Grosz later recalled, 'unless it served as a weapon in the political arena.'[2]

By this point, Grosz had become one of the central figures in the Berlin Dada movement. Dada had begun as a night of noise and nonsense in a Zurich nightclub in 1916. The club's name, 'Cabaret Voltaire', signified the movements aims—combining the anarchic spirit of the cabaret with the sharp-eyed skepticism of the Enlightenment. Dada quickly opened branches in Paris, New York and Berlin, adapting to its surroundings wherever it went. In Paris, for example Dada was an absurd, existential protest—a revolt against sanity in a world gone insane. In Berlin, it took a more constructive approach—pointing fingers and naming names. The Berlin Dadaists could have no use for a movement that simply hoped to smash the world up, because it seemed to them that their world was already pretty well smashed. Berlin Dada became a program of action, designed to shake people out of their stupor.

Following the form of other Dada invasions, the Berlin contingent put on Dada 'revues'—nights of artistic entertainment—

or so the punters thought. 'They came expecting to see a show,' Grosz later recalled in his memoir, 'we simply told them the truth.' Raoul Hausman would walk out on to the stage, point to the audience, and say, 'Would you just look at this big crock of shit before us!'[3] The Berlin Dadaists threw themselves into the life of the city—chewing it up, vomiting it back out, and presenting it on a plate for the populace. They sliced up the newspapers and magazines and stuck them back together in frightening new combinations, to show people what they were really looking at over their morning coffee.

Not all of Dada's targets were political or social. Among its countless announcements, broadsides and manifestos came a curious document called *Dadaistisches Manifest*, authored by Richard Huelsenbeck, demanding an end, not to war-mongering, fascism, racism or any of the other countless problems of the day, but to *expressionism*. What, Huelsenbeck asks of the German people, have these *expressionists* done for you lately?

Have the expressionists satisfied our expectations for
an art of the present day?
   No No No![4]

The problem with expressionism, the Dadaists felt, was that it was too emotional. The Dada painter Francis Picabia insisted that painters who use emotional themes in their work (love, heartbreak, tragedy) are guilty of manipulating their audience, and that you, the art-lover, are an idiot if you'll allow yourself to be fooled by such a cheap trick. Feelings, Picabia wrote in 1920, are a dime a dozen:

You are always looking for an emotion that has
already been felt, just as you like to get an old pair of
trousers back from the cleaners, which seem new, as
long as you don't look too close. Artists are cleaners,
don't be taken in by them.[5]

If emotional art is a con, then the whole German romantic tradition becomes deeply suspect. The dadaists mercilessly sent it up in their Pan Germanic Poetry Contest. Eleven poets appeared on stage, reciting poetry at the top of their lungs. 'They made gestures, brushed tears from their eyes, held hands over their hearts.'[6] Who will win? the audience wondered. Who has the greatest sorrow, the heaviest heart, the most serious case of *einsamkeit*? In the end, the dada judges declared the contest a draw.

Romanticism was bad enough, but expressionism—a kind of uber-romanticism in which emotion becomes the artist's only consideration—was much worse. Kokoschka painted a whole world viewed entirely through the prism of the artist's feelings. His portraits of other people were, essentially, self-portraits—an attempt to represent the emotions stirred in him by other people, rather than the people themselves. 'Therefore,' concluded Dada theoretician Johannes Baargeld, 'Kokoschka can now with certainty be considered the inventor of the automechanical leech "self-help".'[7]

For the dadaists, expressionism, by peddling art as emotional therapy, was counterproductive. Expressionist art turned pain into an aesthetic spectacle, thereby making it beautiful. The spectator settles into his easychair, confident that he understands suffering. Meanwhile, out on the street, the world gets worse, and suffering continues. Expressionists, Huelsenbeck declared, are people 'who prefer their armchair to the noise of the street.'[8] Expressionist art inspires *contemplation*, where for Grosz and the dadaists, art—if it was to be of any use at all in the world—must inspire *action*.

Distress Cries Aloud

EMO HAS A fondness for expressionism—which makes sense, since both represent romanticism run riot, the expression of feelings elevated above every other concern. The very first emo band, Rites of Spring, adorned the cover of their 1991 album *End on End* with an expressionist woodcut—a perfect visual equivalent for the music inside.[1] The sleeve of Saves the Day's *In Reverie* also featured expressionist prints. The booklet illustrations show Kokoschka-like femme fatales drawn with violent gestures and a gloomy young man with haunted eyes above sunken cheeks, his mind being slowly strangled by his own heart.[2]

Expressionism has also proved useful to what Neil Strauss calls 'the eyeliner punk pack'. The Alkaline Trio promoted their 2008 album *The Agony and the Irony* by posing for photos in front of what looks like the set from *The Cabinet of Dr Caligari*.[3] AFI signalled the beginning of its transition from cartoon punk to gothic revival with an expressionist-style illustration of a graveyard at midnight on the cover of *The Art of Drowning*.[4] Inside is more emotional art—one drawing shows a haunted-looking young man standing in a bleak cityscape wearing a Misfits-style 'Devilock'—Munch as a punk. My Chemical Romance prefers a more meticulous, comic-book style of art for their sleeves. But their band logo is expressionist to the core—the letters are formed from violent brushstrokes, as though painted in a great burst of inspiration, or as a cathartic release from some enormous psychic pain. The expressionists talked of 'the charging of every action with significance and soul'—everything, from a great triptych to the title page of a hastily written pamphlet— was to be done with passion and emotional force.[5] The message of My Chemical Romance's logo is exactly this: we are sincere, emotional people, everything we do is intense.

My Chemical Romance's videos and performances also bear a strong resemblance to expressionist theatre—which flourished during the same period as the art movement and began with a play written by a painter—Kokoschka's 'Murderer, Hope of Women'. Photos from a production of

Ernst Toller's expressionist play *Die Wandlung*, staged in Berlin in 1919, look uncannily like stills from My Chemical Romance's tour film, *The Black Parade Is Dead*. One image from Toller's play shows four soldiers in corpse-paint making violent, agonised gestures against the backdrop of a flaming wreck. The figure in the middle, with his shock of white hair, black make-up under the eyes, and panicked expression, could *be* Gerard Way.[6]

The story of *Die Wandlung* also has a familiar ring about it. The play tells the story of Friedrich, a young man with a heart full of dreams. His early optimistic view of life is completely shattered by the war. His dreams are full of armies of skeletons marching through the darkness, troop trains full of undead soldiers. Friedrich returns home, and tries to make art. He is busy working on a statue representing victory when he is interrupted by two war cripples begging for alms. This pathetic display shocks our hero into a new conception of life. 'Fuck art!' he says, smashing the statue to bits, 'I've gotta make a difference!' Much soul-searching ensues, until finally Friedrich realises what he must do. He grabs some kind of megaphone and rushes out into the city square, shouting:

> *You are all of you no longer men and women; you are distorted images of your real selves. And yet you could still be men and women, still be human, if only you had faith in yourselves and in humanity!*[7]

Inspired by Friedrich's call to arms, the broken, beaten and damned join together and sing a revolutionary anthem. But Friedrich knows that singing alone will not change the world. 'Go to your rulers and proclaim to them with the organ tone of a million voices that their power is but an illusion,' he urges. 'Now march! March forward into the light of day!'[8]

Toller's play puts the lie to the dadaists' assertion that all expressionists prefer their armchairs to the noise of the street.

Die Wandlung is just one example of a politically committed variety of expressionism that flourished in the wake of the war. Just like the dadaists, most expressionist painters had their outlook and conception of art profoundly altered by the First World War. Some, it's true, retreated into themselves—but others believed that the emotional impact of their art could be used to bring about real change in the world. In 1919 Max Pechstein designed the cover for a collection of expressionist statements and manifestos entitled *An alle Kunstler!* ('To All Artists!') A romantic young man, his face gaunt, his limbs straining, crawls out of the wreckage of a smouldering, oppressive city-scape. One hand reaches for the sky, the other clutches his own burning heart, which lights up the picture with dazzling red flames—the hero's sole guide in the wilderness.[9] The message is: the world must be saved, and the artist, having brought the community together with his appeals to the spirit, will lead the way. Three years earlier, Hermann Bahr had written:

> *Never yet has any period been so shaken by horror, by such a fear of death. Never has the world been so silent, silent as the grave. Never has man been more insignificant. Never has he felt so nervous. Never was happiness so unattainable and freedom so dead. Distress cries aloud; man cries out for his soul; this whole pregnant time is one great cry of anguish. Art too joins in, into the great darkness she too calls for help, she cries to the spirit; this is expressionism.*[10]

This was undoubtedly stirring stuff in 1916. But as the inter-war period dragged on, and the prospect of another conflict began to loom on the horizon, the romantic rhetoric of expressionism began to sound suspiciously vague. It was all very well to talk about crying out into the great darkness, or to speak—as the Blauer Reiter group did—of bringing about 'spiritual renewal' through art—but what were artists actually doing to help the situation?[11] To Georg Lukacs, writing in 1934, such expressionist hogwash reflected 'a general estrangement from the concrete problems of the economy, a concealment of the connections between society, economy and ideology, with the result that these questions are increasingly mystified.'[12] Marxist critics like Lukacs believed— as punk-era critics later would—that it was the task of the modern artist to identify actual problems in society, reveal the hidden causes of these problems, and propose solutions. Ernst Toller realised this. Art and theatre, he felt, could not simply go on saying 'everything is collapsing, and this is how I feel about it' Toller felt that art must follow up its emotional appeals by providing concrete ideas for a new society.

But Toller was unusual. Most expressionist art in the interwar period seemed merely to give voice to feelings of crisis and chaos in a time of crisis and chaos. The world is falling apart, and the expressionist says to his public, 'it feels like the world is falling apart'. 'Yes!' says the sensitive aesthete, 'I feel the same way.' The result is an army of people full of feeling, but with no real idea how to help the world. This, expressionism's critics believed, could only lead to trouble.

Rock Stars Are Fascists, Too

IN 1924 A lonely, angry dreamer—a failure as an artist, a failure as a revolutionary—sat in his prison cell and considered what it would take to make his people rise up and build a better world. He came to the conclusion that, while intellectuals and politicians might attach great importance to *ideas*, what really moved the masses was *emotion*.

> ... *all great movements are popular movements,*
> *volcanic eruptions of human passions and emotional*

sentiments, stirred either by the cruel goddess of
Distress or by the firebrand of the world hurled among
the masses.[1]

This, in turn, led him to understand the importance of propaganda. Keeping the people informed would cause them to think too much, and nothing would be done. But propaganda, if used correctly, could stir those 'human passions' necessary to bring about radical change:

Its effect for the most part must be aimed at the
emotions, and only to a very limited degree at the so-
called intellect.[2]

In place of rational solutions to the problems of an increasingly complex world, he would offer people feelings, images, myths and symbols. These he felt confident they would accept, because the real choices before them were so difficult.

The author, Adolf Hitler—writing in his memoir *Mein Kampf*—was using language that we have become quite well acquainted with in this story so far. His preference for 'emotional sentiments' over the 'so-called intellect' and his belief in the power of 'human passions' all have a familiar ring about them, as does his insistence elsewhere on the restoration of myth and symbols as a cure for modern soul-sickness. Nazism, as Bertrand Russell points out, is really just the logical outcome of romantic philosophy applied on a mass scale.[3] Nazism sees the romantic worship of passion and intensity, the elevation of the individual genius above the herd, and the feeling for nature and landscape, turned into politics.

This explains why Joseph Goebbels, Hitler's Propaganda minister, made a serious attempt to cultivate expressionism as a national style. 'The fascists, with some justification, see expressionism as a heritage they can use,' wrote Lukacs in 1934.[4] Expressionism, after all, was just the latest permutation of the romantic movement—and what could be more authentically German than romanticism? Goebbels was something of a romantic himself; he wrote his doctoral thesis on Romantic Drama, and in 1929 he wrote a sentimental novel set in the Alps called *Michael*.[5] Goebbels recognised in the expressionists' landscape paintings a similarly sentimental feeling for the fatherland which, he believed, would make them ideal for propaganda purposes. He cannot have failed to see, also, that the rhetoric of expressionist protest art: 'the world is in chaos; we must unite!'—was exactly the kind of emotional bait a fascist leader could use to drum up support. The expressionist call to arms bypassed the 'so-called intellect' and went straight for the heart.

Although Hitler's innate conservatism would quickly cause Nazism and expressionism to part ways, Goebbels' patronage left the style tainted by association for decades to come. David Bowie must have known this at the time he became interested in expressionist art, but had thus far done nothing to distance himself from the work's overtones. In fact, Bowie, much to fans and critics' horror, had already embraced fascism. In 1975 he was living as a virtual recluse in Los Angeles, studying the occult and Nazi theology. The following year he returned to Britain after touring America, and made what looked to many like a Nazi salute to his fans waiting outside Victoria Station. Later, while working on *The Idiot* in Paris, Bowie told *Rolling Stone*'s Cameron Crowe:

> *I'd adore to be prime minister … and yes, I believe very strongly in fascism. The only way we can rid ourselves from the sort of liberalism that's hanging foul in the air at the moment is to speed up the progress of a right-wing, totally dictatorial government and get it over with as soon as possible. People have always responded better under a regimental leadership.*[6]

Bowie had a typical Nietzschean artist's sense of morality in that he didn't really have one. His duty, to paraphrase Dave Gahan, was always to beauty—it would never occur to him to alter a line in a song or an image in his show because it could be seen as 'immoral'. If it sounded good, if it looked good, if it meant something to him, it was in. This is no less than we expect of a romantic artist. 'The artist's feeling,' declared the German painter Caspar David Friedrich in 1818, 'is his law.'[7]

But Friedrich never played the Hammersmith Palais. Bowie did, and here his insistence on subjectivity took on a new significance. He'd created art in defiance of all moral laws. Now it seemed that there were thousands of people who recognised the truth of that art, who agreed with the things he was saying. Society is going to the dogs, morality is bunk, nothing is true, everything is permitted. 'Yes, yes!' said the thousands of Ziggy clones in the audience. What conclusions could he draw from this? Obviously, he was even more special than he thought he was. He was blessed with a unique ability to express the unconscious desires of this community he'd created. It wasn't as though they'd elected him, and he never had to ask them what they wanted—he seemed to be able to 'express' them directly. There was no need for voting or debate or any other boring democratic process. Ideas like his would never survive in a democracy, because they are too bold, too unique. But here he was, with thousands of kids who all seemed to want the same thing in front of him. Imagine what they could do...[8]

As long as it was confined to the realm of music and art, Bowie's philosophy was sound—nobody ever wrote a song like 'Starman' by ballot. When he started imagining his art turned into action, the rock star was on shakier moral ground, but Bowie had already decided morality was something he could do without. Now, there was nothing to stop him from making a flat-out admission that he admired fascism. With his highly aesthetic view of the world, the amoral rock star had found in Hitler a political figure he could relate to. 'Rock stars are fascists too,' he told Crowe. 'Adolf Hitler was the first rock star.'

Twenty years later, AFI showed us what Bowie's rock-star-as-dictator might look like in their video for 'Miss Murder'. While recording the song, AFI invited members of their fan community, the Despair Faction, to take part in the sessions. The Despair Faction's 'whoa-oh's and 'hey's can be heard in the song's chorus, suggesting a political rally, and the video expands on this idea. We see Davey Havok, his black fringe combed down over his face, singing in front of what looks like a Nazi rally at Nuremberg. Huge banners hang down in the background, and torches light up the faces of his fans, who raise their arms in salute to their leader.[9] 'Miss Murder' is disturbing, and arguably in poor taste. But Havok at least deserves points for honesty, for being bold enough to follow the implications of his art to their conclusion. Thousands of people, attuned to his thoughts, singing his words. If this weren't just a recording studio or a rock concert, if this were the real world, imagine what we could *do*...

The Black Parade Is Dead

FOR MY CHEMICAL Romance, *The Black Parade* was a conscious attempt to embrace the dynamics of large-scale stadium rock. Gerard Way, as a confirmed Freddie fan, had doubtless watched Queen's performance at Live Aid many times and wondered—as any performer would—what it would be like to do that. To stand on stage in front of thousands of people and hold every single one of them in the palm of your hand, to have them hanging on every word you sing, every gesture you make. At the famous benefit concert in 1985, Freddie Mercury lead the audience in a vocal warm-up. 'Ay-o!' he sang. Seventy-two thousand people sang 'Ay-o!' back.[1] Mercury went on to sustain this for about ten times as long as anyone would have thought possible, his confidence was supreme, his manipulation of the crowd was breathtaking. Later, he had seventy-two thousand people clapping in unison to Radio Ga Ga—just like the worker drones in the song's *Metropolis*-inspired video. Watching it on DVD is a thrill, being there would have been incredible. But to be the singer, to be Freddie Mercury on that day in front of that crowd, would be to feel superhuman, to feel that anything was possible.

At the Hammersmith Palais, at Mexico's Palacio de los Deportes, and at the final show of the tour on 9 May 2008 at Madison Square Garden, Gerard Way must have known something of what it was like to be Freddie at Live Aid—to wield that power, to stand in front of tens of thousands of people and have them say, 'you express us better than we can express ourselves, we surrender to you.' But Way is not exactly like Freddie. He won't be satisfied by the knowledge that he's united his audience in a collective feeling. He wants to take that feeling and do something with it—and not just vocal warm-ups. He wants to make a difference. And on the Black Parade tour it must have felt to him as though this might really happen. He'd created an army—an army that he would have to lead. It was, after all, his unique insight, his extraordinary ability to identify what was wrong with their world and how to make it right, that had brought them together in the first place. Thousands of kids, a secret army of the broken, beaten and damned ready to follow them anywhere, do anything.

Fascism, as Herbert Read has observed, turns on a subtle combination of sadism and masochism. After any revolution, there is an opportunity for freedom—old institutions have been trashed, the field is open, anything is possible. Ideally, Read says that the outcome of this should be a form of communism—people co-operating with one another to build the kind of world they want to live in. But since this is so difficult to do, in most cases people will settle for the far easier option of being lead. They start looking around for a strong leader. Lo and behold, the people's masochistic desire to be bossed around finds its ideal companion in the leader, whose sadistic desire to impose his will on others makes him the logical choice.

The problem, in the case of *The Black Parade*, is that Gerard Way is not a sadist—he just doesn't have the stomach for it. The line 'teenagers scare the living shit out of me' is only partly delivered in character. It's also a sincere statement on Gerard's part, an admission that he realises his audience virtually demands of him that he tell them what to do, and that this terrifies him to his soul. The band aren't cut out to be sadists either—they can play at being 'a little shittier to the audience' as guitarist Ray Toro puts it; but like Roger Waters after the famous spitting incident, they're too sensitive to keep it up.

But as Toro later admitted, the Black Parade got out of control. Having set the thing in motion, the band members felt compelled to act out the roles required of them. They'd created a monster, dreamed a comic-book army of the undead into existence. Now, like Frankenstein, they found this thing knocking on their door every night, demanding that its parents recognise their demon offspring. The pressure was intense, the sense of responsibility enormous. Somewhere in South America, Ray Toro said to himself, 'Fuck, this shit is trying to kill us!'[2]

At this point, rock history began to repeat itself. *The Black Parade* is in many ways a twenty-first century retelling of Bowie's *The Rise and Fall of Ziggy Stardust and the Spiders from Mars*. Both are loosely structured concept albums which end with the tragic and symbolic death of the hero. And both required a change of identity for the performers themselves in bringing it to life. The Ziggy Stardust concerts were Ziggy concerts, not Bowie concerts—he played a role on stage, a role that allowed him to be 'a little shittier to the audience'. For My Chemical Romance it was the same. They didn't just perform The Black Parade, they *became* The Black Parade.

If there was any problem with Ziggy Stardust it was that it worked too well. By presenting the Passion of Ziggy onstage, Bowie created a cult, a religion with devotees who proclaimed the resurrected Ziggy their leader. 'I began to think he was a new kind of messiah,' recalled one teenage Bowie fan in 1976. 'I really thought he had some kind of infinite wisdom.' 'Julie', speaking to Fred and Judy Vermorel for their book of fan fantasies, *Starlust*, went on. 'Bowie was magic and he was supreme. He had the qualities of a type of ruler.'[3]

Bowie had always perceived these qualities in himself, and would admit to them again in the future. But sometime in 1973 his megalomania had been fatally undermined by his drug use and his low self-esteem. He was too much of a nervous wreck to lead anybody anywhere, and the thought of all those grabbing hands reaching out to him filled him with horror. Life seemed to be imitating art. At this point Bowie realised he'd written an escape clause into his new religion. His fans wanted Ziggy, and he was Ziggy. But since Ziggy was just a character, it would be easy enough for Bowie to kill Ziggy (for real this time) and escape through the back door to live another day. This is exactly what he did at the Hammersmith Odeon on 3 July 1973. 'Not only is it the last show of the tour,' he said, looking down at his devotees from the stage, 'but it's the last show we'll ever do.' 'Noooooo!' screamed the kids.[4]

Sometime in 2008, the members of My Chemical Romance realised that, just as Bowie had done thirty-five years earlier, they had to kill the monster they'd created—their army of the undead had to die. Onstage at Mexico's Palacio de los Deportes, Gerard Way roared, 'the Black Parade...is dead!'[5] 'Noooooo!' screamed the kids. Then, after playing the last show of the tour, the band packed up their floats and banners and threw Colleen Atwood's uniforms in the laundry basket; perhaps hoping—like Spider Man ridding himself of the black suit—that the evil fascist impulses that had come over them on tour were somehow contained in its fabric and would simply come out in the wash. (Ray Toro's is still in the garage—'I don't want to bring it into the house!' he said.) My Chemical Romance looked forward to being an ordinary rock band again, and playing ordinary rock shows in front of relatively small groups of fans. The army of the broken, the beaten and the damned that Gerard had called into existence, which now seemed to be massing its ranks in every city in the world, would have to lead itself.

To imagine Gerard Way in this moment is to imagine two great romantic heroes in one person. Gerard was both Napoleon Bonaparte declaring himself emperor, and Ludwig van Beethoven, tearing up his manuscript in disgust at his own violation of 'the rights of man'. The truth was that Gerard—as much as he liked the idea of having his own army—could not be the leader of a mass movement. The cult of leadership is nice for politicians and leaders of military coups, but not much good for people, and no good at all for artists. Leadership implies a mass who must be lead, and a mass denies individuals their right to be solitary. An artist like Gerard can't accept this, since solitude is what got him the gig in the first place.

Rivers Cuomo: Emotion recollected in tranquillity.

Insulation and Disaffection

IN HIS 1964 book, *To Hell With Culture*, the English art critic Herbert Read tackled a question which is central to any understanding of romantic poetry—or any other kind of emotional art. That is, Read asked himself: what good is self-expression? By the late twentieth century, the importance of self-expression was almost taken for granted by the artistic avant-garde. Read himself, in one of his many long-running arguments with his friend, the sculptor and typographer Eric Gill, had been bold enough to suggest that it might be the sole purpose of art. But searching himself, Read realised that it didn't make sense. Artists would not be tolerated in society if they didn't contribute something useful to it—and what use could society have for self-expression? By simply expressing themselves while everybody else was working, artists would effectively be saying: 'I am more important than everybody else'. Society should, in theory, have no reason to put up with such behaviour.[1]

And yet we can't quite tell these selfish individuals to get lost. On *The Red Album*, Rivers Cuomo's stance is exactly the one described above. In fact, he's gone further. He insisted that he be allowed to express himself and told us in no uncertain terms that this makes him better than you and me— 'the greatest man that ever lived'. Then he dared us to look him in the eye and tell him we don't like it. We have to admit we cannot. How did he get away with this blatantly antisocial self-expression? The story of *Pinkerton* provides a clue. In 1995, Rivers Cuomo had gone deep into his own emotional world. He came back with an album of pure self-expression, an album so completely driven by the need for self-revelation that, to many listeners, it barely seemed to have songs. It should, in theory, have been as useful to society as a brick thrown out of a window into a crowd. Who would want a thing like that? Surprisingly, quite a lot of people wanted it. Weezer's difficult second album became, over the next decade, a sort of secret road map with which the lonely and alienated could find one another. It identified something many people had in common—something which was emotional, irrational and deeply disturbing—but instantly familiar to those concerned. Listening to *Pinkerton*, these individuals began to understand that the strange, unnameable things that nagged at them as they did their jobs or went to school were not delusions, but secret truths. There were others, they realised, who felt alienated from society, who felt like life might be a struggle for which there is no reward, who felt like screaming for no reason at all. Realising this, they no longer felt alone.

Read would say that what Cuomo did with *Pinkerton* was to reveal 'the collective instincts which underlie the brittle surface of convention and normality.' This kind of thing, he argued, is very, very useful to society. 'It is the artist's business,' he wrote in *To Hell With Culture*, 'to make the group aware of its unity, its community.'[2] Artists, he reasoned, only think they're expressing themselves. What they're in fact doing is expressing life—the secret life of their society. With the artist's map of this invisible country in their hands, individuals become connected to one another in ways that a society based on money and production can neither predict nor replicate. The alienating effects of modern life are reversed, a fragmented world is put back together again for the length of a song. The artist's *real* job, Read insisted, is not self-expression, but *life*-expression.[3]

Having figured out what society could expect from modern artists, Herbert Read next asked himself what modern artists could expect from society, what conditions they required in order to be able to do what they do. In Rilke's *Letters to a Young Poet*, and in Wordsworth's *Preface to the Lyrical Ballads*—two documents which neatly bookend the romantic movement—he discovered the answer. 'Poetry,' wrote Wordsworth in 1800, 'takes its origin from emotion recollected in tranquillity.' Here, Wordsworth, like Rilke, seemed to be saying that the poet's insights about the nature of life could only be attained by his remaining at one remove from that life. Therefore the artist's job description, Read concluded, could be said to be:

*To communicate something as essential as bread, yet
to be able to do so only from a position of insulation
and disaffection.*[4]

Rivers Cuomo knows instinctively that this 'position of insulation and disaffection' is the first requirement of his work. He created a cure for loneliness by identifying and isolating certain emotional tendencies in certain people between the ages of sixteen and twenty-one. But he didn't find out what those things were by studying demographics or doing surveys or talking to teenagers in focus groups. He didn't ask his fans what they wanted either (if he had, you can bet they wouldn't have asked for anything like *Pinkerton*). In fact, he didn't really talk to *anyone* in the period when he was making Weezer's second album. He discovered the things that would later bind Pinkerton's community together by studying the lessons of his dreams. And to do that, he had to be alone.

Cuomo's art—like Wordsworth's—comes from emotion recollected in tranquillity. 'Probably most anyone doesn't go through a week without getting upset about something,' he explained to Jenny Eliscu in 2002, 'and that's what I do. I wait for those moments, and then I pounce.'[5] But while emotions might be a dime a dozen, tranquillity—the contemplative calm required to identify those emotions and catch them before they melt away into the air—is not easy to come by in the modern world. In Los Angeles, it's almost impossible. But Cuomo has always found a way. Locking himself in the garage, breaking his own leg, taking a vow of celibacy, 'partying by himself', blacking out the windows in his apartment—all of these, for the Weezer singer, were simply ways of maintaining the position of insulation and disaffection his job requires.

The irony in all this for the rock and roll poet is that the isolation he needs to do his job is constantly threatened by the community his poetry has created. As the cult of *Pinkerton* grew during the late 1990s, the group sought to elect a leader—and naturally they turned to the genius who had made the group aware of its unity. Cuomo 'expressed the group', therefore he ought to be at its head. He ought to, at the very least, acknowledge his constituents by tossing them a bone every now and then. But Cuomo did not accept this role. He hadn't accepted it the first time around, when the success of *The Blue Album* had required of him that he be the spokesperson for 'geek-rock' (whatever that was); and he wouldn't accept it this time around either. He went to extraordinary lengths to alienate his new fans, to make it clear he would not, under any circumstances, be the godfather of emo.

Cuomo was not just being perverse. He refused to be a part of the group he'd created because he saw that if he did, his alone-ness would be compromised. But by refusing to give up his solitary status, Cuomo struck a blow for solitude, not just for himself, but for everyone. Because in those moments when a group forms and the group wants to be lead, it's not just the artist's independence that's at risk, but the independence of his fans as well. *Pinkerton* created a community of people who did not feel at home in society. It would make no sense to then turn those people into a 'mass'— since it was everything 'mass' that they revolted against in the first place. They had rejected the world of the average, the reasonable, the world of 'what's best for everyone'; and attached themselves to this strange, particular sense of truth that the artist had revealed. Now they were banding together, organising, massing. The world of 'what's best for everyone' would be the logical outcome of this process, the *Pinkerton* fans would become more like each other. Cuomo, who had already seen this three years earlier—when he'd looked out into the crowd and seen thousands of kids wearing his glasses—could see where things were headed.

Gerard Way: The saviour of the broken, the beaten and the damned.

Leave Them Kids Alone.

BRUCE SPRINGSTEEN HAD the best possible training for a rock and roll poet. Because he was painfully shy and socially awkward as a young man, he went into himself. Here, he found words—floods of words—endless poems about youth, freedom, landscape, faith and love. He thought he was expressing himself, if he thought about it at all. It was only later, when people started to hear those songs, that he understood what he was really doing. Talking to Springsteen in 1999, *Mojo*'s Mark Hagen remarked, 'I've never been to one of your shows or listened to one of your LPs, without it connecting with something in me I didn't know I felt.' Springsteen replied:

> *That's the writer's job. The writer collects and creates those moments from out of his own experience and the world he sees around him. …and you present those things to your audience, who then experience their own inner vitality, their own centre, their own questions about their own life, and their moral life. …That's what you're paid for—somebody says, "Hey, I'm not alone."*[1]

Sometime in 1985, sitting in his seat (or maybe standing, punching the air) at New Jersey's Bradenburg Arena, Gerard Way was one of those 'somebody's.[2] Fifteen years later, following his own apprenticeship of loneliness, introspection and overlong poetry, Way would start getting paid to do the same thing. He would discover, like Springsteen, that it's not as easy as it looks. It's hard enough in the rehearsal room, or in some tiny club in front of an audience of your peers. It gets harder when your records start to sell and your audience goes from hundreds, to thousands to hundreds of thousands. Sometime before the recording of *The Black Parade*, Gerard realised, as Springsteen had realised around the time of *Born to Run*, that his actions had implications. 'I'd meet these kids that were outsiders,' said the singer. 'And I realised they're looking to us for the answer. It started to scare me.'[3]

In the stadium, ideas are amplified along with sounds. And in the same way that you can't turn the volume up on a record without cracks and pops getting louder too, My Chemical Romance found that as their ideas were broadcast on a larger scale, the flaws and contradictions that had always been there were amplified in proportion. The romantic ideals that drive the band and its music, the things that put the romance in My Chemical Romance, were forced to account for themselves. How can we look death in the face and still say yes to life? How can we reject society without dying of loneliness? And how can we insist on our right to self-expression when the world is falling apart?

Incredibly, the band chose not to pull back from these questions, but to go further into them—to embrace the contradictions at the heart of their songs and the movement those songs had created, and to watch as the consequences played themselves out in the real world. They created a teenage revolution—not a revolution in the name of civil rights, an end to violence, more drugs, less bombs, more fun or free love. Their revolutionary war was waged in the name of loneliness. The members of The Black Parade were standing up—to paraphrase Dostoyevsky—for their own caprices, and for having them guaranteed where necessary. The world was treated to the extraordinary spectacle of thousands of kids demanding the right to be sad. British fans organised a day of action to protest the unfair tactics of the *Daily Mail*'s counter-offensive strike on sadness. They held up banners saying: 'We're not a cult, we're a fucking army!'[4] What were they all doing there? asked one reporter. A fifteen-year-old My Chem fan explained, 'We're all alone together.' At this point, it became Way's job to show how this mind-boggling idea might work out in practice. He couldn't be a leader—he couldn't say to say to his fans 'it's ok to be weird and lonely and different to everyone else' and then deny them their alone-ness. But he couldn't pretend that what he'd created was of no importance either. He had to honour the movement he'd set in motion, and demonstrate, through his art, how its aims might be accomplished. It might seem like a lot to ask of a rock star—but nobody is better qualified. After all, it was his idea.

It's tempting to say that the idea of a world where everybody is 'alone together' is one that could only have been dreamed up by a teenager. Teenagers, who are selfish, amoral, sentimental, obsessed with childhood, dreams and the significance of their own emotions. Only a teenager could elevate these principles above the sensible, utilitarian ones on which our modern society is based. But all of these things are equally important to the artist. A poet like Springsteen or Gerard Way needs them in order to do his job: 'to communicate something as essential as bread, yet to be able to do so only from a position of insulation and disaffection.' When institutions, politicians, society and rational thought itself let the poet down, his faith and creative power can only be restored by returning to the world of childhood, imagination, memory, and emotion—to the small 'h' humanity of a lyric like 'when I was a young boy'. And since the world will not recognise these things, the poet is forced to become a revolutionary. The poet, as Herbert Read writes, 'is compelled to demand, for poetic reasons that the world be changed. We cannot say it is an unreasonable request: it is the first condition of his existence as a poet.'[5]

Now, in the twenty-first century, the romantic poet has found new recruits to his cause. Emotional teenagers are the natural allies of the poet. They want the same things—dreams, nostalgia, intense emotions, solitude. They already understand, like the poet, that there is no political party on earth that can guarantee their happiness because they demand a kind of happiness that a society based on production and money doesn't understand. This is Thomas Carlyle's 'passion incapable of being translated into action'. This is passion that can find no useful outlet in society since it refuses to recognise or participate in a society which has proven itself consistently incapable of providing for real human needs. For such individuals, 'Welcome to the Black Parade'—a song which denounces modern life, asserts the importance of dreams, solitude and emotions, and demands the creation of a new world in which those things are recognised—is a call to arms which cannot be ignored.

'Welcome to the Black Parade' is thrilling and irresistible because it dares to imagine that art might change everyday life. Gerard Way could not, in good faith, sing that song unless he believed poetry was that important, that life could be fundamentally altered by a set of words. But the singer believes this because he has to. He believes it because he knows that if it it's not true, then art is useless. Gerard Way is not just engaging in some scene-politics pissing contest when he says that 'Emo is a pile of shit'. For Way, emotion is important. The poetry of 'Welcome to the Black Parade' takes its origin from emotion recollected in tranquillity, and the poet wants you to feel what he felt when he wrote it. But where, for an emo band, the mission would be accomplished at this point, for Gerard Way it's just the beginning. He knows that if the process stalls here, the promise of a better world glimpsed in the last thirty seconds of the song will never be more than thirty seconds of noise on the radio. He can't commit himself to politics, because he's demanding the kind of freedom no political party on earth can allow. He can't get bogged down in the kind of Marxist analysis advocated by the post-punk positivists; if he does, the poetry that drives his music will disappear. But he can't accept the notion that music begins and ends with the sharing of feelings, as though rock and roll were a giant talk show or group therapy session. If art has no power to improve life, then art—as Herbert Read says—will never be anything more than 'self-expression'.[5] Which is another way of saying that until we start taking poets and their irrational demands seriously, *everything* will be emo.

Notes

Emotional People

1. Jason Pettigrew, 'Dead to see another day', *Alternative Press*, July 2008.
2. Gerard Way, 'My Chemical Romance brand emo "shit".' NME News, nme.com. September 2007.
3. Ronen Kaufmann, 'Blood Runs Deep', *Alternative Press*, July 2008.
4. Tim Karan, 'Blood Runs Deep', *Alternative Press*, July 2008.
5. Andy Greenwald, 'Emo: We Feel Your Pain', in Michael Sia (ed.), *Spin: 20 Years of Alternative Music*, Three Rivers Press, New York.
6. Gwyn Tyme, 'My Chemical Romance', Musicpix.net, May 2005.

Buzzcocks

1. Jon Savage, *England's Dreaming*, Faber and Faber, London, 1991.
2. Buzzcocks: 'What do I Get?', Manchester—So Much to Answer For: The Peel Sessions, Strange Fruit LP, 1990.
3. Annie Zaleski, 'Blood Runs Deep', *Alternative Press*, July 2008.

The Cure

1. Dave Thompson, *In Between Days: An Armchair Guide to the Cure*, Helter Skelter, London, 2004.
2. Ibid.
3. Ibid.
4. Ibid.
5. Ibid.

Weezer

1. Rivers Cuomo, Sleevenotes for *Alone: The Home Recordings of Rivers Cuomo*, Geffen CD, 2007.
2. Ed Masley, '10 Essential "Disappointing Albums"', *Alternative Press*, July 2008.
3. Rivers Cuomo, op. cit.
4. Andy Greenwald, *Nothing Feels Good: Punk Rock, Teenagers and Emo*, St Martin's Press, New York, 2003.
5. Harry Thomas, 'Not So Serious Rivers Cuomo', *Rolling Stone*, June 2001.
6. Chris Mundy, 'Weezer's Cracked Genius', *Rolling Stone*, September 2001.
7. Songmeanings.com, 2002.

8. Ibid.
9. Rob Mitchum, 'Weezer: Make Believe', album review, Pitchfork.com, May 2005.

The Classics

1. William J. Long, *Outlines of English and American Literature*, Gutenberg.org
2. Robert Barnard, *A Short History of English Literature*, B. Blackwell, New York, 1984.
3. Walter Horatio Pater, *Essay on Style*, Gutenberg.org

Troublemaker

1. Steve Kandell, 'Heck on Wheels', *Spin*, June 2008.
2. Weezer, 'Troublemaker', *The Red Album*, Geffen CD, 2008.
3. Rivers Cuomo, Sleevenotes for *Alone: The Home Recordings of Rivers Cuomo*, Geffen CD, 2007.
4. Weezer, 'Dreamin'', *The Red Album*, Geffen CD, 2008.

Wordsworth

1. William Wordsworth, 'Expostulation and Reply' in Wordsworth, William, *Lyrical Ballads, with other poems*, (1800 edition) Gutenberg.org
2. William Wordsworth, 'The Tables Turned' in Wordsworth, William, *Lyrical Ballads, with other poems*, (1800 edition) Gutenberg.org

Civilisation

1. Norman Davies, *Europe: A History*, Pimlico, London, 1997.
2. Nicholas Dent, *Rousseau*, Routledge, New York, 2005.

The French Revolution

1. Thomas Carlyle, *The French Revolution: A History*, Gutenberg.org, 2006.
2. Graeme Fife, *The Terror*, Portrait, London, 2004.
3. Mathew Arnold, *Selections from the Prose Works of Matthew Arnold*, ed. Johnson, William Savage, Gutenberg.org, 2004.
4. Roger Sharrock, *Selected Poems of William Wordsworth*, Heinemann, London, 1968.
5. Rupert Christiansen, *Romantic Affinities*, Pimlico, London, 2004.
6. Eric Hobsbawm, *The Age of Revolution: Europe 1789–1848*, Weidenfeld and Nicolson, London, 1962.
7. William Wordsworth, 'The French Revolution' in Sharrock, Roger (ed.), *Selected Poems of William Wordsworth*, Heinemann, London, 1968.

8. William Wordsworth, 'The Prelude, or, Growth of a Poet's Mind' in Ernest de Selincourt (ed.), Oxford University Press, London,1960.
9. Ibid.

The Story Is in the Soil

1. Gavin Edwards, 'Rock's Boy Genius', *Rolling Stone*, October 2002.
2. Bright Eyes, 'I Believe in Symmetry', *Digital Ash in a Digital Urn*, Saddle Creek CD, 2005.
3. Bright Eyes, 'Road to Joy', *I'm Wide Awake, It's Morning*, Saddle Creek CD, 2005
4. Norman Davies, *Europe: A History*, Pimlico, London, 1997.
5. Rupert Christiansen, *Romantic Affinities*, Pimlico, London, 2004.
6. William Vaughn, *Romanticism and Art*, Thames and Hudson, London, 1994.
7. Ludwig Van Beethoven, *Beethoven's Letters, 1790–1826*, Gutenberg.org, 2004.
8. Bright Eyes. 'Road to Joy', op. cit.
9. Triple j interview, Zan Rowe
10. Ibid.

A Motion and a Spirit

1. William Wordsworth, 'Tintern Abbey', in Sharrock, Roger (ed.), *Selected Poems of William Wordsworth*, Heinemann, London, 1968.
2. William Wordsworth, 'Tintern Abbey' in William Wordsworth, *Lyrical Ballads, with other poems*, (1800 edition) Gutenberg.org
3. William Wordsworth, 'Preface to the Lyrical Ballads' in William Wordsworth, *Lyrical Ballads, with other poems*, op. cit.

Romantic

1. Brian Howe, 'Bright Eyes: Noise Floor' (review), Pitchfork.com, October 2006.
2. Isiah Berlin, *Against the Current: Essays in the history of ideas*, Hogarth Press, London, 1979.
3. Robert Barnard, *A Short History of English Literature*, B. Blackwell, New York, 1984.
4. William Wordsworth, 'The Tables Turned' in Roger Sharrock (ed.), *Selected Poems of William Wordsworth*, Heinemann, London, 1968.
5. Ibid.

Disenchanted

1. My Chemical Romance, 'Disenchanted', *The Black Parade is Dead*, Warner / Reprise DVD, 2008.
2. My Chemical Romance, 'Welcome to the Black Parade', *The Black Parade*, Warner / Reprise CD, 2006.
3. Ibid.
4. Alex De Jonge, *Dostoyevsky and the Age of Intensity*, Secker and Warburg, London, 1975.
5. Wordsworth, 'The Prelude', Oxford University Press, London, 1964.
6. Ibid.
7. Herbert Read, *To Hell With Culture*, Routledge, London, 2002.
8. William Vaughn, *Romanticism and Art*, Thames and Hudson, London, 1994.

Paint It Black and Take It Back

1. Dan Stapleton, 'My Chemical Romance', *Rolling Stone*, February 2007.
2. Shirley Halperin, 'Coldplay talk "Viva la Vida"'. Ew.com., June 2007.
3. Tom Prideaux, *The World of Delacroix 1798–1863*, Time Incorporated, New York, 1966.
4. Ibid.
5. William Vaughn, *Romanticism and Art*, Thames and Hudson, London, 1994.
6. Tom Prideaux, op. cit.
7. Shirley Halperin, 'Coldplay talk "Viva la Vida"'. Ew.com., June 2007.
8. Mtv.com 'Buzzworthy', June 2007.

Napoleon

1. Norman Davies, *Europe: A History*, Pimlico, London, 1997.
2. Eric Hobsbawm, *The Age of Revolution: Europe 1789–1848*, Weidenfeld and Nicolson, London, 1962.
3. H C Robbins Landon, *Beethoven: A Documentary Study*, Thames and Hudson, London,1974.
4. Bertrand Russell, *History of Western Philosophy*, Routledge, London, 2006.
5. Hobsbawm, op. cit.
6. Russell, op. cit.
7. Hobsbawm, op. cit.
8. Davies, op. cit.
9. William Vaughn, *Romanticism and Art*, Thames and Hudson, London, 1994.
10. Davies, op.cit.

11. Johann Wolfgang von Goethe, *The Sorrows of Young Werther*, Gutenberg.org, 2004.
12. Thomas Carlyle, Introduction to Johann Wolfgang Von Goethe, *Truth and Fiction relating to my life*. Gutenberg.org, 2004.
13. Ibid.
14. Hobsbawm, op. cit.

This Tragic Affair

1. My Chemical Romance, 'Famous Last Words', *The Black Parade*, Warner / Reprise CD, 2006.
2. Tom Rawstorne, 'Why no child is safe from the sinister cult of emo', Dailymail.co.uk, May 2008.
3. Rupert Christiansen, *Romantic Affinities*, Pimlico, London, 2004.
4. Thomas Carlyle, Introduction to Johann Wolfgang Von Goethe, *Truth and Fiction relating to my life*. Gutenberg.org, 2004.
5. Johann Wolfgang Von Goethe, *The Sorrows of Young Werther*, Gutenberg.org, 2004.
6. Ibid.
7. Ibid.
8. Ibid.
9. Ibid.
10. Ibid.
11. Ibid.
12. Ibid.
13. Ibid.
14. Ibid.
15. Ibid.
16. Ibid.

Passion Incapable of Being Converted into Action

1. William Vaughn, *Romanticism and Art*, Thames and Hudson, London, 1994.
2. Gerhart Hoffmeister, 'Reception in Germany and Abroad' in Lesley Sharpe, *The Cambridge Companion to Goethe*, Cambridge University Press, Cambridge, 2002.
3. Ibid.
4. Ibid.
5. Barker Fairley, *A Study of Goethe*, Oxford University Press, London, 1950.
6. Hoffmeister, op. cit.
7. Thomas Carlyle, Introduction to Johann Wolfgang Von Goethe, *Truth and Fiction relating to my life*. Gutenberg.org, 2004.
8. Johann Wolfgang Von Goethe, *The Sorrows of Young Werther*, Gutenberg.org, 2004.
9. Carlyle, op. cit.

Sentimentalists

1. Rupert Christiansen, *Romantic Affinities*, Pimlico, London, 2004
2. Walter Benjamin, 'Goethe' in Michael Jennings (ed.), *Walter Benjamin: Selected Writings Volume 2, Part 1*, Harvard University Press, Cambridge, Mass., 2005.
3. Christiansen, op. cit.
4. Johann Wolfgang Von Goethe, *The Sorrows of Young Werther*, Gutenberg.org, 2004.
5. Martin Swales, 'Goethe's Prose Fiction' in Lesley Sharpe, *The Cambridge Companion to Goethe*, Cambridge University Press, Cambridge, 2002.

Across the Sea

1. Weezer, 'Across the Sea', *Pinkerton*, Geffen CD, 1996.
2. Weezer, 'Butterfly', *Pinkerton*, Geffen CD, 1996.
3. Chris Mundy, 'Weezer's Cracked Genius', *Rolling Stone*, September 2001.
4. Ibid.
5. Andy Greenwald, *Nothing Feels Good: Punk Rock, Teenagers, and Emo*, St Martins Press, New York, 2003.
6. Ibid.
7. John Weightman, *The Concept of the Avant-Garde: Explorations in Modernism*, Alcove Press, 1973.
8. Greenwald, op. cit.
9. Greenwald, op cit.
10. Posted in 'The Despair Faction', despairfaction.com, November 2007

Love Like Winter

1. Neil Strauss, 'AFI: Decemberunderground' (album review), *Rolling Stone*, June 2006.
2. Alex De Jonge, *Dostoyevsky and the Age of Intensity*, Secker and Warburg, London, 1975.
3. Davey Havok, 'Decemberunderground', AFI official website, afireinside.net
4. Austin Scaggs, 'Davey Havok: Q&A', *Rolling Stone*, June 2006.
5. AFI, 'Summer Shudder', *Decemberunderground*, Interscope / Universal CD, 2006.
6. AFI, 'Love Like Winter', *Decemberunderground*, Interscope / Universal CD, 2006.
7. The Making of 'Love Like Winter' Part 1. YouTube.com

Alone and Palely Loitering

1. Robert Gittings, *John Keats*, Penguin, London, 1968.
2. Ibid.

3. John Keats, 'La Belle Dame sans Merci' in Robert Gittings (ed.), *Selected Poems and Letters of Keats*, Heinemann, London, 1966.
4. Ibid.
5. Gittings, op. cit.
6. Ibid.

A Forest

1. Dave Thompson, *In Between Days: An Armchair Guide to the Cure*, Helter Skelter, London, 2004.
2. The Cure, 'A Forest', *Standing on a Beach*, Warner CD, 1986.
3. The Cure, ibid.

Lemonade

1. Robert Gittings, *John Keats*, Penguin, London, 1968.
2. John Keats, 'Ode on Melancholy' in Robert Gittings (ed.), *Selected Poems and Letters of Keats*, Heinemann, London, 1966.
3. Rivers Cuomo, Sleevenotes for *Alone: The Home Recordings of Rivers Cuomo*, Geffen CD, 2008.
4. Rivers Cuomo, 'Lemonade', *Alone: The Home Recordings of Rivers Cuomo*, op. cit.
5. Rivers Cuomo, Sleevenotes for *Alone: The Home Recordings of Rivers Cuomo*, op. cit.
6. Ibid.
7. Rivers Cuomo, 'Buddy Holly', *Alone: The Home Recordings of Rivers Cuomo*, Geffen CD, 2008.
8. Andy Greenwald, *Nothing Feels Good: Punk Rock, Teenagers, and Emo*, St Martins Press, New York, 2003.
9. Jenny Eliscu, 'Rivers Cuomo's Encyclopedia of Pop', *Rolling Stone*, June 2002.
10. Alpha, Centri, posted on Songmeanings.com, August 2002.
11. Brian Hiatt, 'The Boys with the Car Crash Hearts', *Rolling Stone*, March 2007.

Anatomy of Mellon Collie

1. William J Long, *Outlines of English and American Literature*, gutenberg.org
2. Amy Hanson, *Smashing Pumpkins: Tales of a Scorched Earth*, Helter Skelter, London, 2004.
3. Smashing Pumpkins, 'Disarm', *Siamese Dream*, Hut / Virgin CD, 1993.
4. Billy Corgan, from transcript of 1993 *Rage* interview, quoted in Starla.org.
5. Richard Kingsmill, *The J-Files Compendium*, ABC Books, Sydney, 2002.

6. Hanson, op. cit.
7. Ibid.
8. Dave Thompson, *In Between Days: An Armchair Guide to the Cure*, Helter Skelter, London, 2004.

Rock and Roll Suicide

1. Paul Du Noyer, 'Contact', *Mojo*, July 2002.
2. David Bowie, 'Ziggy Stardust', *The Rise and Fall of Ziggy Stardust and the Spiders from Mars*, RCA LP, 1972.
3. W A Mozart, *Don Giovanni*, CBS Masterworks, 1979.
4. Ibid.
5. David Bowie, 'Rock and Roll Suicide', *The Rise and Fall of Ziggy Stardust and the Spiders from Mars*, RCA LP, 1972.
6. AFI, 'Miss Murder', *Decemberunderground*, Interscope CD, 2006.
7. AFI, 'Prelude', *Decemberunderground*, Interscope CD, 2006.
8. Matt Diehl, *My So-Called Punk*, St Martin's Griffin Press, New York, 2007.

Screamin' Lord Byron

1. David Bowie, 'Blue Jean' (music video, dir. Julian Temple), *Best of Bowie*, EMI DVD, 2002.

Lord Byron

1. Robert Gittings, *John Keats*, Penguin, London, 1968.
2. Peter Quennell, *Byron: The Years of Fame*, Penguin, London, 2001.
3. Ibid.
4. George Gordon Byron, 'Childe Harold's Pilgrimage' in *The Poetical Works of Lord Byron*, Murray, London, 1948.
5. Ibid.
6. Quennell, op. cit.
7. Colin Wilson, *The Misfits: A study of sexual outsiders*, Grafton Books, London, 1989.
8. Quennell, op. cit.
9. Wilson, op. cit.
10. Quennell, op. cit
11. Quennell, op. cit.
12. Ibid.
13. Ibid.
14. George Gordon Byron, *Selected Poetry and Prose of Byron*, W H Auden (ed.), Signet Classics, New York, 1966.
15. Ibid.
16. *Selected Poetry and Prose of Byron* W H Auden (ed.), op. cit.
17. Bertrand Russell, *History of Western Philosophy*, Routledge, London, 2006.

18. Quennell, op. cit.
19. Ibid.

Give Them Blood

1. David Bowie, 'Ziggy Stardust', *The Rise and Fall of Ziggy Stardust and the Spiders from Mars*, RCA LP, 1972.
2. Norman Davies, *Europe: A History*, Pimlico, London, 1997.
3. My Chemical Romance, 'Blood', *The Black Parade*, Warner / Reprise CD, 2006.
4. Smashing Pumpkins, 'Bullet With Butterfly Wings', *Mellon Collie and the Infinite Sadness*, Hut / EMI CD, 1995.
5. X V Scott, 'My Chemical Romance' posted on mychemicalromanceweb.yaia.com

The Vampyre

1. Martin Swales, 'Goethe's Prose Fiction' in Lesley Sharpe, *The Cambridge Companion to Goethe*, Cambridge University Press, Cambridge, 2002.
2. Gerhart Hoffmeister, Gerhart, 'Reception in Germany and Abroad' in Lesley Sharpe, *The Cambridge Companion to Goethe*, Cambridge University Press, Cambridge, 2002.
3. Johann Wolfgang von Goethe, *Faust (Part Two)*, Penguin, London, 1959.
4. George Gordon Byron, *Selected Poetry and Prose of Byron*, W H Auden (ed.), Signet Classics, New York, 1966.
5. Frederic Raphael, *Byron*, Thames and Hudson, London, 1982.
6. Mary Shelley, *Frankenstein* in Peter Fairclough (ed.), *Three Gothic Novels*, Penguin, London,1986.
7. Rapahel, op. cit.
8. Christopher Frayling, *Vampyres: Lord Byron to Count Dracula*, Faber and Faber, London, 1991.
9. Christopher Sandford, *Bowie: Loving the Alien*, Warner Books, London, 1996.

Goths

1. David Johnson, 'Dean Street' in Hanif Kureshi and Jon Savage (eds), *The Faber Book of Pop*, Faber and Faber, London, 1995.
2. George Gimarc, *Post-Punk Diary 1980–1982*, St Martin's Press, New York, 1997.
3. Johnson, op. cit.
4. Susan Colon, 'The Gloom Generation', *Details* magazine, July 1997.
5. *Sounds* magazine, August 1983.
6. Dave Thompson and Jo-Anne Green, Interview with Ian Astbury, *Alternative Press*, November 1994.

7. Norman Davies, *Europe: A History*, Pimlico, London, 1997
8. John Ruskin, *Stones of Venice*, Gutenberg.org, 2003.
9. Horace Walpole, *Letters of Horace Walpole*, Gutenberg.org, 2003.
10. Ibid.
11. Michael Gamer, Introduction to Horace Walpole, *The Castle of Otranto*, Penguin, London, 2001.
12. Ibid.
13. Ibid.
14. Ibid.
15. Davies, op. cit.

Rocky Horror

1. Michael Gamer, Introduction to Horace Walpole, *The Castle of Otranto*, Penguin, London, 2001.
2. Ibid.
3. Simon Reynolds, *Rip it Up and Start Again: Post-punk 1978–1984*, Faber and Faber, London, 2005.
4. Austin Scaggs, Davey Havok Q&A, *Rolling Stone*, June 2006.
5. Gerard Way, MTV 'VMA Virgins' interview, 2005.
6. Misfits video [YouTube]

Vincent

1. 'Vincent', Cinema 16, American Short Films, Warp DVD, 2006.
2. Ibid.
3. Ibid.
4. Mark Salisbury, *Burton on Burton*, Faber and Faber, London, 1997.
5. Ibid.
6. Ibid.

Frankenstein

1. *Bride of Frankenstein*, Universal DVD, 2001.
2. Ibid
3. Mary Shelley, *Frankenstein* in *Three Gothic Novels*, Penguin, London, 1986.
4. Ibid
5. Bertrand Russell, *History of Western Philosophy*, Routledge, London, 2006.
6. George Gordon Byron, *Selected Poetry and Prose of Byron*, W H Auden (ed.), Signet Classics, New York, 1966.
7. Mary Shelley, op. cit.
8. Russell, op. cit.
9. Mary Shelley, op. cit.
10. Ibid.

11. Smashing Pumpkins, 'Disarm', *Siamese Dream*, Virgin CD, 1993.
12. Billy Corgan, from transcript of 1993 *Rage* interview, quoted in Starla.org
13. Mary Shelley, op. cit.

Edward Scissorhands

1. Mark Salisbury, *Burton on Burton*, Faber and Faber, London, 1997.
2. Ibid.
3. Ibid.
4. Ibid.
5. Ibid.
6. *Edward Scissorhands*, Twentieth Century Fox DVD, 2007.
7. Salisbury, op. cit.
8. *Beetlejuice*, Warner Brothers DVD, 2000.
9. Ibid.
10. Ibid.

'The Dark Side of Human Things

1. Rupert Christiansen, *Romantic Affinities*, Pimlico, London, 2004.

Mystery

1. Simon Reynolds, *Blissed Out*, Serpents Tail, London, 1990.
2. Ibid.
3. Ibid.
4. Karen Armstrong, *A History of God*, Vintage, London, 2000.
5. Yasmine Gooneratne, *Alexander Pope*, Cambridge University Press, Cambridge, 1976.
6. Voltaire, *Candide: or, Optimism*, Penguin, London, 1947.
7. Norman Davies, *Europe: A History*, Pimlico, London, 1997
8. Nicholas Dent, *Rousseau*, Routledge, New York, 2005.
9. Armstrong, op. cit.
10. Nick Cave, 'The Secret Life of the Love Song' in *Nick Cave: The Complete Lyrics*, Penguin, London, 2007.

Utopia

1. Antoine Nicolas de Condorcet, 'Sketch' in John Carey (ed.), *The Faber Book of Utopias*, Faber and Faber London, 1999.
2. Toby Creswell, *1001 Songs: The Great Songs of All Time*, Hardie Grant Books, Melbourne, 2005.
3. Gang of Four, 'Love Like Anthrax', *Entertainment!*, EMI LP, 1980.
4. Simon Reynolds, *Blissed Out*, Serpents Tail, London, 1990.
5. Ibid.

Utopiate

1. Nick Cave, 'The Secret Life of the Love Song' in *Nick Cave: The Complete Lyrics*, Penguin, London, 2007.
2. Simon Reynolds, *Blissed Out*, Serpents Tail, London, 1990.
3. Clinton Walker, *Stranded: The Secret History of Australian Independent Music*, Pan McMillan, Sydney, 1996.
4. Nick Cave, 'Zoo Music Girl' in *Nick Cave: The Complete Lyrics*, Penguin, London, 2007.
5. Nick Cave, 'Hamlet Pow Pow Pow!' in *Nick Cave: The Complete Lyrics*, Penguin, London, 2007.
6. Janine Barrand, *Nick Cave Stories*, Victorian Arts Centre Trust, Melbourne, 2007.
7. Reynolds, op. cit.
8. Barrand, op. cit.
9. Nick Cave, 'Mutiny in Heaven' in *Nick Cave: The Complete Lyrics*, Penguin, London, 2007.
10. Ibid.

The Degraded Present

1. Nick Cave, 'Release the Bats' in *Nick Cave: The Complete Lyrics*, Penguin, London, 2007.
2. Simon Reynolds, *Rip it Up and Start Again: Post-punk 1978–1984*, Faber and Faber, London, 2005.
3. Keith Cameron, 'Siouxsie Sioux—The Mojo Interview', *Mojo*, October 2007.
4. Andy Greenwald, *Nothing Feels Good: Punk Rock, Teenagers, and Emo*, St Martins Press, New York, 2003.
5. Alex De Jonge, *Dostoyevsky and the Age of Intensity*, Secker and Warburg, London, 1975.
6. Siouxsie and the Banshees, 'Spellbound', *Juju*, Polydor CD, 1989.
7. Norman Davies, *Europe: A History*, Pimlico, London, 1997

Blasphemous Rumours

1. Depeche Mode, 'Blasphemous Rumours', *Some Great Reward*, Mute LP, 1984.
2. Dave Thompson, *Depeche Mode: Some Great Reward*, Sidgwick and Jackson, London, 1995.
3. Depeche Mode, 'Blasphemous Rumours', op. cit.
4. Thompson, op. cit.

Paradise Lost

1. Mary Shelley, *Frankenstein* in *Three Gothic Novels*, Penguin, London, 1986.
2. Ibid.

3. Ibid.
4. Ibid.
5. Karen Armstrong, *A History of God*, Vintage, London, 2000.
6. Ibid.

The Disappearing God

1. Karen Armstrong, *A History of God*, Vintage, London, 2000.
2. Bertrand Russell, *History of Western Philosophy*, Routledge, London, 2006.
3. Armstrong, op. cit.
4. Ibid.
5. Robert Gittings, *John Keats*, Penguin, London, 1968.
6. Ibid.
7. Ibid.

The Age of Simple Faith

1. Depeche Mode, 'Stripped', *101*, Mute LP, 1988.
2. Eric Hobsbawm, *The Age of Revolution: Europe 1789–1848*, Weidenfeld and Nicolson, London, 1962.
3. John Ruskin in Elizabeth Gilmore Holt, *From the Classicists to the Impressionists: Volume III of A Documentary History of Art*, Doubleday Anchor, New York.
4. William Morris, *The House of the Wolfings*, Gutenberg.org, 2005.
5. *The Pre-Raphaelites*, Tate Gallery, London, 1973.
6. Ibid.
7. Ibid.
8. Ibid.

Faith

1. 24 Hour Museum Staff, 'Rare Wordsworth Manuscript Secured by Wordsworth Trust', 24hourmuseum.org.uk, April 2007.
2. Karen Armstrong, *A History of God*, Vintage, London, 2000.
3. William Wordsworth, 'Tintern Abbey' in William Wordsworth, *Lyrical Ballads, with other poems*, (1800 edition) Gutenberg.org
4. The Cure, 'All Cats Are Grey', *Faith*, 7 Records LP, 1981.
5. The Cure, 'Faith', *Faith* 7 Records LP, 1981.
6. Ibid.
7. The Cure, 'The Holy Hour', *Faith*, 7 Records LP, 1981.
8. The Cure, 'Faith', *Faith*, 7 Records LP, 1981.

World in My Eyes

1. Matthew Arnold, 'Dover Beach' in *Matthew Arnold: Selected Poems*, Crofts Classics, New York, 1951.

2. William J. Long, *Outlines of English and American Literature*, Gutenberg.org
3. Arnold, op. cit.
4. Ibid.
5. Depeche Mode, 'Nothing', *101*, Mute LP, 1988.
6. James Thomson, 'City of Dreadful Night' in John Hayward (ed.), *The Penguin Book of English Verse*, Penguin, London, 1958.
7. Depeche Mode, 'Black Celebration', *101*, Mute LP, 1988.
8. Depeche Mode, 'World in My Eyes', *Violator*, Mute LP, 1990.
9. Depeche Mode, 'Personal Jesus', *Violator*, Mute LP, 1990.

We Can Be Heroes

1. David Bowie, 'Heroes', *Heroes*, RCA LP, 1977.
2. Peter and Leni Gillman, *Alias David Bowie*, Henry Holt and Co., London, 1987.
3. David Bowie, 'Heroes', op. cit.
4. Michael Tanner, *Wagner*, Harper Collins, London,1996.
5. Ibid.
6. Ibid.
7. Ibid.
8. Ibid.
9. Ibid.
10. Ibid.
11. Ibid.
12. Ibid.
13. Ibid.

Wagnerian

1. www.theatreworldawards.org
2. Don Root, 1980s Rock 'n' Roll knowledge cards, Pomegranate Communications, Petaluma CA, 2006.
3. OscarWilde, *The Picture of Dorian Grey*, Gutenberg.org
4. *New York Times*, 22 June 1874.
5. Phil Hardy, *The Faber Companion to Twentieth Century Popular Music*, Faber and Faber, London, 1995.
6. Philip Dodd, *The Book of Rock*, Pavilion Books, London, 2001.

Born to Run

1. Greil Marcus, *In the Fascist Bathroom*, Penguin, London, 1993.
2. Mark Hagen, 'The Midnight Cowboy', *Mojo*, January 1999.
3. Robert Spillane, *An Eye for an I: Living Philosophically*, Michelle Anderson Publishing, Melbourne, 2007.
4. Bruce Springsteen, 'Born to Run', *Born to Run*, CBS LP, 1975.
5. Ibid.

6. Ibid.
7. Michael Tanner, *Wagner*, Harper Collins, London,1996.
8. Bruce Springsteen, 'Thunder Road', Born to Run, CBS LP, 1975.
9. Ibid.

Pressure

1. Peter and Leni Gillman, *Alias David Bowie*, Henry Holt and Co., London, 1987.
2. Daryl Easley, 'Under Pressure' in *Mojo Classic: Queen, The Inside Story*, 2005.
3. Ibid.
4. Queen and David Bowie, 'Under Pressure', *Greatest Hits*, Elektra LP, 1981.
5. Arthur Schopenhauer, *Essays and Aphorisms*, Penguin, London, 2004.
6. Ibid.

Schopenhauer

1. R J Hollingdale, Introduction to Arthur Schopenhauer, *Essays and Aphorisms*, Penguin, London, 2004.
2. Ibid.
3. Barker Fairley, *A Study of Goethe*, Oxford University Press, London, 1950.
4. Robert Spillane, *An Eye for an I: Living Philosophically*, Michelle Anderson Publishing, Melbourne, 2007.
5. Ibid.
6. Robert Gutman, *Richard Wagner: The Man, His Mind and His Music*, Penguin, London, 1971.
7. Arthur Schopenhauer, *Essays and Aphorisms*, Penguin, London, 2004.

Pinkerton

1. William Ashbrook, *The Operas of Puccini*, Oxford University Press, Oxford, 1985.
2. Ibid.
3. Ibid.
4. Ibid.
5. Ibid.

Butterfly

1. William Ashbrook, *The Operas of Puccini*, Oxford University Press, Oxford, 1985.
2. Ibid.
3. Weezer, 'Butterfly', *Pinkerton*, Geffen CD, 1996.

4. Weezer, 'Tired of Sex', *Pinkerton*, Geffen CD, 1996.
5. Arthur Schopenhauer, *Essays and Aphorisms*, Penguin, London, 2004.

Satisfaction

1. Andrew Loog Oldham, *2Stoned*, Vintage, London, 2002.
2. Ibid.
3. Arthur Schopenhauer, *Essays and Aphorisms*, Penguin, London, 2004.
4. Robert Gutman, *Richard Wagner: The Man, His Mind and His Music*, Penguin, London, 1971.
5. Toby Creswell, *1001 Songs: The Great Songs of All Time*, Hardie Grant Books, Melbourne, 2005.
6. Schopenhauer, op. cit.

Boredom

1. The Stooges, 'No Fun', *No Fun*, Elektra LP, 1980.
2. The Stooges, '1969', *No Fun*, Elektra LP, 1980.
3. Jon Savage, *England's Dreaming*, Faber and Faber, London, 1991.
4. Jon Savage, *Time Travel*, Vintage, London, 1996
5. Ibid.
6. Magazine, 'Song From Under the Floorboards', Virgin LP, 1980.
7. Savage, *Time Travel*, op. cit.
8. Michael Bracewell, *The Nineties: When Surface was Depth*, Flamingo, London, 2003.
9. Savage, *Time Travel*, op. cit.
10. Magazine, op. cit.

Notes from Underground

1. Morrissey, 'Live at the Olympia Theatre, Paris, 11 April 2006', YouTube.com
2. Ibid.
3. Fyodor Dostoyevsky, *Notes from Underground*, London: Penguin, London, 1972.
4. Ibid.
5. Ibid.
6. Ibid.

How Soon Is Now?

1. Toby Creswell, *1001 Songs: The Great Songs of All Time*, Hardie Grant Books, Melbourne, 2005.
2. Creswell, op. cit.
3. Andrew Loog Oldham, *2Stoned*, Vintage, London, 2002.
4. Ibid.

5. The Rolling Stones, 'Not Fade Away', *Rolled Gold*, Decca LP, 1979.
6. The Smiths, 'How Soon is Now', *Meat is Murder*, Rough Trade LP, 1985.
7. Ibid.
8. Simon Reynolds, *Blissed Out*, Serpents Tail, London, 1990.
9. Ibid.

Why Bother?

1. Andy Greenwald, *Nothing Feels Good: Punk Rock, Teenagers, and Emo*, St Martins Press, New York, 2003.
2. Get Up Kids, *Something to Write Home About*, Zomba CD, 1999.
3. Trevor Kelley and Leslie Simon, *Everybody Hurts: An essential guide to emo culture*, HarperCollins, New York, 2007.
4. Greenwald, op. cit.
5. Ibid.
6. The Smiths, 'How Soon Is Now', *Meat is Murder*, Roughtrade LP, 1985.

The Crystal Palace

1. Walter Benjamin, 'Goethe' in Michael Jennings (ed.), *Walter Bengamin: Selected Writings Volume 2, Part 1*, Harvard University Press, Cambridge, Mass., 2005.
2. 'World's Fairs' exhibition, National Gallery of Victoria, December 2007.
3. Fyodor Dostoyevsky, *Notes from Underground*, London: Penguin, London, 1972.
4. Ibid.
5. Ibid.
6. Ibid.
7. Ibid.
8. The Smiths, 'Shoplifters of the World Unite', *World Won't Listen*, Rough Trade LP, 1986.

The Broken, the Beaten and the Damned

1. The Smith, 'Unloveable', *World Won't Listen*, Rough Trade LP, 1986.
2. Gerard Way, 'Future of Music' Q&A, *Rolling Stone,* November 2007.
3. Gerard Way, Wikiquote, wikipedia.com

Teenagers

1. My Chemical Romance, 'Teenagers', *The Black Parade*, Warner / Reprise CD, 2006
2. Antoine Nicolas de Condorcet, 'Sketch' in John Carey (ed.), *The Faber Book of Utopias*, Faber and Faber, London, 1999.

3. Anthony Burgess, *A Clockwork Orange*, Penguin, London, 2002.
4. William Blake, *Poems of William Blake*, gutenberg.org
5. George Gordon Byron, *Life of Lord Byron with his Letters and Journals*, Thomas Moore (ed.), gutenberg.com
6. Pink Floyd, 'Pigs on the Wing', *Animals*, CBS LP, 1977.
7. Sylvie Simmons, 'Goodbye Blue Sky' in *Mojo Special Edition: Pink Floyd*, 2004.
8. Pink Floyd, 'Another Brick in the Wall: Part 2', *The Wall*, CBS LP, 1979.
9. My Chemical Romance, 'Teenagers', op. cit.
10. Bertrand Russell, *History of Western Philosophy*, Routledge, London, 2006.

I've Gotto Get Out of the Basement

1. George Koroneos, 'My Chemical Romance Interview', February 2006, lifeinabungal.com
2. Gerard Way, 'Future of Music' Q&A, *Rolling Stone,* November 2007.
3. Andy Greenwald, *Spin* magazine, May 2005.
4. Jenny Eliscu, 'Teen Titans', *Rolling Stone*, July 2005.
5. Weezer, 'In the Garage', *The Blue Album*, Geffen CD, 1994.
6. Eliscu, op. cit.

Myths of the Near Future

1. Karen Armstrong, *A History of God*, Vintage, London, 2000.
2. Isiah Berlin, *Against the Current*, Hogarth Press, London, 1979.
3. Alex De Jonge, *Dostoyevsky and the Age of Intensity*, Secker and Warburg, London, 1975.
4. Eric Hobsbawm, *The Age of Revolution: Europe 1789–1848*, Weidenfeld and Nicolson, London, 1962.
5. Ibid.
6. Carl E. Schorske, *Fin-Du-Siecle Vienna*, Vintage Books, New York, 1981.
7. Ibid.
8. Ibid.

Gustav Klint

1. Carl E. Schorske, *Fin-Du-Siecle Vienna*, Vintage Books, New York, 1981.
2. Ibid.

Nietzsche

1. Colin Wilson, *The Outsider*, Pan, London, 1970.
2. Rudiger Safranski, *Nietzsche: A Philosophical Biography*, Granta, London, 2002.

3. Wilson, op. cit.
4. Ibid.
5. Ibid.
6. Robert Gutman, *Richard Wagner: The Man, His Mind and His Music*, Penguin, London, 1971.
7. Friedrich Nietzsche, 'Attempt at a Self-Criticism' in Friedrich Nietzsche, *The Birth of Tragedy*, Penguin, London, 2003.
8. Wilson, op. cit.

A Night at the Opera

1. My Chemical Romance, 'The End', *The Black Parade*, Warner / Reprise CD, 2006.
2. Martin Aston, 'In the Lap of the Gods' in *Mojo Special Edition: Queen*, 2005.
3. Mark Cunningham, *Good Vibrations: A History of Record Production*, Castle, London, 1996
4. Ibid.
5. *Mojo Special Edition: Queen*, op. cit.
6. Queen, 'Bohemian Rhapsody', *Greatest Hits*, Elektra LP, 1981.
7. Gerhart Hoffmeister, 'Reception in Germany and Abroad' in Lesley Sharpe, *The Cambridge Companion to Goethe*, Cambridge University Press, Cambridge, 2002.
8. Queen, 'Bohemian Rhapsody', op. cit.
9. Friedrich Nietzsche, *The Birth of Tragedy*, Penguin, London, 2003.
10. Ibid.
11. My Chemical Romance, 'The End', *The Black Parade*, Warner / Reprise CD, 2006.

The Wisdom of the Woods

1. Colin Wilson, *The Outsider*, Pan, London, 1970.
2. Friedrich Nietzsche, *The Birth of Tragedy*, Penguin, London, 2003.
3. The Chemical Brothers, 'Salmon Dance', *We Are The Night*, Virgin CD, 2007.
4. Nietzsche, op. cit.
5. Ibid.
6. Ibid.
7. Ibid.
8. Wilson, op. cit.
9. Ibid.

Personal Jesus

1. Friedrich Nietzsche, *The Gay Science*, Penguin, London, 2003.
2. Friedrich Nietzsche, *Thus Spoke Zarathustra* Penguin, London, 2003.

3. Ibid.
4. Ibid.
5. Phil Sutcliffe, 'Never Let Me Down Again', *Mojo Special Edition: Depeche Mode + The Story of Electro-Pop*, 2005.
6. Depeche Mode, 'Strangelove', *Music For the Masses*, Mute LP, 1987.
7. Sutcliffe, op. cit.
8. Bertrand Russell, *History of Western Philosophy*, Routledge, London, 2006.
9. Nietzsche,, *Thus Spoke Zarathustra*, op. cit.
10. Depeche Mode, 'Walking in My Shoes', *Songs of Faith and Devotion*, Mute CD, 1993.
11. Marilyn Manson, 'Beautiful People', Interscope CD, 1996.
12. Tom Bryant, 'Twilight of the Gods' in *Kerrang!*, December 2004.
13. Colin Wilson, *The Outsider*, Pan, London, 1970.
14. Nietzsche, *Thus Spoke Zarathustra*, op. cit.
15. Depeche Mode, 'Condemnation', *Songs of Faith and Devotion*, Mute CD, 1993.

Stronger

1. Friedrich Nietzsche in R J Hollingdale (ed.), *A Nietzsche Reader*, Penguin, London, 2003
2. Kanye West, 'Stronger', Def Jam CD, 2007.
3. Hollingdale, op. cit.
4. West, op. cit..
5. Ibid.
6. Ibid.
7. Ibid.
8. 'Kanye West Throws Diva-Like Tantrum in Europe', *Rolling Stone*, March 2006.
9. Ibid.
10. Hollingdale, op. cit.
11. Mario Praz, *The Romantic Agony*, Oxford University Press, London, 1978.
12. Rudiger Safranski, *Nietzsche: A Philosophical Biography*, Granta, London, 2002.
13. Ibid.

Also Sprach Zarathustra

1. Peter Guralnick, *Careless Love*, Abacus, London, 2001.
2. Michael Kennedy, Richard Strauss, J M Dent and Sons, London, 1988.
3. E C Snow, Sleevenotes for Richard Strauss, *Also Sprach Zarathustra*, Decca LP.

4. Friedrich Nietzsche, *Thus Spoke Zarathustra*, Penguin, London, 2003.
5. Ibid.
6. Guralnick, op. cit.
7. Nietzche, op. cit.
8. Guralnick, op. cit.
9. 'Man or Superman?', *Mojo*, January 2007.
10. Greil Marcus, *Dead Elvis: A Chronicle of a Cultural Obsession*, Penguin, London, 1991.
11. Douglas Brinkley, 'All Shook Up', *Los Angeles Times*, September 2000, latimes.com

Homo Superior

1. Chris Charlesworth, *David Bowie: The Archive*, Omnibus Press, London, 1987.
2. David Bowie, 'Oh You Pretty Things', *Hunky Dory*, RCA LP, 1971.
3. Paul Du Noyer, 'Contact', *Mojo*, July 2002.
4. Ibid.
5. Mick Watts, 'Oh You Pretty Thing' in Hanif Kureshi and Jon Savage (eds) *The Faber Book of Pop*, Faber and Faber, London, 1995.
6. Ibid.
7. Friedrich Nietzsche in R J Hollingdale (ed.), *A Nietzsche Reader*, Penguin, London, 2003
8. Herbert Read, *To Hell With Culture*, Routledge, London, 2002.
9. David Bowie, 'Star', *The Rise and Fall of Ziggy Stardust and the Spiders from Mars*, RCA LP, 1972.
10. Colin Wilson, *The Outsider*, Pan, London, 1970.
11. Friedrich Nietzsche, *Thus Spoke Zarathustra*, Penguin, London, 2003.
12. David Bowie, *Moonage Daydream*, Hardie Grant Books, Melbourne, 2002.
13. Ben Fisher, 'But Boy Could He Play Guitar', *Mojo*, October 1997.
14. Bowie, op. cit.

Destroyer

1. Gordon Gebert and Bob McAdams, *Kiss and Tell*, Pitbull Publishing, New York, 1997.
2. Gerard Jones, *Men of Tomorrow*, Basic Books, New York, 2004.
3. Jenny Eliscu, 'Teen Times', *Rolling Stone*, July 2005.

Such a Special Guy

1. Weezer, 'Pork and Beans', *The Red Album*, Geffen CD, 2008.
2. Andy Greenwald, *Nothing Feels Good: Punk Rock, Teenagers, and Emo*, St Martins Press, New York, 2003.

3. Friedrich Nietzsche, *On the Genealogy of Morals*, Great Literature Online 1997–2008, www.classicauthors.net
4. Weezer, 'Troublemaker', *The Red Album*, Geffen CD, 2008.
5. Ibid.
6. Rainer Maria Rilke, *Letters to a Young Poet*, W W Norton and Co., New York, 1962.
7. Ibid.
8. Ibid.
9. Weezer, 'Troublemaker', op. cit.
10. Weezer, 'The Greatest Man that Ever Lived', *The Red Album*, Geffen CD, 2008

Expressionism

1. Oskar Kokoschka, *My Life*, Thames and Hudson, London, 1974.
2. Ibid.
3. Wolf-Dieter Dube, *Expressionism*, Praeger, New York, 1973.
4. Carl E. Schorske, *Fin-Du-Siècle Vienna*, Vintage Books, New York, 1981.
5. Ibid.
6. Mark Salisbury, *Burton on Burton*, Faber and Faber, London, 1997.
7. Siegfried Kracauer, 'Caligari by Siegfried Kracauer' in R V Adkinson (ed.), *The Cabinet of Dr Caligari*, Lorrimer, London, 1972.
8. . Ibid.
9. Dube, op. cit.
10. Ibid.
11. Kracauer, op. cit.
12. Ibid.

The Pain Threshold

1. A Alvarez, *The New Poetry*, Penguin, London, 1963.
2. Carl E. Schorske, *Fin-Du-Siècle Vienna*, Vintage Books, New York, 1981.
3. Notes from permanent exhibition at Arnold Schoenberg Center, 6 Schwartzen-bergplatz, Vienna, May 2007.
4. Ibid.
5. Allen Shawn, *Arnold Schoenberg's Journey*, Farrar, Strauss and Giroux, New York, 2002.
6. Arnold Schoenberg, 'Pierrot Lunaire', Chandos CD.
7. Liza Minnelli, 'My Chemical Romance', *Interview*, April 2007.
8. Dan Stapleton, My Chemical Romance, *Rolling Stone*, February 2007.

Sprechstimme

1. Allen Shawn, *Arnold Schoenberg's Journey*, Farrar, Strauss and Giroux, New York, 2002.
2. Richard Kingsmill, *The J-Files Compendium*, ABC Books, Sydney, 2002.
3. Saves The Day, 'Jukebox Breakdown', *Stay What You Are*, Vagrant CD, 2001.
4. My Chemical Romance, 'Blood', *The Black Parade*, Warner / Reprise CD, 2006.

Everything Collapses

1. Christopher Isherwood, *Goodbye to Berlin* in *The Berlin Novels*, Minerva, London, 1997.
2. Ibid.
3. Ibid.
4. David Bowie, 'Time', *Aladdin Sane*, RCA LP, 1973.
5. George Grosz, *George Grosz: An Autobiography*, University of California Press, Berkely, 1998.
6. Barney Hoskyns, 'When the Kids Had Killed the Man: David Bowie and the Death of Ziggy Stardust', posted in *Rock's Backpages*, rocksbackpages.com, June 2008.
7. Iggy Pop, 'Nightclubbing', *The Idiot*, RCA LP, 1977.
8. The Sex Pistols, 'God Save the Queen', *Never Mind the Bollocks*, Virgin LP, 1977.
9. Richard Kingsmill, *The J-Files Compendium*, ABC Books, Sydney, 2002.
10. Siouxsie Sioux, Foreword by Siouxsie Sioux, *Mojo Special Edition: Bowie*, 2003.
11. Jon Savage, *England's Dreaming*, Faber and Faber, London, 1991.
12. Norman Lebrecht, *The Complete Companion to Twentieth Century Music*, Simon and Schuster, London 2000.
13. Savage, op. cit.
14. Susan D'arcy, *Liza Minnelli*, LSP Books, Surrey, 1982.

Life Is a Cabaret

1. Liza Minnelli, 'Life is a Cabaret', *Cabaret*, MRA DVD, 2002.
2. Ibid.
3. Ibid.
4. Ibid.
5. Peter Conrad, *Modern Times Modern Place: Life & Art in the Twentieth Century*, Thames and Hudson, London, 1998.
6. Henry Edwards and Tony Zanetta, *Stardust: The David Bowie Story*, Bantam, London, 1987.
7. Jon Savage, *England's Dreaming*, Faber and Faber, London, 1991.

Mother War

1. Liza Minnelli, 'My Chemical Romance', *Interview*, April 2007.
2. Ibid.
3. Ibid.
4. Ibid.
5. My Chemical Romance, 'Mama', *The Black Parade*, Warner / Reprise CD, 2006.
6. Ibid.
7. Andy Greenwald, *Spin* magazine, May 2005

Artists are Cleaners

1. George Grosz, *George Grosz: An Autobiography*, University of California Press, Berkely, 1998.
2. Ibid.
3. Ibid.
4. Hannah Hoch, 'Aller Anfang ist Dada!' Exhibition, Berlinische Galerie, Alte Jakobstrasse, Berlin, May 2007.
5. Dawn Ades, 'Dada and Surrealism' in Nikos Stangos (ed.), *Concepts of Modern Art*, Thames and Hudson, London, 1990.
6. Mel Gordon, *Dada Performance*, PAJ Publications, New York,1993.
7. Ibid.
8. Jason Gaiger, 'Expressionism and the Crisis of Subjectivity' in Steve Edwards and Paul Wood (eds), *Art of the Avant-Gardes*, Yale University Press, London, 2004.

Distress Cries Aloud

1. Andy Greenwald, 'Emo: We Feel Your Pain', in Sia, Michael (ed.) *Spin: 20 Years of Alternative Music*, Three Rivers Press, New York.
2. Saves the Day, *In Reverie*, Dreamworks CD 2003.
3. Everett True, 'Salutation Begins at Home', *JMag* no. 20, August 2008.
4. AFI, *The Art of Drowning*, Nitro CD, 2003.
5. Wolf-Dieter Dube, *Expressionism*, Praeger, New York, 1973.
6. Hugh Frederick Garten, *Modern German Drama*, Methuen, London, 1959.
7. Ibid.
8. Ibid.
9. Jason Gaiger, 'Expressionism and the Crisis of Subjectivity' in Steve Edwards and Paul Wood (eds), *Art of the Avant-Gardes*, Yale University Press, London, 2004.
10. Ibid.
11. Ibid.
12. Ibid.

Rock Stars Are Fascists, Too

1. Adolf Hitler, *Mein Kampf*, Pimlico, London, 1992.
2. Ibid.
3. Bertrand Russell, *History of Western Philosophy*, Routledge, London, 2006.
4. Martin Gaughn, 'Narrating the Dada Game Plan' in Steve Edwards and Paul Wood (eds), *Art of the Avant-Gardes*, Yale University Press, London, 2004.
5. Joachim Fest, *The Face of the Third Reich*, Weidenfeld and Nicholson, London, 1970.
6. Nick Kent 'Into the Abyss', *Mojo Special Edition: Bowie*, 2003.
7. Caspar David Friedrich in Elizabeth Gilmore Holt, *From the Classicists to the Impressionists: Volume III of A Documentary History of Art*, Doubleday Anchor, New York, 1966.
8. Kent, op. cit.
9. AFI, 'Miss Murder', (video) YouTube.com.

The Black Parade Is Dead

1. 1985 Live Aid Concert, WEA DVD, 2004.
2. Jim Sharples, 'In Memoriam', *Big Cheese* magazine, April 2008.
3. Fred Vermorel and Judy Vermorel, 'Julie: "He's got a lot to answer for"' in Hanif Kureshi and Jon Savage (eds), *The Faber Book of Pop*, Faber and Faber, London, 1995.
4. David Bowie, 'Rock and Roll Suicide' (Live version), *Ziggy Stardust: The Motion Picture*, RCA LP, 1982.
5. My Chemical Romance, *The Black Parade Is Dead*, Warner / Reprise DVD, 2008.

Insulation and Disaffection

1. Herbert Read, *To Hell With Culture*, Routledge, London, 2002.
2. Ibid.
3. Ibid.
4. Ibid.
5. Jenny Eliscu, 'Rivers Cuomo Encyclopaedia of Pop', *Rolling Stone*, June 2002.

Leave Them Kids Alone

1. Mark Hagen, 'The Midnight Cowboy', *Mojo*, January 1999.
2. Liza Minnelli, 'My Chemical Romance', *Interview*, April 2007.
3. Timothy Gunatilaka, 'My Chemical Romance Saves Lives', *Spin*, January 2007.
4. Guardian.co.uk, May 2008.
5. Herbert Read, *To Hell With Culture*, Routledge, London, 2002.

Index

www.ingramcontent.com/pod-product-compliance
Lightning Source LLC
Chambersburg PA
CBHW022133020426
42334CB00015B/880